INEVITABLE PEACE

Inevitable Peace

CARL JOACHIM FRIEDRICH

GREENWOOD PRESS, PUBLISHERS
NEW YORK

The distance that the dead have gone
Does not at first appear;
Their coming back seems possible
For many an ardent year.

And then, that we have followed them
We more than half suspect,
So intimate have we become
With their dear retrospect.

EMILY DICKINSON

PREFACE

When, in the summer of 1945, the charter of the United Nations became a reality, I was tempted to write a brief study to celebrate the one hundred fiftieth anniversary of Immanuel Kant's *Eternal Peace*. For it was during the summer of 1795 that the aging philosopher of critical rationalism wrote his celebrated essay, which was published on Saint Michael's Day of that year. Königsberg, the city where he lived and worked, lies in ruins. None of the bitter and ironical judgments which he repeated throughout his life in condemning war do full justice to the indescribable horror which the folly of Prussian and German militarism has finally brought upon the people who had more reason than any other to heed the sage counsel of their greatest philosopher. The summer of 1945 seemed one of those dramatic moments in history which like a flash of lightning throw into sharp outline and perspective the dark panorama of human history. But the task I had conceived grew beyond its first limited objective. Earlier efforts in this field of political philosophy became linked with the new purpose, and at long last the present volume emerged. It is meant to be a contribution to the history of the idea of universal order under law, that is to say: peace.

The task is difficult, and only an analysis as rigorous and exacting as we can make it will avail us in such an endeavor. But I shall feel well repaid for my inadequate efforts if I succeed in opening up a discussion of theoretical issues which have lain dormant too long, buried under the mountains of a Kantian scholarship which has been preoccupied with the critic of Reason. That

Kant was basically a political philosopher moved by an intense hope for and a clear vision of one world can be realized only by him who takes into full account his central preoccupation with the problem of peace. It is my fervent hope that even the Germans, so long the learned misinterpreters of Kant's genuine philosophy, will at long last give due attention to the true meaning of their greatest political thinker.

Three books have recently come to my attention which I wish might have been at my disposal while I was developing the central theme of this book. They bear an intimate relation, albeit a controversial one, to the present enterprise. The first is *Fate and Freedom* (1945), by Jerome Frank. Frank, with a masterly and deft touch, draws attention to the moral implications of the idea of "inevitableness." Unfortunately, Frank's book is affected by the war-time notion that an idea is true because it is held by Americans or false because it is held by their enemies. While this may sometimes be the case, it is obscurantism from a philosophical standpoint. As a result of this blind spot, Frank fails to give due weight to the strong voluntaristic elements in Marx, Engels, and their followers. And while I fully sympathize with the aspersions he casts upon Hegel, I must say that Frank seems to be unaware of the fact that by 1860 Hegel was philosophically dead in Germany, that his real influence between 1870 and 1914 was in England and America, where the Neo-Hegelians flourished, and that his "dialectics" has facets which Frank does not seem to suspect.

The identification of Hegel with Imperial Germany is even more marked in *The Meeting of East and West* (1946), by F. S. C. Northrop. But my main objection to this in many ways remarkable volume is its inclination to treat systems of ideas culturally and anthropologically. Having, in typical Spenglerian fashion, accepted the division of the world into warring cultural groups with clashing ideologies as philosophically relevant, Northrop then struggles manfully to reunite it by combining complementary aspects of these philosophies. In this effort, he lays primary emphasis upon the purely cognitional side of man's nature, as may be seen from his statement of what he believes to be his contribution to the concept of personality. He writes:

> Thus, there is all the difference in the world, morally and politically, whether one believes Locke's theory that a person is a mental substance, or Hume's theory that he is a mere association of sense data, or Buddha's theory that he is primarily the aesthetic continuum, or the theory to which this long inquiry has led; the theory, namely, that a person, like anything else in the universe, is the aesthetic component of the nature of things joined to the theoretic components of the nature of things by the two-termed relation of epistemic correlation.[1]

I prefer yet another concept to these, and that is the concept of the person implied in Kant's categorical imperative: "Act so that you employ man both in your own person and in the person of everyone else at all times as an end in itself, not merely as a means." This conception is not enough, as we shall show, but surely the capacity for autonomous and responsible action in the light of reason is as important in any theory of "personality" as as either the aesthetic or the theoretic component of which Professor Northrop writes. If, instead of getting himself blinded by an approach to *German* idealism, he had more fully explored the truth and relevancy of the critical rationalism of Kant,[2] he would have had at his disposal a universal conception of moral man.

The third remarkable book which came too late to be given real thought before this study was brought to its present (and I believe temporary) conclusion is *The Open Society and Its Enemies*, by Karl R. Popper. Volume I, *The Age of Plato* and

---

[1] Page 466.
[2] As far as the theoretic component of Kant's philosophy is concerned, Professor Northrop is keenly aware of the genuine contribution of the critique of our rational faculties; but to the practical aspect he has not given comparable and adequate weight. Like his "pragmatist" colleagues, he sees Kant through Hegelian eyes.

Volume II, *The High Tide of Prophecy: Hegel, Marx, and the Aftermath*, were published in 1945. On the negative side, Popper has made a profound and penetrating contribution which gets beyond anything so far written to show the weakness of "elitist" doctrines of the "good society." [3] But, unhappily, Popper seems to be misled into an uncritical radicalism in the opposite direction, although we cannot be certain until his concluding volume appears. At present, the implication of his analysis seems to be that that government is best which governs least—a palpably unsound doctrine. I am afraid that his enthusiasm for Hayek augurs ill for his constructive suggestions.[4]

All three authors would, I believe, have gained from a fuller grasp of the critical rationalism of Immanuel Kant. Northrop rightly speaks from time to time of the pre-Kantian and the post-Kantian method and philosophizing. Too many Americans, especially philosophers and social scientists, are still in the pre-Kantian mental frame. Kant's position was not "idealism" as customarily understood; it could just as readily be called or miscalled "pragmatism." It could also be called rationalism. Kant's philosophy has been identified with all of these metaphysical positions. Actually he is preoccupied with the "Prolegomena of *every* metaphysics which in the future may want to present itself as a science," as the title of one of his best books puts it. I propose to call his position "critical rationalism."

It has often been observed that Kant is a "technical" philosopher. If that means that he is careful, it is very true. But if it is supposed to suggest that he is writing about things which do not concern the common man, it is very wrong indeed. What

---

[3] Some of these issues were adumbrated in chapter ii of my book, *The New Belief in the Common Man* (1942).

[4] See my essay on Hayek's approach to planning and democracy in the *American Political Science Review*, xxxix (1945), 575ff, as well as Herman Finer's *The Road to Reaction* (1946), which unfortunately weakens a brilliant and sound line of reasoning by ill-tempered abuse of the opponent. Shades of Schopenhauer?

clearer proof can there be than that he, rather than Locke, Hume, Hegel, Descartes, Voltaire, Mill, not to mention lesser worthies, wrote the most penetrating philosophical analysis on peace that has been written to date? It is not definitive. It is not at all adequate. It is written out of and in relation to the dynastic wars of the eighteenth century. But it was Kant who proclaimed Rousseau the Newton of the moral realm, and who greeted the French Revolution with unqualified enthusiasm in spite of the Terror, and stuck to his view that it was a proof of man's moral aspiration. It was Kant who never wavered in his conviction that to work for peace was man's moral duty, to enjoy peace his natural end, and to achieve it his probable destiny.[5]

There is a simple, homespun quality about Kant, a twinkle of gentle irony, which lends to his discussion of politics a common sense which is the very antithesis of the wordy abstractions of Hegel. It is hoped that the inclusion in the present volume of Kant's *Eternal Peace* and some pages from his thought on history will give the reader a glimpse of another side of Kant—a man who could readily be depicted walking through a New England village, questioning the wordy politician and the earnest clergyman to see "what it is all about."

It remains for me to acknowledge with gratitude the help which I have received. Continuing inspiration has come to me from the students in my seminars on political theory. Their enthusiasm has carried me over many a "dead point" when the wheel would turn no more. There are also many friends with whom I have discussed one idea or another. I have tried to repay my debt, wherever I could, by proper references to their work.

[5] If only Mr. Jerome Frank had looked a bit beyond what he could read in the literature on Hegel concerning Kant, how readily he might have saved himself from his extravagances about the "inevitabilist" Kant and Marx. Their profound moral faith, so closely akin to what Frank believes to be an American ideal, he missed almost completely. Frank is right, however, in questioning the "asceticism" of their approaches. Both Kant and Marx were "secular monks," and the joy of living was only dimly recognized in their thought.

But when preliminary labors extend over many years, how am I ever to do justice to those who allowed me to share their insight, their knowledge, their wit and humanity? Quite a few, like my farmer neighbors in Vermont, are not learned men; many have struggled with the reestablishing of peace in Europe and Asia after studying "military government" with me and with others. I feel that the only way to express my gratitude to them is to try my best at this undertaking. But I must mention especially Mrs. Dorothy Smith, who as my research assistant has helped at all the stages of the final writing, including the index and the proofs. She and Mrs. Shom Edmonds, my secretary, are responsible for the fact that the manuscript actually reached the printer. To Little, Brown and Company and to Mr. A. L. Hampson I am indebted for permission to quote the poem by Emily Dickinson which appears on page v.

The book is dedicated to Liesel, who died in the midst of a war she hated with all the intensity of a generous heart. Brutality of any kind she could not understand. One of the last things she did was to gaze with incredulous horror at some pictures in *Life* showing the mangled bodies of the victims of a race riot. The fierce aversion to all violence which the natural child feels seems a more convincing token of the eventual establishment of a reign of universal peace than all philosophies of history and all categorical imperatives. It is the ascetic strain in Kant, in Marx, and in many other intellectuals which makes them give too little weight to the sympathetic emotion—the great Eros who inspires, creates, and builds the brotherhood of man with man.

Concord, Massachusetts   CARL JOACHIM FRIEDRICH
January 5, 1947

CONTENTS

KANT'S WORKS CITED

In view of the great divergencies in translations of the several works by Immanuel Kant, it has seemed necessary to establish a uniform code of reference for the works cited. Listed below are the translations used for the respective works throughout. Page references will be given to Ernst Cassirer's edition, *Immanuel Kants Werke*, in eleven volumes (Berlin: B. Cassirer, 1912-1922), cited below as *Werke*.

Critique of Pure Reason—Kritik der reinen Vernunft (2nd ed., 1787), vol. III of *Werke.*

Idea for a Universal History—Idee zu einer allgemeinen Geschichte in weltbürgerlichter Absicht (1784), in vol. IV of *Werke.*

Fundamentals of the Metaphysics of Morals—Grundlegung zur Metaphysik der Sitten (1785), in vol. IV of *Werke.*

Prolegomena—Prolegomena zu einer jeden künftigen Metaphysik, die als Wissenshaft wird auftreten können (1783), in vol. IV of *Werke.*

Critique of Practical Reason—Kritik der praktischen Vernunft (1788), in vol. V of *Werke.*

Critique of Judgment—Kritik der Urtheilskraft (1793), in vol. V of *Werke.*

Eternal Peace—Zum Ewigen Frieden. Ein philosophischer Entwurf (1795), in vol. VI of *Werke.*

Theory and Practice—Ueber den Gemeinspruch: Das mag in the Theorie richtig sein, taugt aber nicht für die Praxis (1793), in vol. VI of *Werke.*

Religion within the Limits of Reason Alone—Die Religion innerhalb dez Grenzen der blossen Vernunft (1793), in vol. VI of *Werke.*

Announcement of the Impending Conclusion of a Treaty for Eternal Peace in Philosophy—Verkündigung eines nahen Abschlusses eines Traktats zum ewigen Frieden in der Philosophie (1796), in vol. VI of *Werke.*

The Argument of the Faculties—Der Streit der Fakultäten (1798), in vol. VII of *Werke.*

Metaphysics of Morals; Part I, Theory of Law; Part II, Theory of Ethics—Die Metaphysik der Sitten; (I) Metaphysische Anfangsgründe der Rechtslehre; (II) Metaphysische Anfangsgründe der Tugendlehre (1797), in vol. VII of *Werke.*

INTRODUCTION

✌ INTRODUCTION ✌

THE CONFLICT OF IDEAS AND THE INEVITABLE WAR

Most people in America and in Europe expect another world war. They differ only as to the length of time that will elapse before it breaks out. Public opinion polls have been conducted which prove this fearful state of mind.[1] The situation contrasts sharply with the mentality after World War I. Then overwhelming public sentiment, at least in the United States, held that the war "to end all wars" had been won for good, and people were willing to go "back to normalcy."

If one inquires into the reason why people, young and old, should so universally expect another war, the answers invariably stress the conflict of ideas between "East and West," meaning thereby the Soviet Union and the Anglo-American world. So general has the notion of this conflict become that it hardly

---

[1] Some material on this question is analyzed in Jerome Bruner, *Mandate from the People* (1944). Cf. also the news release of the American Institute of Public Opinion Research, August 14, 1946, for a poll of prominent citizens on their attitude toward general peace, and *World Opinion,* vol. I, no. 3 (July 1946), for results of the AIPOR poll conducted in Europe by Dr. Gallup. The following table shows the comparative vote of people polled in France, Britain, and the United States answering the question: "Do you believe there will be a war in the next 25 years?"

	France	Britain	U.S.
Yes	50%	48%	69%
No	27%	28%	19%
No opinion	23%	24%	12%

See also the National Opinion Research Center report no. 29, "Can the UNO Prevent Wars?" for general polls conducted between 1943 and 1945.

seems necessary to give any supporting evidence. The American press has been resounding with such views; commentators and columnists have lent their weighty support; and even those opposing the general pessimism have usually stressed the ideological conflict as a vital factor. This is not to deny that there have been dissenting voices upholding the view that the problem of ideological conflict is irrelevant to that of amicable relations, but for the most part this view is a survival of wartime propaganda which stressed the "nationalist" change of outlook in the Soviet Union, talked rather insistently about the "Russians," and even sought to sentimentalize the situation by reviving Czarist symbols.[2] A small group of writers of very conservative hue have simply refused to change from the traditional view of war as a war between national states. Such writers have, of course, a strong attachment to "non-intervention" as a cornerstone of national foreign policy. To them it seems clear that—in spite of the United Nations and Quadripartite arrangements which shape policy for the United States in most vital areas—the "sovereignty" of national states, and more especially of the United States, can not, must not, and is not to be interfered with. It is not surprising that their opponents look upon them as "unrealistic."

There can be little doubt that a war *may* be "caused," at least in part, by a clash of ideas.[3] Historians will attest the recurrence of such wars, unless they are doctrinaire economic determinists. In the latter case, all ideological elements are, of course, reduced to their economic and class basis; their presence is not denied, but they are treated as wholly dependent variables in the total equation of war-producing factors. It is not without interest that the official doctrine of the Soviet Union is still dominated by this

[2] A striking example is Maurice Hindus, *Mother Russia* (1943). It is well known that films and other popular arts, including even the "national anthem" of the Soviet Union, were affected by the trend. See Frederick L. Schuman, *Soviet Politics at Home and Abroad* (1946), chapters ix, xi, and xii.

[3] On the problem of "causes" of war see Appendix 1.

view. In his election speech of February 9, 1946,[4] Marshal Joseph Stalin opened his analysis of the future by these words:

It would be incorrect to think that the war arose accidentally or as the result of the fault of some of the statesmen. Although these faults did exist, the war arose in reality as the inevitable result of the development of the world economic and political forces on the basis of monopoly capitalism.

After a straightforward summary of the Marxist-Leninist theory of war, Stalin recapitulated his view by saying:

Thus, as a result of the first crisis in the development of the capitalist world economy, arose the First World War. The Second World War arose as a result of the second crisis.

Stalin nevertheless recognized a difference between the first and the second world war, by introducing the idea of "freedom-loving peoples," whom the Fascists had sought to enslave.

In view of this circumstance the Second World War, against the Axis Powers, as distinct from the First World War, assumed from the very beginning an Anti-Fascist liberating character, having also as its aim the reëstablishment of democratic liberties.

While these sentences will cause a wry smile to appear on the faces of those who refuse to face the fact that the Soviet Union employs the word "democratic" in one sense, while we employ it in another, the real significance of these phrases lies in their heralding clearly and unmistakably the ideological conflict which worries us, and which causes the expectation of war both here and abroad. At the same time, Stalin's remarks show that the leaders of the Soviet Union do *not* expect a war to result from such ideological conflicts, but rather from the clash of eco-

[4] *New York Times*, February 9, 1946. Stalin's interview concerning the prospect of war now was reported by *World Report*, October 8, 1946, pp. 43, 44.

nomic forces inherent in monopoly capitalism. They also seem to fear a war initiated by the capitalist powers to check the growth of the Soviet Union and the spread of Communism. It is hard for Westerners to believe that this fear is real, because they do not understand Soviet mentality. The very confidence of the Soviet leaders in their system's ultimate triumph inspires their fear of aggressive designs harbored by the capitalist powers. Agreeing with the most alarmist groups in the United States and Western Europe, they ask: "How can the leaders of capitalism be so stupid as not to try to stop the forward march of Communism while it must still appear a promising venture to them?" In this connection, American and British solicitude about the voting rights and other "liberties" of such peoples as the Bulgarians and the Poles is viewed as an ideological screen for aggressive designs arising from threatened economic interests, the interests of the capitalist class.[5] Thus clashes, which to Americans bear the earmark of the "irrepressible conflict" of a world half slave and half free in terms of freedom and democracy as they interpret them, to the Soviet Union are attempts to regain or maintain the economic controls of capitalist exploiters.

All this is familiar enough. And yet, there is something very puzzling about this rising propensity of Western thought to accept ideological conflict as an inevitable cause of war, and more especially the kind of war which the atomic age has ushered in. For this trembling, terrified belief in a fate which will devour civilization in the very act of trying to preserve itself is little short of grotesque in its illogical self-contradiction. Indeed, this view is so incoherent as to suggest a need for psychological analysis. It may seem fanciful to intimate that the prevalence

---

[5] See Paul M. Sweezey, *The Theory of Capitalist Development* (1943), especially ch. xvii, for a succinct statement of the orthodox Leninist position on these issues. Cf. also Stalin's "Report on the Work of the Central Committee to the Eighteenth Congress of the Communist Party of the Soviet Union," reprinted in *Leninism—Selected Writings by Joseph Stalin* (International Publishers, 1942), pp. 434ff.

of a belief in the inescapable doom of ideological conflict is a sublimation of a powerful sense of guilt regarding the world war just passed. It seems that all those who failed to do their utmost to restrain the Fascist powers at a time when it was still possible to do so without fighting a major war (and who can conscientiously say that he did all he might have done?) are now escaping into the self-excusing belief that a war is inevitable between clashing ideologies. The tremendous danger which results from this mass escapism and psychotic sublimation lies in their paralyzing effect upon future effort. In short, the ideological underpinnings of *The Wave of the Future* have been reinforced by the victory over the Fascists, although cold logic does not support such a conclusion.[6] Indeed, logic should lead people to argue that a decided effort of free men determines the future itself to a considerable degree. But the subconscious sense of guilt about the war just past provides a powerful emotional basis for escapist self-hypnotism about the "irrepressible conflict."

The issue, however, goes deeper. Let us grant, someone may say, that many people are emotional when they expect what they fear, because of their previous experience of fearing it. Yet they are being engulfed—helpless victims of historical forces which have swept over them in the past and will sweep over them again. Is it not true, after all, that the ideology of the Soviet Union is aggressively world-wide in its aspirations, filling with fanatical zeal its devotees and followers? Is it not a fact that throughout the Western world there exists today a fifth column of Communist parties who are prepared to sacrifice their country for the greater glory of the victory of world-wide Soviet Communism? It would be silly to deny such patent facts. Maybe the French Communist party can make and will make a foreign policy independent of Moscow, but there are few who will believe it until the French Communists have proved their claims by

---

[6] See *The Wave of the Future* (1940), by Anne Morrow Lindbergh, and my article, "We Build the Future," in *Atlantic Monthly*, January 1941.

many independent actions. In any case, the Communist parties in many weaker countries hardly advance such assertions and the prospect of such collaboration between Communists in all countries and the Soviet Union may as well be faced squarely. In what sense does it lend credence to the belief in an inevitable war?

Certain gentle persons in our time have been startled by the suggestion that "ideas are weapons." The phrase is reminiscent of a Fascist slogan which proclaimed: "We cheat with ideas." Hitler's *Mein Kampf* is full of sentiments supporting the notion that ideas are weapons, and nothing but weapons. That ideas are nothing but weapons is the cynical aspect of the doctrine. One might readily recognize that ideas may be used as weapons, and often have been so used; but as long as one retains the notion that they may also be attempts at stating the truth, a certain measure of faith in human integrity is retained. Max Lerner put this very nicely when he wrote:

> Ideas are necessarily weapons. But they will be effective only if the uses to which they are put are life-affirming. If the craftsmen in ideas have a belief in the possibilities of human society and a sense of the dignity of ordinary people, that will be the best safeguard of those ultimate standards of validity that we call science and truth.[7]

However, in putting the matter thus, Lerner abandoned the central tenets of his preceding discussion. Here a dichotomy between an instrumental and a manipulative approach to ideas had been suggested. This dichotomy did not turn upon the "ultimate standards of validity," but rather stressed the humanist respect for the common man as contrasted with the manipulative approach which "sees the common people as so much ma-

---

[7] *Ideas Are Weapons* (1939), p. 12. Lerner's insistence upon the necessity of bearing in mind the needs of the common man and his call for a more sensible balance between the rational and irrational appeals to the common man are thoroughly sound, but not as novel as would appear from his phrasing. An attempt to carry forward the problems involved was made in my book, *The New Belief in the Common Man* (1942).

terial to be used." This manipulative approach Lerner held to be characteristic of totalitarian regimes.

Leaving the Fascist states aside as not central to the issue we are exploring, we are stranded as far as the ideological conflict with the Soviet Union is concerned when we attempt the smooth formulation of criteria such as "life-affirmation," and "the dignity of ordinary people." For it is precisely over the question, What is life-affirming? and the related question, What is in keeping with the dignity of the common man? that our clash with the Soviet Union arises. The deep gulf which separates the Soviet Union from the Hitler regime and other Fascist systems, on account of their divergent ends and avowed purposes, cannot deceive the students of comparative government when it comes to the many striking similarities between these totalitarian states in matters of method and procedure. And in nothing are they more strikingly similar than in their skillful use of ideas as propaganda, backed by terror when necessary. When Stalin proclaimed the Soviet Union the "true democracy" he made it amply clear that he did not desire the USSR to be confused with such other presumably false democracies as are found in the capitalist world. The "true democracy" which is characterized by the rule of one party representing in its own view the proletarian masses and manipulating them in the proletariat's own interest —such a democracy is neither a constitutional government nor a democracy in the traditional Western sense.[8] But that does not in any sense deprive it of a vigorous conviction that the ideas which it has written on its banner are valid and true. Indeed, so fierce is the Soviets' conviction in this matter that those who grasp the full meaning and significance of these ideas believe that they are thereby justified in doing all that a Platonic guardian or philosopher-king was entitled to do, including lying to and regi-

[8] See my *Constitutional Government and Democracy* (1946), for a discussion of the problem. A sketch of the development of constitutional democracy is contained in chapter i.

menting the common man.[9] In short, the seemingly helpful dichotomy between the instrumental and the manipulative approach breaks down completely. Like so many essentially rhetorical distinctions, their plausibility depends upon a self-deception by which we attribute to ourselves praiseworthy motives for doing what we condemn in those whose motives we suspect. We cannot escape from the threatening implications of ideological conflict by word magic, which at one point calls the idea we are using to fight our enemies an "instrument" and at another point calls the idea which the enemy uses in fighting back a "manipulative device."

What is really needed to resolve our problem is a new and different approach to it. Obviously, if the conflict is a conflict of ideas in the first place, the first step would seem to be to clarify the ideas which are at issue. Democracy, the common man, freedom, and all the other ideological issues need to be examined in their relation to the issue of war and peace. If the clash is clearly an open clash between Marx and the Marxists on one hand and the bourgeois world and capitalism on the other, it behooves us to inquire into the antecedents of both, but more particularly of the bourgeois ideas on war and peace. It is a curious and noteworthy fact that the United Nations Charter, agreed upon by both the bourgeois world and the Soviet Union, embodies essentially the ideology of the bourgeois world. The theory of war in terms of which the Charter is written is not that of Stalin and the Marxists, but closely resembles that of the Covenant of the League of Nations. Else it would concentrate upon the problems which according to Marxist doctrine lie at the root of all

---

[9] It is at times forgotten by modern Platonists that both in the *Republic* and in the *Laws* Plato grants that the governing class is entitled to lie "for the good of the *polis*." See *Republic* III.389B, 414 B-C and *Laws* II 663. By way of contrast, it may be observed that Kant denied the right to lie, and made truthfulness an "absolute" derivative of the categorical imperative. See below, end of this chapter.

modern war: capitalism in all its economic and governmental and social ramifications. Now it may be objected that such a charter would have been wholly inacceptable to the United States and other Western powers. True enough. But we are here merely noting *what* the ideology is, and not *why* it is what it is, or whether it could or should be different. To repeat, there can be little doubt that the United Nations Charter is ideologically rooted in the bourgeois heritage of the Christian West. Its emphasis on law, on peaceful progress, on civil liberties, on judicial methods—these and many other features are unmistakable tokens of the Charter's ideological ancestry.

There are a number of different ways in which light can be shed upon the pattern of such an ideological edifice. You may take the ideas one by one and trace their history. Or you may attempt to evaluate each basic concept dialectically, and thus bring it into full focus. In the study here presented we are following a different approach. We asked ourselves, Which writer or philosopher has most fully and profoundly presented the thought which underlies the charter of the United Nations? We asked this question because the ideas are stated in an imprecise and popular fashion in the Charter itself, and much guesswork would be involved in restating them in a form more suitable to the critical analysis we are seeking to make. Moreover, it is our profound conviction that perspectives and insights are gained by selecting a thinker to represent the bourgeois world in its great ideological bout with the proletarian world which is represented by Karl Marx and his followers. In answer to this question, we suggest that much the most penetrating analysis of the problem of war and peace in terms consonant with the Charter's approach was made by Immanuel Kant. Kant, furthermore, has the symbolical advantage of belonging to the age of the great bourgeois revolution, of which he himself was an ardent and life-long partisan. The deep kinship between Kant's puritanical pietism and the Wilsonian (American) puritanism was frequently noted after the establishment of the League.[10]

But there is another and even more significant typological relationship. Kant, to whom peace appeared as the highest political good, and who proclaimed the dictum "There shall not be war" to be a direct application of the categorical imperative, is indeed a representative type of the bourgeois at the height of the bourgeois age.

Elsewhere in this study, we shall note other revealing aspects of Kant's doctrine, such as his vigorous insistence that private property is a first and basic principle of natural law. Like Locke and Hume, to whose philosophy his is so closely linked, Kant never seriously questioned the inherent necessity of a system of controls of material possessions, and he consequently saw the problem of peace in term of maintaining, by force if necessary, the existing pattern of "mine and thine." Yet, like the bourgeois civilization of which he was the philosophical spokesman, he laid the basis for transcending such a scheme of things. For not only the recognition of class struggle as a factor of progress in his philosophy of history (Chapter II, below), but also the deep moral regard for the intrinsic worth of the common man (Chapter VI), provides a bridge to the workers' civilization into which we are moving with such speed since the turn of the century (Chapter VIII). Hence Kant, like every thinker of pan-human scope, is not only a representative and symbolic figure of his age, but transcends it and achieves universal significance. This is as true of philosophical insight as of other great creative achieve-

---

[10] For the great significance of Calvinist theology in the shaping of thought conducive to the functioning of constitutional democracy, see Charles Borgeaud, *The Rise of Modern Democracy in Old and New England* (tr. 1894). Some years ago, in my Introduction to *Johannes Althusius' Politica Methodice Digesta* (1932), I showed how this "representative" thinker and expounder of Calvinist political ideas anticipated the "institutional implications" of Calvinist orthodoxy.

ments. It has been claimed that "Kant's categorical imperative finds its musical parallel in Beethoven's music." [11]

But are we not straying far afield when we select a German philosopher as the representative thinker of the bourgeois world? I think not. Karl Marx and Friedrich Engels also were Germans. The claim to truth of a given philosophy can not in any case be gauged by the collective belonging of the person expounding it. But in the case of Kant, unique and special considerations have to be taken into account. Besides his vigorous response to the French Revolution, and preceding it, Kant's thought evolved within the framework of a constant exchange of thought between himself, Rousseau, and Hume. This study will deal with several vital phases of this fellowship of the three near contemporaries. It would be too much to say that Kant was engaged in reconciling the ideas of his two great partners. Kant goes too far beyond both for that. The central place which the idea of peace —everlasting peace—occupies in Kant's philosophy demonstrates clearly how far he went beyond Hume and Rousseau; for they both remained within conventional eighteenth-century thought regarding peace and war. But even so, these three thinkers— born within twelve years of each other, Hume in 1711, Rousseau in 1712, and Kant in 1723—between them overturned the rationalism which had reigned for a hundred years, since about the middle of the seventeenth century. Thus the hopeful and senseless optimism of typical thinkers of the rationalist age, men like the Abbé Saint-Pierre and Voltaire, with their faith in the enlightenment of despots, was replaced by a new recognition of the irrational in men. This appreciation of the "limits of reason," while rooted in a theory of knowledge, had its focus in practical (moral) thought. In their moral and political philosophy, which

[11] Hugo Leichtentritt, *Music, History, and Ideas* (1938), p. xxiv. While not capable of rational proof, such an intuition suggests the universality of the highest good.

occupies an understandably central place in their thought, Hume, Rousseau, and Kant stress different phases of the non-rational springs of man's action. It was convention and tradition in the case of Hume, feeling and the communal spirit in Rousseau, duty and the categorical imperative in Kant.

The concatenation of Hume, Rousseau, and Kant illustrates well how misleading the national approach to philosophy and the history of ideas can be. Unfortunately, the rampant nationalism of our age, together with the urgent requirement of war propaganda, have popularized this approach enormously. But it can not be gainsaid that certain insights may be gathered by taking English, or French, or German philosophy in their sequel. These insights are, however, more nearly on the literary side. This might be expected, since the idea of a "national spirit," so generally believed in since the Romantics first expounded it, has borne its richest fruits in the interpretation of literature, where the "genius of the language" rules supreme. Mathematics, on the other hand, has gained little from such an approach; and only demented minds obsessed with the "folkish" mania would talk of a German, or French, or Jewish mathematics.[12] Philosophy stands somewhere midway between mathematics and literature. Truth and relevancy are both involved in its teachings. It expounds ideas which are claimed to be true, but they are also meant to be relevant to a given situation confronting the philosopher and his audience. This is especially true of political philosophy. Unfortunately, truth-claims and claims to relevancy often conflict with each other. Abstractly considered, untrue ideas obviously can not be relevant to any situation. But in the history of political thought, erroneous ideas have often triumphed, because of their greater relevancy. Time and again, the most egregious errors have prevailed, because they fitted a particular political need and therefore fulfilled the propagan-

[12] Oswald Spengler, in his *Decline of the West* (1926), exemplifies the length to which this speculative "cultural" pluralism can be carried.

distic requirements of a group, class, or nation which happened to be in the ascendancy. Bodin's doctrine of sovereignty, Grotius' doctrine of war, and Hegel's idea of constitutional liberty are three noteworthy examples of a long list of falsehoods which served to make their authors famous and influential, in their lifetime and beyond.

It is easy, in the light of such a record, to succumb to the cynical conclusion that the truth-claims of political and moral philosophy are altogether irrelevant. Such a cynical approach has often been expressly stated or implied in the past generation, especially in America. It has even been hailed as a "Copernican revolution" in the study of the history of ideas.[13] We are told that an "unmasking of ideologies" is the vital task, and that a completely "naturalistic approach" to ideas is wanted. Such a naturalistic approach is said to be characterized by an examination of "four converging strains which must be seen in focus: the man and his biography, the intellectual tradition, the social context and the historical consequences, that is to say the "successive audiences." [14] It is hard to perceive what the Copernican aspect of this "revolution" is supposed to be; for when has the history of ideas not been treated by its masters in this way? If we take any of the classic studies of great political thinkers and their ideas—Morley on Rousseau, Ferrara on Machiavelli, Chauviré on Bodin—we find them treating of these four aspects. But why call such aspects of a man and his ideas "converging strains"? What is to be understood by "seeing converging strains in a focus"? These are glittering and vague phrases which can not alter the fact that we still have to differentiate clearly

[13] This suggestion is made by Max Lerner, *Ideas Are Weapons,* p. 6. His reference is so casual that I presume he took his clue from John Dewey, whose claims to having initiated a Copernican revolution are discussed in a later chapter (see Chapter II, footnote 2).

[14] Lerner, p. 6. The phrase "unmasking the ideologies" was coined by Karl Mannheim, who in his *Ideology and Utopia* (1936) develops an analogous approach.

between the truth and the relevancy of ideas in history, or, to put it more critically, "claims" to truth and relevancy.[15] "The unmasking of ideologies," which sounded so titillating, even shocking, to an age which quaked at the muckraking in the realm of practical politics, is indeed a worth-while part of the study of ideas. But it is not nearly as novel as the author of that wounding phrase thought it was. What is more, such "unmasking" does not free us from the task of exploring the claim to truth on its merits. For an idea may have been expounded as a partisan ideology and yet be true, as far as we can see, while another idea may have been set forth detachedly and yet be false. It is not necessary to believe in one's own ability to discover absolute and final truth in order to recognize one's obligation to look for truth. Truthfulness, as Kant said, remains a virtue, no matter how critical one becomes regarding one's ability to attain the truth.[16]

It is in this general perspective that the more refined as well as the cruder attempts must be examined which seek to sidetrack a consideration of ideas by labeling their authors as belonging to a group which happens temporarily to be in disfavor. Kant's ideas are no more untrue because Kant was a German than Marx's are untrue because he was a Jew. Nor are they true for that reason. All this may seem too obvious for one to be troubled by it. Yet it goes to the very heart of our problem of inevitable war and peace, especially in so far as that inevitability is proclaimed in terms of a conflict of ideas. A world order depends for its viability upon the underlying pan-human capacity of the human mind to examine claims to truth in terms of universal standards of value. If such universal standards do not exist, no universal order can be expected. Fortunately for man-

[15] For all this discussion, Kant's essay which the translations call *Theory and Practice* is of basic importance.

[16] Kant insists upon this time and again. It is given a central position in his essay *Verkündigung eines nahen Abschlusses eines Traktats zum ewigen Frieden in der Philosophie* (1796), *Werke*, vi, 501ff.

kind, there are few propositions that are less doubted by the majority of mankind than that men can argue with each other about truth and untruth, provided they learn each other's language.

And yet, the "cultural" approach which dominates our thought on man and society has given rise to very subtle and ingenious disquisitions which would subdivide the world, and even European-American civilization, into watertight national compartments. What is expounded inside these "national" compartments must be relevant only to that particular nation, and have no universal significance. Thus German thought is labeled by some general adjective such as "egotistic" or "subjective" carrying a negative connotation, and by this familiar name-calling device the ideas of the particular thinker are disposed of. Perhaps the most penetrating effort along this line was made by George Santayana in his *Egotism in German Philosophy* (1916). This brilliant essay, written during World War I, acquired well-deserved fame and exercised far-reaching influence.[17] It abounds with poignant, if sententious, judgments; it is studded with shrewd insights. It is without a doubt one of the best studies of certain phases of the German intellectual tradition. Moreover, the author protects himself against the obvious objection of oversimplification by stating at the outset (p. 1) that he is not really dealing with German philosophy:

---

[17] Discussion in a great many authors seems barely more than echoes of Santayana's essay. The references to Kant in Lewis Mumford's *The Condition of Man* (1944) are serviceable illustrations. Mumford suggests here that "the overbearing subjectivism of Luther's thought" was "later unsuccessfully sublimates in the metaphysics of Immanuel Kant." Mumford in turn links Calvin to Descartes; how easy it is to get lost in these facile hints about influence! There is more Calvin than Luther in Kant, though some of both (see below, Chapter IV). In what sense Luther is more subjective than Calvin, Kant than Descartes, we are not told; indeed the term remains undefined. Yet on p. 320 Mumford rightly links Kant's *Eternal Peace* to the ideology of the United States. Since this essay, as we shall show, is centrally related to Kant's thought, American ideology would likewise be "sublimated overbearing subjectivism"—a paradoxical suggestion, to say the least.

What I propose in these pages to call German philosophy is not identical with philosophy in Germany . . . We should very likely discover
that the majority of intelligent Germans held views which German
philosophy proper must entirely despise, and that this philosophy seemed
as strange to them as to other people.

Nevertheless, Santayana proceeded to call it German philosophy.
Time and again he speaks of the Germans as thinking this and
that, and to make doubly sure that we do not miss the political
bias and prejudice, he tells us that German philosophy was never
his chief interest, and yet that "under its obscure and fluctuating
tenets I felt something sinister at work, something at once hollow and aggressive."

Before we specifically turn to Kant as representative of this
"hollow and sinister" German philosophy, two observations are
called for. First of all, it seems to this writer that Santayana's
strictures are well deserved by the Hegelian and other Romantic
idealist schools. They are equally or even more justified when
he decries Nietzsche. But such strictures do not support his prop-
agandistic purpose well, because to Hegel and Schelling correspond Spinoza and Berkeley; and to Nietzsche, Carlyle and
Sorel. These egotistical and subjectivist trends are a common
feature of European thought, and they found their rather com-
mon-sense echo in the transcendentalism of New England, more
especially in Emerson. Santayana, in his prejudice, pays hardly
any attention to these fellow subjectivists. He does not worry
about the fact that Bismarck acknowledged Spinoza as his "philosopher," as indeed he might, since the central tenet of Spinoza's
political and moral philosophy is that "the big fishes devour the
little fishes by natural right." Still, it remains true and sound
that Hegel and Nietzsche exaggerated the "self" above all else.
So far, so good.

The other observation is this: the historical fact which was
almost an accident—that Kant chose to call his system "critical
idealism," while the Romantic schools that followed called theirs

"idealism"—has obscured the fact that the role of ideas (with which we are here concerned) in Kant's philosophy is almost the reverse of that in Hegel and the Romantics. The emphasis on the "critique" of reason ought to have served as a warning that the emphasis is upon the "critical" aspect, which insists that experience and the reality which is experienced are something different and apart from the ideas we have of them. I wish that we might shift to using the word "idea-tism" for Kant's position, to describe his ideatic criticism, which amounts to critical realism. In short, Kant's position did not contain the "seeds" of Romantic "egotism," but rather their antidote.

In the light of these two observations, Santayana's treatment of "German" philosophy appears rather partial. It is a well-known rhetorical device[18] to take the part for the whole, say that you do not mean the whole, but a part, but then proceed to employ the name of the whole in speaking of the part in an effort to "persuade the jury."

In keeping with this manner of discretion, Santayana includes a discussion of Kant, albeit a friendly, even respectful one, in his book, under the heading of "Seeds of Egotism in Kant." This chapter contains many sound observations, but it reveals a basic misunderstanding of Kant's position. In commenting upon the *Critique of Pure Reason*, Santayana alleges that its "theory of knowledge proclaims that knowledge is impossible. You know only your so-called knowledge, which itself knows nothing; and you are limited to the autobiography of your illusions." [19] This statement would be much more accurate in describing Hume's position than Kant's, and it is precisely this position which Kant sought to overcome. Without inquiring now as to whether he succeeded—a matter which will be more fully dealt with later

---

[18] See Aristotle, *Rhetoric,* II.xxiii.4.

[19] This kind of statement is equally applicable to Berkeley, for example, as well as to Hegel. It is more true of Descartes than of Kant. Views of this sort have cropped up wherever men have thought deeply about the problem of knowledge; for example, the Bhagavad-Gîta is full of it.

on—we know that Kant had the most profound sense of the objectivity of a dual world of natural phenomena and moral noumena which he unforgettably put down in the famous sentence:

Two things fill me with ever-renewed wonder: the starred heaven above me and the moral law within me.

Since Kant is himself so very explicit about the objective reality of heaven and man, the without and the within, our propagandist philosopher has to go in for the humpty-dumpty kind of "interpretation" by which so many Germans have also tried to escape from the full impact of the Kantian philosophy of critical rationalism. Santayana writes:

The postulates of practical reason, by which Kant hoped to elude the subjectivity which he attributed to knowledge, are no less subjective than knowledge, and far more private and variable . . . In the categorical imperative *we see* something native and inward to the private soul . . .[20]

We, that is to say Santayana, see the categorical imperative as something subjective. Very well, then: who is the subjectivist? Santayana himself did not quite believe what he said; for on the next page the purely private and subjective categorical imperative has become "the conscience of the eighteenth century, which had become humanitarian without ceasing to be Christian, the conscience of the Puritans passing into that of Rousseau." Was the conscience of a whole century, the conscience withal of a great religious faith, "something subjective"? To the unbeliever, yes. But this thoroughgoing skepticism, with its ensuing animal faith, is the egotistical doctrine, not the philosophy which rationalizes "the moral law within." I am not a Kantian, but as a historian of ideas I strenuously object to such sophistical turning of an author's words and meaning around in his own mouth.

As one groping for the truth, and determined to examine with

---

[20] *Egotism in German Philosophy,* pp. 61-62.

due care all honest claims to truth on their merits, I object even more strenuously to being barred from examining the intrinsic worth of the philosophy which has given us the most coherent, viable, and comprehensive philosophy of peace which the bourgeois world has produced. Only by a determined effort to ascertain the framework within which this peace philosophy was conceived can we hope to fathom the depth and determine the limitations of an institutional development which corresponds to this philosophy's general tenets. That framework is partly provided by the general philosophy of Kant, and partly by the antecedents of its central ideas. Thus Kant's emphasis on effective organization—that is to say, government—as the solution to the problem of war must be our first concern. Why did he, of all people, perceive clearly that peace cannot be lasting unless it is provided with an institutional sanction against war? How did Kant's radical dualism, dividing the world into a naturalistic determinism and a spiritualistic freedom, enable him to proclaim "peace" as both the inevitable end and the inexorable duty of mankind's development? How were progress in history and self-realization for all men everywhere resolved in the higher unity of the "end of mankind," its immanent destiny? Why did Kant, as against Hume and Rousseau, undertake to recapture the tenets of natural law, so ancient in their inception, so gravely endangered by the thoroughgoing criticism of its rationalist foundations? How did Kant restate the natural law in a critical spirit, so that its idea could be held more universally valid than Christian rationalism had thought possible? How did Kant manage to transcend the divisive implications of Rousseau's notion of limitless popular sovereignty and the general will by his conception of the categorical imperative? How did Kant transcend a purely utilitarian approach to peace and war by his concept of duty, as contrasted with happiness as man's motivation? These are the issues which have to be dealt with. It would be unwise to pretend that they are easy or simple issues. For many people they do not even constitute problems. As such people flounder about in their vague fears of the "irrepressible conflict," as they look at the Soviet Union and its dogmatic declarations in favor of a universal order of Communism as the only safe and sound basis for a lasting peace—and feel defeated—they shrink from the one road to a resolution of these clashes of ideas: thought. Here we reach the concluding task: How does Marx believe peace can be achieved? Upon what foundations is his political philosophy built? Are they different from Kant's or are they the same? How does Marx' approach differ from that of other socialists, such as Saint Simon, Proudhon, or Veblen? How does it differ from the approach of anarchists, such as Thoreau and Tolstoy? For to all these thinkers the peace problem was of central importance. Yet none evolved a coherent peace philosophy which can stand as a rival to Kant's thought on universal peace.

In conclusion, we return to our starting point. What precisely is the import of a conflict of ideas? How meaningful is it to fight wars over them? Here too Kant may guide us to the truth for our time, even if he does not have it. He himself, in his spirit of playful mockery, wrote a short paper a year after *On Eternal Peace*. In dealing with a writer who did not like his critical philosophy he wrote an essay, *Announcement of the Impending Conclusion of a Treaty for Eternal Peace in Philosophy*. His hopes have not so far been fulfilled in the realm of ideas, any more than in that of practical politics. Yet, there is today a much wider critical appreciation of the human side of ideas, of their ideological aspect. Kant's appeal was to understanding and truthfulness.

A pacific union which is so constructed that it will be concluded as soon as the parties understand each other, may be proclaimed as *nearly* concluded.[21]

[21] This statement, in the essay mentioned (*Werke,* vi, 512), suggests clearly that Kant believed his "critical" limitation of reason to provide a basis for abandoning all dogmatic controversy.

Kant, having said this much, pleads for truthfulness:

It may well be that not all is true that a man considers so; but in all that he says he must be truthful . . . The trespassing against this duty of truthfulness is called lying . . .

After distinguishing between the "inner lie" of lying to oneself or God, and the "outer lie" of lying to one's fellow men, Kant observes that there are two kinds of lying, whether internal or external: (1) when one maintains that as true which one knows to be untrue, and (2) when one maintains something as certain of the uncertainty of which one is subjectively aware. Kant continues:

Lying is the real rotten spot in human nature . . . If in philosophy we were to take earnestly the maxim: Thou shalt not lie, we would not only bring on eternal peace in philosophy, but we would secure it for all our future.

If we will only make sure that we understand, and after understanding will not misrepresent the ideas held by others, we will achieve that tolerance which makes peace rather than war inevitable. For the claim to truth of rival ideas cannot be tested by arms; for force, being a natural phenomenon, as Kant says, can never determine a question of right which belongs to the normative realm. Maybe it is true that Kant in his clear dualism of the realm of nature and the realm of right and norm followed Calvin.[22] I doubt it. But whatever its ancestry, the idea that right is separate and apart from power and force is essential to lasting peace, because it eliminates war as a serviceable means for settling any conflict of ideas between man and man.

Kant's moral teaching shaped the creed of Friedrich Schiller,

[22] So stated by Santayana, *Egotism in German Philosophy,* p. 57. The problem is considered below in greater detail, especially at p. 88. There is undoubtedly a strong link between Kant and Calvinism, but it is *not* the dualistic aspect, for Calvinists inclined toward a monistic identification of all laws. Cf. my Introduction to *Johannes Althusius' Politica,* p. xcivff.

who sang: "Be embraced now, all ye millions . . ." The concluding movement of Beethoven's Ninth Symphony culminates
in the immortal melody which Schiller's ode of universal brotherhood inspired. Natural feeling here rises to the challenge of the
highest political good which the moral nature of man requires
him to realize as the essential condition for the never-ending task
of self-fulfillment. As this feeling is converted into action—as
more and more men come to realize the compelling force of the
categorical imperative's corollary and conclude "There shall not
be war"—peace—real, lasting, universal peace—becomes inevitable. It is a strange doctrine to consider in 1947, and few men
believe it fully today; yet it is a doctrine which transcends the
conflict of East and West, of the bourgeoisie and the proletariat,
of capitalism and Communism. Its historical antecedents, its
philosophical framework, its kinship to the ideology of the
United Nations surely are of profound interest to all who have
an abiding interest in human betterment and mankind's onward
march.

INEVITABLE PEACE

WAR AS A PROBLEM OF GOVERNMENT:
KANT'S ESSAY ON ETERNAL PEACE
AND THE UNITED NATIONS CHARTER

The year 1945, which witnessed the final rout of the forces of Fascist and National Socialist reaction in Europe, was the year which witnessed the drafting of a charter for a new world of united nations. The same year was also the one hundred fiftieth anniversary of the appearance of Immanuel Kant's *Eternal Peace*. The wizened little man with the giant mind, so provincial in his personal life as never to have left his native city of Königsberg, so universal in his sympathy as to feel himself a fellow of the American and French revolutionaries, hammered out in his seventy-first year a brief discourse of prophetic insight. He sought to show and to prove as best he could that peace— eternal, universal peace—was not only desirable (which had been proved by many others before him), was not only conceivable (that too had been proved repeatedly), but was necessary and inevitable.

Clothed in the quaint and involved eighteenth-century German which was just emerging from medieval Latin, *Eternal Peace* is nevertheless as inspired as anything Kant wrote. And far from being a marginal by-product of his old age, this little treatise flows from the very core of Kant's feeling. It develops more fully ideas which crop up again and again in other places in his writings on ethics and social philosophy. It rests squarely upon Kant's extraordinary philosophy of history.

What is more, looking back from San Francisco in 1945, we can test his ideas by the intervening century and a half, and we can say, "He was right." Or rather, that he was more nearly right than anyone else at that time or since.

It is an extraordinary spectacle, the picture of this quiet and "unpolitical man," challenging in a detached, albeit mocking voice each of the main pillars of the Prussia of Frederick the Great. "You are a dying branch of humanity," he seems to say to the men in power; "you are digging your own grave." Yet never was it more true that the prophet counts for little in his own country.

Time and again German writers, from Hegel down to our time, have tried to interpret away Kant's vigorous dislike of war-like enterprise.[1] The gentle skepticism admitting some doubt as to the prospects of establishing eternal peace which Kant's critical mind injects into the discussion has been blown up into the proposition that Kant considered peace, and more particularly eternal peace, only an unattainable ideal, comparable to the moon which guides the lonely wanderer at night.[2]

How untrue this interpretation is in fact, we shall see later on. It has, however, served as a basis for statements which make Kant an integral part of the "glorification-of-war" school which presumably has dominated German thought.[3] Against such

---

[1] Thus Dr. Willy Moog, *Kant's Ansichten über Krieg und Frieden* (1917), goes so far as to allege, without any supporting evidence, that "Kant fehlt auch nicht das Verständnis für den Wert des nationalen Staates." More accurately, O. Pfleiderer had pointed out, though with apparent regret, that Kant lacked an appreciation for the "people in arms," and for the thought that such a "people in arms" is "the best means for maintaining peace." Cf. O. Pfleiderer, *Die Idee des Ewigen Friedens* (Berliner Rektoratsrede, 1895).

[2] See Ludwig Stein, *Das Ideal des "ewigen Friedens" und die soziale Frage* (1896), p. 29. Such misinterpretations are the result of tearing special formulations from their context, more particularly to make into a complete dichotomy the Kantian distinction of *Sein* and *Sollen*. Much more accurate is the estimate of Fichte, who in his *Grundlage des Naturrechts* points out that the importance of Kant's essay lies in its insisting upon the convergence of the design of nature and the dictate of moral duty.

[3] This fate is shared by Fichte, in spite of the latter's unequivocal enthusiasm for Kant's idea of eternal peace. However, Fichte later turned toward a strident nationalism. See H. C. Engelbrecht, *Johann Gottlieb Fichte* (1933), especially ch. vii.

views, which are a perversion of all the patent facts, we hope to show that for Kant the full development of the autonomous personality is the goal of civilization, and this goal cannot be reached except through the establishment of a universal rule of law, that is to say, a scheme of organization which would guarantee universal and eternal peace. But he is very far from assuming that the mere desirability of eternal peace insures its eventual advent. His clear differentiation between the realm of being and the realm of norms, to which correspond the realm of the phenomena and the realm of the noumena, forces him to go beyond such facile preaching. The Abbé Saint-Pierre (1658-1743) had preached that sermon well enough. In his *Projet pour rendre la paix perpétuelle en Europe* (1713-1717), the Abbé, who had been secretary to the French delegation at the peace conference of Utrecht, suggested the foundation of a permanent international organization to maintain a rule of law between nations. The states should renounce war, establish arbitral procedures for the settlement of disputes, and maintain a common police force. This organization was to be an alliance of princes, however, and not of free peoples. Rousseau, who prepared an extract and summary with comments, considered such a project ridiculous and quoted approvingly Frederick the Great's sardonic comment that all was well with the plan and nothing lacking but the will to adopt it.[4]

Kant censures this inclination to ridicule:

Even though this idea may seem utopian, it is the inevitable escape from the want into which human beings bring each other. It must force the states to the resolution (hard as it may seem) to which savage man was forced equally unwillingly, namely: to surrender his brutal freedom and to seek rest and security under a lawful constitution.[5]

[4] See below, Chapter VI.
[5] *Idee zu einer allgemeinen Geschichte* (*Werke,* IV, 159). See also Chapter II below.

But the realization of this "goal" would be beyond hope, were there not a convergence of natural conditions and moral tasks. Thus Kant puts the whole problem within the broader framework of a philosophy of history which is at the same time a theory of war. This is extremely important, because without a sound knowledge of war a sound peace structure can no more be erected than a sound health program without a sound knowledge of disease.

"Through the wars," Kant wrote,

through the excessive and never realized preparation for them, through the want which hence every state even in the midst of peace must feel, nature drives man to make attempts, at first quite inadequate, to leave the lawless state of savages, and to enter a league of nations; where each state, even the smallest, may expect his security and his rights—not from its own power or its own legal views, but alone from this great league of nations (*foedus amphictyonum*), from a united power, and from the decision according to laws adopted by the united will.[6]

Thus man's search for happiness combines with man's moral duty to produce "what reason could have told him without so much sad experience, many devastations, retreats, and even complete exhaustion."

This convergence of the ideal and material motivation constitutes the complete reality. Against the hardheaded cynics of his day, as of ours, who tried to argue that "this may be true in theory, but does not fit practice," Kant had explicitly developed the proposition that what is sound in theory must have practical application. Just as sound physics is the basis of sound engineering, so sound political theory is the basis of sound statecraft;[7] but this means, of course, that the theory must be comprehensive enough to include both ideal and material motivation.

[6] *Idee zu einer allgemeinen Geschichte* (*Werke*, IV, 159).
[7] *Ueber den Gemeinspruch* (*Theory and Practice*), *Werke*, VI, 357ff.

It is hardly surprising that, starting from this general outlook, Kant should have been heartily in sympathy with the American and French revolutionaries. Indeed, it is not too much to say that Kant "belongs" to this tradition, ideologically speaking. In spite of its excesses, the French Revolution seems to him in line with mankind's higher moral purpose.[8] His strong response to the views of Rousseau, whom he at one point called the "Newton of the moral world," had led him to a vigorous espousal of the cause of the common man.

Kant's attitude toward the French Revolution has been described as wavering, and has been explained by "considering him as a representative of his class." It is valuable to consider the class background of political theorists, but so broad a description of Kant's as "bourgeois" explains very little. Virtually all political writers and philosophers were (and are) of the middle class, with insignificant exceptions. The striking differences between Hobbes and Rousseau, between Kant and Hegel, between Bentham and Marx, are not variables dependent upon their respective class positions. Creative thought, like other creative enterprises of man, evolves in accordance with its own inherent needs: the problemata, or stumbling stones, are not found exclusively or even primarily in the material world. Kant, like Rousseau, had a workingman's background.

His complete abandonment of the idea of an intellectual elite, so dear to the eighteenth-century philosophers, is of course central to Kant's idea of the autonomous moral personality and its freedom. His vigorous rejection of paternalism, no matter how enlightened, stands in forceful contrast to the thought of men like Voltaire and the early Bentham, both of whom looked toward the enlightened despot, advised by the philosophers, for the amelioration of society. Not so Kant. To him who stressed the moral element within each man's make-up as the faculty of

---

[8] See Chapter VI below, and also Reinhold Aris, *History of Political Thought in Germany from 1789 to 1815* (1936), ch. ii.

freedom, the common man was endowed with as much dignity as the most exalted. Nor is it too much to say that these views reflected a deep personal feeling in Kant. He hated to be considered a "genius." He insisted that the difference between men is not great. He was generally regarded as the most modest of men, very much averse to personal display or vain presumption.[9] His was the judicial spirit of the scientist who humbly acknowledges himself the servant of the exacting mistress Truth.

And yet this modesty hides a greater conceit than personal vanity ever pretends. The belief in the common man's capacity to master his own fate is the key expression of that strident expectancy which found its fullest expression in America. It is moving to find the cumbrous yet glowing passage from Kant's *Idea for a Universal History*[10] reappearing in Walt Whitman's inspired song against war and for peace:

As I pondered in silence,
Returning upon my poems, considering, lingering long,
A Phantom arose before me, with distrustful aspect,
Terrible in beauty, age and power,
The genius of poets of old lands,
As to me directing like flame its eyes,
With finger pointing to many immortal songs,
And menacing voice, What singest thou? it said;
Knowst thou not, there is but one theme for ever-enduring bards?
And that is the theme of War, the fortune of battles,
The making of perfect soldiers?

Be it so, then I answer'd,
I too, haughty Shade, also sing war—and a longer and greater one
    than any,
Waged in my book with varying fortune—with flight, advance, and
    retreat—Victory deferr'd and wavering,

[9] Among many personal estimates of Kant's character, the following are among the best: Bruno Bauch's "Die Persönlichkeit Kants" in his *Zu Kants Gedächtnis* (1904); Georg Simmel's *Kant* (5th ed., 1921); Karl Vorländer's *Immanuel Kant* (1924); and Kurt Borries' *Kant als Politiker* (1928).

[10] Quoted above. See footnotes 6 and 7.

(Yet, methinks, certain, or as good as certain, at the last,)—The field
   the world;
For life and death—for the Body, and for the eternal Soul,
Lo! I too am come, chanting the chant of battles,
I, above all, promote brave soldiers.[11]

There can be little question that the Charter of the United
Nations in many respects fulfills those conditions which Immanuel Kant had formulated as essential to the establishment of
a world-wide organization. Nor would he be as disturbed as
some among us that the organization turned out to be a league
rather than a Union. He suggests in his *Theory and Practice*[12]
that a universal cosmopolitan constitution might end up in the
most terrible despotism, and thus be even more dangerous to
freedom than war. He thinks the analogy of some very large
states suggests this possibility. (He does not mention them, but
it is more than likely that he had France and Russia in mind.)
In this case, the desperate need for international order will force
the states and nations into a federation which would operate according to an accepted law of nations.

This close parallel between the underlying ideas of the new
Charter and Kant's philosophical approach to the problems of
lasting peace suggests the possibility that considerable perspective on the United Nations may be gained by examining in
greater detail the pattern of ideas in which the Kantian position
is cast. A huge literature on Kant has tended to obscure the close
relationship between his insistence upon peace as the goal of civilization and the remainder of his philosophy. Kant has been
called the secular fulfillment of Luther; he has also been called
the secular fulfillment of Calvin.[13] He has likewise been labeled
with every conceivable tab from idealism to skepticism. From

---

[11] "As I pondered in silence," from *Leaves of Grass*.
[12] *Ueber den Gemeinspruch* (*Werke*, vi, 395).
[13] Friedrich Paulsen, *Kant, der Philosoph des Protestantismus* (1899); Hans
Rust, *Kant und Calvin* (1928); Bruno Bauch, *Luther and Kant* (1904); Ernst
Katzer, *Luther und Kant* (1910).

his seminal base have sprung a great many different systems. It would be rash to assume that where so many have found such divergent emphases there is likely to be agreement upon the interpretation here set forth. But it may be worth while at this particular time for someone with primary interest and competence in the history of political ideas and jurisprudence to reassess the Kantian position from the viewpoint, strict as well as restricted, of political philosophy. The writer has gradually come to the conclusion that Kant's whole system is much more closely related to his basic political outlook and his sense of the broad revolutionary developments of his time than has commonly been assumed. Heine's jocular remark that Kant's work on ethics, his *Critique of Practical Reason,* was an afterthought, has been generally rejected. But the more widely held notion that Kant's views on law and government, and more especially his ideas on peace and war, are peripheral to his thought, is untenable in the light of our broader insight into what *mattered* to Kant. For it was peace and freedom, in the most personal sense, that occupied the center of his hopes and fears; and peace and freedom were the themes to which his philosophizing returned again and again. And since the Prussia of Frederick the Great— perhaps even a bit more than the enlightened despotism of mid-eighteenth-century Europe generally—was built upon an explicit (and in fact cynically frank) denial of both peace and freedom, Immanuel Kant was indeed confronted with the task of lifting the entire world of enlightened despotism off its axles.

The result was not only a devastating critique of reason, the heavenly city of the eighteenth-century philosophers, but at the same time the construction of the most profound philosophical foundation for a regime of freedom under law for all men that the bourgeois age produced. For beyond Kant lie the revolutionary speculations of Marx, Marxism, and the many currents which his basic challenge set in motion. Hence the task which we are facing is threefold: to show how the ideas on peace are

anchored in the totality of the Kantian philosophical system, to
trace the relationship of some central concepts through antecedent and contemporary thought by contrast and comparison,
and to set Kant's scheme into critical perspective by showing its
relationship to the major succeeding approaches to the problems
of peace and world order.

The title of Kant's essay is cast in the most unpretentious
form, although the suggestion of eternity is challenging in the
extreme. It has been the tradition in England and America to
soften eternity into durability, and thus to speak of a "lasting,"
or perpetual, rather than an eternal, peace. This gives the Kantian position at once a more practical and a less exalted mold.
But the German *zum* is nearly untranslatable in its tentativeness
and caution; for it implies merely a contribution to the discussion, some thoughts, a hunch. "Concerning Eternal Peace" comes
nearest to rendering the idea.

The reader is at the outset struck by the tone of gentle irony
which is obviously intended to disguise the bitter seriousness of
the topic in hand.

Whether the above satirical inscription [*Zum Ewigen Frieden*], once
put by a certain Dutch innkeeper on his signboard on which a graveyard was painted, holds of men in general, or particularly of the heads
of states who are never sated with war, or perhaps only of those philosophers who are dreaming that sweet dream of peace, may remain undecided. However, in presenting his ideas, the author of the present
essay makes one condition. The practical statesman should not, in case
of a controversy with the political theorist suspect that any danger to
the state lurks behind the opinions which such a theorist ventures
honestly and openly to express. Consistency demands this of the practical statesman, for he assumes a haughty air and looks down upon
the theorist with great self-satisfaction as a mere theorizer whose impractical ideas can bring no danger to the state, since the state must
be founded on principles derived from experience. The worldly-wise
statesman may therefore, without giving himself great concern, allow
the theorist to throw his eleven bowling balls all at once. By this "sav-

ing clause" the author of this essay knows himself protected in the best manner possible against all malicious interpretation.[14]

The evident mockery calls immediate attention to the fact that Immanuel Kant lived in a rigidly authoritarian state, the Prussia of Frederick the Great. For even though the man who pragmatically proclaimed that "in my domains every man must go to heaven in his own way" [15] was far from the rigidities of modern totalitarian governments, the field of government and politics was largely *terra incognita,* and the academician was largely confined to the vague abstractions and metaphysical speculations of the "natural law." By the time Kant wrote his essay, *Eternal Peace,* he had already been involved in a sharp conflict, and his general and pronounced sympathy for the French Revolution had earned him the epithet of a Jacobin. The essay itself, upon its appearance, elicited from so liberal a mind as Wilhelm von Humboldt the comment that "ein manchmal wirklich zu grell durchblickender Demokratismus ist nun meinem Geschmack nicht recht gemäss: so wenig als gewiss auch dem Ihrigen." [16] It is important to bear this setting in mind, because it suggests that one should be alert to any innuendoes between the lines and should proceed on the hypothesis that Kant will go as far as he dares to in the direction of advocating popular government—a hypothesis which is important in interpreting several key ideas, as we hope to show.[17]

The organization and structure of *Eternal Peace* is rather curious. It is divided into two sections, of which the first contains the "preliminary" articles of eternal peace while the second con-

---

[14] See Appendix 1 for a complete translation of the essay from which this introductory paragraph was taken.

[15] Cf. Thomas Carlyle, History of Friedrich the Second, Vol. III, p. 242. The original was a marginal note as follows: "Hier muss ein jeder nach seiner Facon selig werden"—a statement typical of enlightened despotism and its concept of toleration.

[16] Letter to Friedrich Schiller, October 30, 1795.

[17] See below, Chapter V, and Karl Vorländer, *Kant,* especially II, 210-238.

tains the "definitive" articles. To these two sections there are appended two postscripts or "additions" and an extended "appendix" which discourses upon the relation between morals and politics. Treaties at the time were cast in such preliminary and definitive articles, and since there was usually a secret article included in each treaty, Kant, too, provides a "secret" article. This secret article displays the irony, to the point of skittishness, with which the philosopher looked at the whole matter. It provides that the principles of the philosophers concerning the conditions of public peace shall be consulted by the states which are ready for war. But since this procedure might seem humiliating to statesmen in their great wisdom, this article will be kept secret. The essay concludes upon a note of tempered confidence: eternal peace is no empty idea, but a task which through gradual solutions will approach steadily nearer to its fulfillment.

The six preliminary articles contain negative conditions for the establishment of peace among states: prohibitions or laws restricting the contracting states. All six constitute explicit rejections of existing practices, especially practices of the despotic monarchical states, including Prussia. As we said before, if Kant appears to knock the pillars out from under monarchical absolutism. Nor is this surprising, since later, in the first definitive article, he insists upon a republican constitution as a prerequisite of a peaceful order.

The six conditions are interrelated, and a full appreciation of them presupposes a reading of the essay as a whole. However, even a mere enumeration shows the drift of Kant's ideas quite clearly. Here they are:

First. No treaty of peace shall be held to be such, which is made with the secret reservation of the material for a future war.
Second. No state having an independent existence, whether it be small or great, may be acquired by another state, through inheritance, exchange, purchase or gift.
Third. Standing armies shall gradually disappear.

Fourth. No debts shall be contracted in connection with the foreign
affairs of the state.

Fifth. No state shall interfere by force in the constitution and government of another state.

Sixth. No state at war with another shall permit such acts of warfare
as must make mutual confidence impossible in time of future
peace: such as the employment of assassins, of poisoners, the
violation of articles of surrender, the instigation of treason in
the state against which it is making war, etc.

Now it can be readily seen that virtually none of these conditions are fulfilled at the present time. Indeed—even without
considering the more detailed elaboration which Kant gives for
each of these preliminary articles, and which in each case sharp-
ens its edge—it is apparent that no time in recent centuries has
been less promising in terms of these conditions than the present
moment. The utterly uncivilized warfare which the Fascist
powers have waged has destroyed both the legal institution and
the psychological foundation of genuine peace. Kant remarks at
the outset, under the first article, that most peace treaties are
really nothing more than armistices. The moment they are made
with the idea of a future war in mind they destroy the very
foundation of genuine peace. The many arguments heard at the
present time in favor of naval bases for the United States are invariably supported by the logic of defense needs, and hence are
made with a view to future wars. No lasting peace is possible
under such conditions, says Kant. He does not say, and we do
not say, that it may not be arguable that such plans be included
in a "peace" settlement, but he does say that if they are, peace in
the real sense—lasting peace—can not be hoped for.

It may round out this summary to add Kant's reason for de-
manding the abolition of standing armies. He feels that such
armies constantly threaten war; they provoke states to excel each
other in the number of armed men; the costs of such a peace

tend to appear more burdensome than a short war; to be hired for
the purpose of being killed lowers men to the level of engines or
tools. Voluntary service of the citizens is something quite different, he thinks. No doubt he would have approved of pre-war
conditions in Switzerland and the United States, but not in
France, Germany, or the U.S.S.R. Is the world moving in the
direction of Kant's third condition, or not?

But perhaps these preliminary articles should be considered as
outmoded, related as they were to the conditions of Kant's time.
Or, as Kant himself puts it in commenting upon the first of
these preliminary articles: "If, however, enlightened conceptions
of political prudence place the true honor of the state into a continuous increase in the power of the state, by whatever means,
why then this judgment appears as doctrinaire and pedantic indeed." Is Kant mocking again? Is he saying in effect that we
can have peace only at the price of abandoning the quest for
power, knowing full well that such a thing is never going to
happen? Surely all those who proclaim it a great step forward
to have enhanced the power of the great powers at the expense
of the small ones will be ready to say that Kant is hopelessly out
of date.

So much for the preliminary articles at this time. There will
be occasions for returning to one or the other. Of the definitive
articles there are only three in all. Kant prefaces his statement
of these articles by a brief paragraph in which he summarizes the
political philosophy which he had developed in the essay *Ueber
den Gemeinspruch*, on the relation of theory and practice,[18] an
essay which is altogether of paramount importance for Kant's
political theory. "The state of peace," Kant writes, "among men
who live together is not a natural state; for the natural state is
one of war, i.e., if not a state of open hostilities, still a continuous

---

[18] *Ueber den Gemeinspruch: Das mag in der Theorie richtig sein, taugt aber
nicht für die Praxis* (1793), *Werke*, VI, 355ff.

threat of such. The state of peace must therefore be established . . ." In a footnote he develops this further by insisting
that the mere presence of another in the state of nature, be it an
individual or a people, is of itself a threat. Therefore, he formulates the postulate that all men who can influence each other
should be under a common civil constitution. Kant envisages
three levels of constitutional order for men: the particular constitution of each nation, the international law binding these several states, and the constitution of the world order under which
men and states are to be considered as citizens. There seems to be
a certain amount of confusion and obscurity here; the sentences
in the footnote are not well constructed. It would seem that
Kant is groping for a firm basis of law for the international order, but is not sure whether it should be applied to individuals or
to states. Presumably, his individualist premises suggest individuals, but his sense of reality[19] makes him apprehensive lest such
a suggestion be considered visionary. How very central the
problem has become that Kant is here confronted with is shown
by the extent of its discussion in recent years, with quite a few
voices insisting[20] that any *real* international organization should
have direct contact with the people. This argument is a reflection, in turn, of the arguments at the time of the drafting of the
American Constitution, which are vividly reflected in the *Feder-
alist*.[21] Indeed, here lies the touchstone for determining whether
a government has been created, or merely a federation or league.
Even a casual examination of the San Francisco Charter shows
beyond the shadow of a doubt that the Charter is a league based
on treaty. At the same time, it contains hints that an evolution

[19] See below, pp. 65-66.
[20] A striking and important line of approach has been developed in Britain
by Lionel Curtis, who in his *World War—Its Cause and Cure* (2nd ed., 1945)
has shown how "empire thoughts" may be converted into "world government
thoughts." See also Clarence Streit, *Union Now* (1939), ch. x and elsewhere.
[21] See especially No. xxx and following where the matter is considered in
relation to taxation.

in the direction of world citizenship may occur. For the Charter several times refers to human rights and fundamental freedoms, and the final draft contains a special provision for the establishment by the Economic and Social Council of a commission "for the promotion of human rights." Because of the variety of basic divergencies among the United Nations as to what is "right," great difficulties may be anticipated in coming to an agreement which is more than a paper declaration,[22] but the value of these provisions may nevertheless be great.

After these introductory remarks, with their superficially Hobbesian flavor,[23] Kant proceeds to formulate his first definitive article: *The Civil Constitution of each state shall be republican.* What does this imply? Obviously, we must inquire into what Kant means by "republican." A first answer is simple: he means a constitution that really *is* a constitution, under which power is exercised according to well-defined laws and these laws are made with the consent of the citizens represented in a legislature.[24] In other words, the antithesis to a republican constitution is a despotic one where all power is concentrated and no real restraints exist. The reason Kant insists upon this requirement of a republican constitution is to be found in his concept of freedom under law. He states: "The constitution which is established (1) according to the principles of freedom of the members of a society as human beings, (2) according to the principles of dependence of all as subjects upon a single, common legislation, and (3) according to the law of equality of all as

---

[22] See my article, "Rights, Liberties, Freedoms," *University of Pennsylvania Law Review,* 91:312ff (December 1942), and my book, *The New Belief in the Common Man* (1942), ch. x.

[23] Hobbes's view of human nature had great vogue among natural law writers during the preceding century. See below, Chapter V, for more detail on this point.

[24] For the problems of constitutionalism and constitutional government, see my *Constitutional Government and Democracy* (1946), *passim,* and the literature cited there.

citizens, such a constitution is republican." Kant developed these ideas more fully in another work, *Metaphysics of Morals*,[25] as he had sketched them in his discourse on *Theory and Practice*. True freedom is that freedom which is compatible with the freedom of all other free men, and right is "the sum of the circumstance according to which the will of one may be reconciled with the will of another according to a common rule of freedom." But these common rules, these laws, are compatible with freedom only if they result from agreement, if they are consented to by the citizens. Self-expression and freedom are linked for Kant through the legal order, or as we would now say, the normative order.[26]

But there is one more point to be noted in connection with Kant's first definitive article, and that is the implied requirement of homogeneity for the international order as such. This requirement is recognized in Article IV, Section 4 of the Constitution of the United States: "The United States shall guarantee to every state in this Union a republican form of government . . ." Here "republican" means also non-monarchical. A similar clause was included in the Covenant of the League of Nations, but it was honored in the breach rather than in the observance.[27]

How far this general principle would carry Kant, or should carry a follower, in providing for popular participation in foreign affairs, it is difficult to say. On the whole, the experiences to date in this field have been somewhat short of encouraging.

---

[25] *Die Metaphysik der Sitten*, the first part of which is entitled *Metaphysische Anfangsgründe der Rechtslehre* (1797), *Werke*, VII, 1-180. Of this work on jurisprudence, Dean Pound has written: "No philosopher, unless it be Aristotle, has left so deep an impress upon the science of law as has Immanuel Kant. Kant marks an epoch in philosophical jurisprudence." (Roscoe Pound, "Law," in *Immanuel Kant 1724-1924*, 1925, edited by E. C. Wilm.) Cf. Chapter IV, below.

[26] See Chapter V, below, for an elaboration of the problems involved in this position.

[27] League of Nations Covenant, Article I.

Mass emotionalism is the most dangerous force generated by democracy. It has provided, and is continuing to provide, the most abundant source of appeal for the professional demagogue.[28] The basic difficulty results from the fact that several of the factors which justify the participation of "the common man" in the shaping of public policy are lacking in the field of international policy. The resulting difficulty is well illustrated by Walter Lippmann's *U. S. Foreign Policy* (1943), in which he formulates a pattern which, whether right or wrong (and I believe it to be wrong), is in its complexity incomprehensible to the average citizen; and yet Lippmann rightly insists that such a pattern has little chance of being followed unless backed by the people at large.[29] Under these conditions, it is likely that even policies with mixed national and international aspects, such as military training, are going to be decided on their domestic aspects. How the people's inchoate desire for the maintenance of peace can be effectively implemented by an understanding of what is required will be an unresolved problem until genuine lawmaking power can be developed on an international level and the majority of mankind offered an opportunity to participate in its shaping.

No such requirement is included in the San Francisco Charter, except that the participating states should be "peace-loving." Since no criteria have been suggested for the meaning of that phrase, it remains obscure. The fact, however, that semi-Fascist states, such as the Arabian kingdoms and Argentina, were urged to declare war upon our enemies if they wished to be participants

[28] The range of concrete problems involved in this development are analyzed in my *Foreign Policy in the Making* (1938). The true title of this attempt to assess the disintegration of the international order between 1918 and 1939 was "War in the Making"; it was written during the winter of 1937-38 and completed just after Hitler's invasion of Austria. It tried to show how a balance-of-power system had worked itself into a League of Nations, and that the search for peace under such auspices was vain.

[29] *U. S. Foreign Policy,* pp. 81ff.

at San Francisco suggests that the term "peace-loving" has the concrete meaning of "being willing to participate in efforts to put down the disturbers of the peace"—a reasonable view.

Historically, leagues have in fact included members of diverse political structure; thus the German Union of 1815 included an autocratic empire—Metternich's Austria; a militaristic and despotic kingdom—Prussia; kingdoms and principalities in constitutional evolution, such as Saxony and Baden; and free cities (that is, republics), such as Hamburg and Bremen. But the Union broke down in the war of 1866 precisely over the rivalry of these divergent structures. One may be justified even in drawing into this discussion the experience in the United States, where a formal requirement for homogeneity in political structure left out of account the problem of slavery with its implicit denial of freedom for a substantial portion of the common men; Kant's definition of a republican constitution would oblige one to deny that those states which permitted slavery were "republican" and hence to conclude that the breakdown of the Union in the Civil War was on Kantian terms to be predicted.

When heterogeneity in structure and social pattern threatens the cohesion of a league there is danger that the league may disintegrate as the rival factions strive for a balance of power. This search for a new balance of power within and around the League of Nations in order to buttress its tottering edifice should provide empirical lessons for the dangers that are looming for the United Nations as long as their organizational pattern remains that of a league. Not only the fear of outsiders, who played such a role in the disintegration of the League of Nations, but internal stresses and strains, may necessitate a balance of power. Appeals to morality[30] are of little avail against such trends. The "moral" propensities of man require an institutional framework for the realization of a "more perfect league." Only a true in-

[30] See E. H. Carr, *The Twenty Years' Crisis* (1939), which concluded on a note of distrust for international organization and an appeal to "morality."

ternational government can free the common man in all mankind to help maintain peace. The idea of a "balance of powers" is based upon philosophical premises which are untenable.[31]

If the first definitive article raises key issues highlighted by experience since Kant's time, the second leads right into the center of the present discussion. Kant puts his second article this way: *International Law shall be based upon a federalism of free states*. Now it is obvious that this is the keynote of both the Covenant of the League of Nations and the United Nations Charter. Both Article 1 and Article 2 of the Charter paraphrase this requirement and elaborate it. The expression "free states," however, which was found in the Covenant, is lacking in the Charter, which contains merely the principle of "the sovereign equality of all its members." This is an important deviation once again from the principle of homogeneity which we have just discussed; for by *free* states Kant clearly means states with a "republican constitution."

Kant's argument in support of this article discourses at length upon the question as to whether a federation or league would be enough, or whether a government, or—as Streit and other Unionists would say, a union—is required. It is obvious from his discussion that Kant favors the union and envisages a government of nations, a comprehensive world state (*Völkerstaat, civitas gentium*) as the "positive idea" and the final goal. It has at times been contended that Kant did not favor the idea of world government because he says in speaking of the league (*Völkerbund*) that it "need not be a world government [*Völkerstaat*]." He then goes on to explain that such a government would be a contradiction, because all nations would, as far as this government is concerned, be as one people. Contradiction to what? To the assumption, obviously, that nations agree to set up this organization. Kant is obviously not entirely clear in his own mind as to how to reconcile the world citizenship of individual

[31] Cf. Quincy Wright, *A Study of War* (1942), ch. xx.

human beings comprised under the world organization with the national citizenship of these same individuals. In any case, however, since people won't accept a comprehensive world state, he says, we will have to be content with the "negative substitute" of an expanding federation which will try to avert war by restraining the hostile tendencies which shy away from the restraint of law. He adds, rightly, that such a substitute leaves us with the constant danger of a new outbreak. In other words, Kant insists unequivocally that a federalism is better than nothing, but far short of a sure means for preventing war. That means can be found in one, and only one, solution: a united government for the world. But, as we have already pointed out, he is not unaware of the fact that such a government raises the specter of a world-wide despotism, and that it may hence be wiser to stick to the federalism.

It is not without interest at this time, in view of the leading role which the United States has played in setting up both the League of Nations and the United Nations, that Kant believes the possibility of realizing such a federalism can be demonstrated as objectively present by referring to the United States. His strong sympathy for the American Revolution has already been alluded to. Now, at this crucial point in his argument, he suggests the "objective reality" of such a federalism to lie in this reflection: "If fortune should so arrange it that a powerful and enlightened people should form itself into a republic (which according to its very nature must incline toward eternal peace), then this republic provides a center for the federative association of other states who may join her and thus make secure the freedom of these states according to the idea of the law of nations and gradually through several such accessions extend itself further and further." History did not quite follow this path during the nineteenth century, but it is clear that Kant nevertheless clearly forecast the role which the United States was eventually to assume.

The third significant point which Kant develops in connection with the second definitive article is his trenchant criticism of the idea of a "law" of war. The argument is straightforward in the extreme: War is contrary to the moral law; objective, i.e., real, law is the specific institutionalization of the moral law, hence there cannot be any place for a "law" of war. Those who have discoursed upon it, like Grotius and Pufendorf, are "miserable comforters." Their codices do not have the least legal force. Nor could they have it, since states do not live under a common external coercion. And yet Kant finds consolation of a kind in the fact that states have at least verbally rendered homage to the idea of law; it seems to him to suggest that there is a higher moral propensity to be found in man, even if it is still slumbering. He is emphatic, however, in insisting that what is right is never decided by success in war, because reason condemns war and makes peace a duty.

The third definitive article suggested by Kant addresses itself to what Kant calls the *jus cosmopoliticum* or law of world citizenship. It is highly significant that Kant, unlike the Covenant of the League of Nations or the United Nations Charter, insists upon the importance of making the individual a member of the world order. In so far as the United Nations Charter is concerned with human rights and fundamental freedom (Articles 1:3; 55c; 62:3; 76c, as well as the Preamble), there is, however, a recognition of the individual's place in the international order. Kant proposed that "the law of world citizenship shall be restricted to conditions of general hospitality." This sounds very strange indeed. What does he mean? He means that conquest and imperialism are incompatible with a world order. People have a natural right to visit foreign countries; they do not have a right to subject them. He lists America, Africa, India as instances of lands where the "civilized" nations of Europe conducted themselves very "inhospitably." And he approves the policy of China and Japan of permitting, after some experience

with such guests, only one European nation to enter, and even
that one only under very strict conditions.

Kant adds one very significant reflection to support his third
article. It is an idea that has become familiar to us in the quotation from Donne:

> No man is an Iland, intire of itselfe; every man is a peece of the Con
> tinent, a part of the maine; if a Clod bee washed away by the Sea, Eu
> rope is the lesse, as well as if a Promontorie were, as well as if a Manor
> of thy friends or of thine owne were; any mans death diminishes me,
> because I am involved in Mankinde; and therefore never send to know
> for whom the bell tolls; it tolls for thee.

When Hemingway suggested that the victory of Fascism in
Spain (and of course, *a fortiori* in Italy and Germany) was of
vital concern to America, he was at one with Kant; for the
latter urged that a violation of law (*Recht*) in one place on this
earth is bound to be felt everywhere. This proposition, so painfully apparent in the Nazis' assault upon the Jews, made Kant
urge a *Weltbürgerrecht,* which in its essence is nothing else than
the equality of all men everywhere, and the unconditional denial of the right of one people to rule over another on any
pretext whatsoever. How Kant imagined this article to be reconciled with his fifth preliminary article, which forbids interference with the constitution and government of another state,
he does not explicitly say. It is to be assumed, however, that he
would question the argument of those who assert that Americans
have no right to concern themselves with the colonial possessions
of other nations on the ground that such concern means interfering with their government. Kant's *jus Cosmopoliticum*
suggests that he would have restricted the idea of non-intervention in such fashion as to enable the world federalism to take
positive steps to protect people against imperialism and minorities against abuse; in short, Kant would have approved heartily
of provisions in the United Nations Charter for protecting

human rights and fundamental freedoms as a step in the right direction. At the same time, it cannot be denied that Kant's ideas on this score are lamentably inadequate in the light of modern developments, and that his third article fails demonstrably in coping with some of our most pressing issues, especially minority protection and the individual's urgent need for a court of international jurisdiction in which he can seek his right. Unfortunately, such a court was not provided by the United Nations Charter either.

This brief outline of Kant's essay suggests the need for a much more thorough exploration of some of the premises upon which his approach to the peace organization and world order is built. More specifically we shall want to inquire into the two worlds of natural necessity and of freedom under law. What are the outstanding characteristics of each of these worlds, and how do they interact? What is this universal moral law which imposes upon each and every one of us the obligation of working for the establishment of a lasting peace? And how is this hidden plan of nature to be interpreted which enables us to interpret history as a slow unfolding of a universal, cosmopolitan order of mankind?

❧ II ❧

THE IDEA OF PROGRESS
IN HISTORY
AND THE ESTABLISHMENT OF
A UNIVERSAL ORDER UNDER LAW

"If it is a duty, and if at the same time there is a well-founded hope that we make real a state of public law, even if only in an infinitely gradual approximation, then the eternal peace which will take the place of the peace-makings (falsely so-called because really just truces) is no empty idea, but a task which, gradually solved, steadily approaches its end, since it is to be hoped that the periods within which equal progress is achieved will become shorter and shorter." With this clumsy, complex sentence Kant concludes his *Eternal Peace*. Yet in all its tentativeness, it shows that Kant was convinced that a universal order of peace could be expected from the coincidence of natural causes and moral norms. Peace, in other words, emerged at the end of both empirical and normative reasoning.

This idea of a consonance of fact and norm is not a new element in Kant's thought, but it does constitute so sharp a challenge to the basic dualism of the Kantian system that its underlying rationale is easily misunderstood or entirely missed. It has always been one of the most baffling features of Kant's philosophy that he at once asserts the utter divergency and incommensurability of the causal nexus of observed phenomena in space and time and the causal nexus of free actions willed by human beings who are undeniably part of this causal nexus of observed phenomena, and that he at the same time posits both as basically experienced by the human individual who through observing or willing is the source of all knowledge. This central humanism in Kant's view of the world has often been attacked as subjectivist, but without justification, since Kant's philosophy is inspired by a deep sense of dependence upon an objective order of things, both factual and normative. The famous line from the *Critique of Practical Reason*, "Two things fill me with ever renewed wonder: The starred heavens above me and the moral law within me," are the expression of an overwhelming feeling that he, the insignificant man Kant, is placed in an objective world which he can master only by understanding its laws. As against the intense subjectivism of Descartes' *Cogito, ergo sum*, Kant seems to place his wonder at the two ordered wholes which his contemplation beholds in order to say *Sum, ergo cogito*.

It is our task to explore these basic constitutive ideas of Kant's philosophy in their relation to his ideas on history. Palpably, the world of history is the story of the men who, whether or not filled with the wonder at the world within and without them, are the bridge between the two orders which Kant considers the prime data of man's experience. For it is our contention that Kant, in the last analysis, is an empiricist. This view is at variance with much of the literature on Kant, and massive quotations from the works of Kant can be brought forward to counter this contention, owing to the special use which Kant made of the word "empirical" as he linked it with the natural order and our experience of it. But in spite of this verbal difficulty, it can be convincingly shown that both the necessary forms of perception of the world of phenomena and the equally necessary forms of free willing are seen by Kant as experiences of man the observer and the free agent.[1]

[1] The interpretation here given that these are matters of experience is shared by Georg Simmel, *Kant* (5th ed., 1921), p. 15: "His [Kant's] basic assumption is the absolute validity of experience. The individual experience may err, but the whole of experience, its principle, cannot." Kant's special use of the word

At this point we feel it to be essential to clarify the relationship between the Kantian view and Dewey's conception of pragmatism.[2] For Dewey has claimed that Kant's view of an experiment is that a "directive idea" "determines a known object" in a way which he describes as "fixed" and "rigidly determinative," whereas, in fact, an experiment is "tentative, conditional." This interpretation we believe to rest upon a complete misunderstanding. No one was more clearly aware of the tentative, hypothetical nature of all experiments, and of the necessity of testing such hypothetical judgments by experience than Kant. When Dewey writes that such an idea "controls an action to be performed, but the consequences of the operation determine the worth of the directive idea," he is speaking in completely Kantian terms. No work of Kant's shows this more conclusively than *Eternal Peace*. In the Appendix he insisted (as, of course, he had often done before) that only what is possible can be morally required, and he recites the dictum of the law *ultra posse nemo obligatur*. That is precisely the reason for the importance of showing the possibility that in peace-making, as in other human affairs, we learn by doing.[3]

When Dewey alleges that "there is accordingly opposition

---

empirisch in contrast to *Erfahrung* has confused the issue in translation; by *empirisch* he means the narrower *sense experience* of the sensualists, as contrasted with the broader concept of experience which includes other varieties, as, for example, those suggested by William James's title *Varieties of Religious Experience.*

[2] I am following, in the discussion here offered, John Dewey's line of argument as presented in *The Quest for Certainty* (1928), one of his outstanding contributions and perhaps the most interesting for anyone concerned with the problem of the relation of theory to social action. Dewey twice comments explicitly upon Kant's views (pp. 58-62 and 287-291). But the entire last chapter, entitled "The Copernican Revolution," is meant as a refutation of Kant, who had claimed to have effected a Copernican revolution which Dewey himself desires to claim for his views.

[3] In this connection a passage from the review of Herder's *Ideen* discussed below (see footnote 26) is of special interest. In it Kant stresses the importance of *actions* as the only reliable basis for interpreting man, because it is in such actions that man reveals his character. (See *Werke,* IV, 191.) The relevant passage occurs in Kant's reply to the anonymous critic of his first review.

rather than agreement between the Kantian determination of objects by thought and the determination by thought that takes place in experimentation," he backs this statement by the further proposition that "there is nothing hypothetical or conditional about Kant's forms of perception and conception." And he adds: "They work uniformly and triumphantly; they need no differential testing by consequences." But what does this prove? The forms of perception are "necessary conditions of all experimentation." Without these no experiment can be conceived, let alone be carried on. This crucial point Dewey seems to have missed; for if we cannot think without adopting certain axioms, such as the axiom of the excluded middle, how can such necessary conditions of all thought be tested by experiment? Dewey writes: "The reason Kant postulates them is to secure universality and necessity instead of the hypothetical and the probable. Nor is there anything overt, observable, and temporal or historical in the Kantian machinery." But how could that be tested by observation which is involved in the process of observing itself? It would seem that Kant did not at all particularly seek to secure universality and necessity, but that he wished to restrict such universality and necessity to those mental operations which are involved in the process of testing truths. To impute to Kant the very rationalistic authoritarianism against which his entire philosophizing was directed may provide one with a specious claim to having initiated the Copernican revolution oneself, but it is utterly misleading as a commentary upon Kant's position. It seems to me that, as far as the world of natural causal sequences is concerned, Dewey's view is essentially that of Kant—as far as it goes. Sentences like "The world as we experience it is a real world," or, "Knowing consists of operations that give experienced objects a form in which the relations, upon which the outward course of events depends, are securely experienced"—sentences like these are entirely in keeping with Kant's view of the world of phenomena which we observe and whose regularities we determine by hypothesis and experiment. Surely the notion that "one problematic situation is resolved and another takes its place" is in no sense at variance with Kant's discussion of judgments based on perception (*Wahrnehmungsurteile*) and judgments based on experience (*Erfahrungsurteile*).

The real difference between Kant's position and that of Dewey occurs in the realm of the "ought," where normative judgments are involved. But it seems to me that the resolution of the difficulty lies in recognizing that Dewey simply is not interested in the problems which Kant takes up in the *Critique of Practical Reason*. To put it bluntly, he has not been "wondering" at the "moral law" within man which the categorical imperative seeks to make explicit, but has considered human conduct as part of the phenomenal world of natural causal sequences. To assume that Kant denied that human conduct could and should be so considered is to misread him completely. Time and again he insists upon the importance of this field of inquiry, and nothing shows this more strikingly than his several sketches of an approach to world history.

It is not usually recognized by people who discourse upon war and peace that any general theory of war implies a general view of history. Nor have they always been aware of the fact that you cannot usefully discuss the problems of how to maintain peace if you have no theory of war. You put yourself into the position of the quack who, in contrast to the doctor, imagines that he can heal without understanding the nature of illness in general as well as the particular disease in hand.[4]

The reason for the necessity of constructing a comprehensive

---

[4] Striking instances of this kind of thoughtlessness are readily found in a good many programs offered at the present time. Regardless of whether the program is feasible, desirable, or necessary for preventing the recurrence of what happened, it contains no convincing analysis of what happened, or any data to show that it is likely to happen again. This is equally true of the advocates of either a "hard" or a "soft" peace.

view of universal history in accounting for war on an empirical basis is simple enough: war has been so common and recurrent a phenomenon that any explanatory theory finds itself sampling vast masses of historical experience.[5] Kant's unequivocal rejection of war from the standpoint of practical reason naturally leads him to ask, What end or purpose is being served by war? What does nature, the artificer of things (*natura daedalus rerum*), mean to accomplish by such reprehensible means? In answer to this question, he undertakes to show that war is part of a *hidden plan of nature* to drive men onward to the establishment of a universal rule of freedom under law, that is to say, a universal, all-inclusive government.

Kant's view is premised clearly on the hypothesis that there is an order of nature. This position is, of course, nothing new. Ever since the sixteenth century, the old Stoic conviction that all nature is functioning according to immutable laws had been making headway, taking in ever broader realms of inquiry.[6] But the application to history of this conception of nature as ordered by universal laws was rather novel. Giovanni Battista Vico (1668-1774) and Montesquieu (1689-1775) are the two outstanding thinkers who during the generation preceding Kant's had sought to show that history unfolds according to laws of universal application. Vico's highly original ideas have received altogether inadequate attention in the English-speaking world, where his declaration that "we know only what we do" and that thus action and truth are intimately linked should have given the pragmatically inclined an inkling that theirs was not as Copernican a revolution as they envisaged.[7] Montesquieu, less

---

[5] For a heroic effort along these lines see Quincy Wright, *A Study of War* (1942), pp. 717ff. Cf. also my review of this magistral work in the *American Journal of Sociology*, XLVIII, 508ff (January 1943).

[6] For a more detailed analysis of this development see Chapters IV and V, below.

[7] Cf. Benedetto Croce, *The Philosophy of Giovanni Battista Vico* (1913), translated by R. G. Collingwood; and C. E. Vaughan, *Studies in the History of Political Philosophy before and after Rousseau* (1925), I, 205-253. Croce stresses the anti-Cartesian emphasis of Vico.

profound and radical than Vico, nevertheless shared his interpretation of history. According to Montesquieu, universal laws govern the vast impersonal forces by which history is shaped. More especially, of course, he interpreted laws as the expression of a general spirit which permeates a given society and which is itself a resultant of various factors, both ideal and material, which operate according to natural necessity. To both Montesquieu and Vico, however, the idea of unilinear progress was quite alien, and it is precisely this idea which is central in the Kantian conception of history.[8]

In positing progress toward an end toward which human history is moving and unfolding, Kant rationalizes and secularizes a key conception of Christian theology. In premising this end as of so ideal a nature as to present man with an infinite task which, while progressively approached, is never wholly fulfilled, he transforms this Aristotelian teleology into the thought patterns of Western mathematics and science. The last great purely Christian eschatology was offered by Bossuet, who attempted to revive the Augustinian idea of a finite progression toward fulfillment of a divine plan. That this idea in turn has roots in the Old Testament admits of no doubt. Indeed, the Jews were unquestionably the creators of the idea of a universal history of man, guided by divine will toward an eventual fulfillment of a reign of peace on earth under the laws of God.

This theological background was clearly suggested by Wilhelm

---

[8] For Montesquieu, see Joseph Dedieu, *Montesquieu* (1913); A. J. Grant, "Montesquieu," in F. J. C. Hearnshaw, *The Social and Political Ideas of Some Great French Thinkers of the Age of Reason* (1930), ch. v; Victor von Klemperer, *Montesquieu* (1914-15). For the problem of history in this period, see also Carl Becker, *The Heavenly City of the Eighteenth-Century Philosophers* (1932), ch. iii. On page 114, Becker comments: "Montesquieu has little reverence for the facts as such; for him they are not fundamental but illustrative, their essential truth is not in themselves but in their implications." He cites Hume's dictum that history's "chief use is only to discover the constant and universal principles of human nature."

Dilthey.[9] It has been brilliantly analyzed by Reinhold Niebuhr in his *Human Destiny* (1943). Curiously enough, Niebuhr does not mention Kant's treatment of the problem, although it is closely akin to his own.[10] Niebuhr describes the end of history as eternal, and he intends this to mean that man, acting freely and according to his will, injects the normative into the stream of history. "In so far as the freedom of man to be creative in history implies a freedom over history itself, there are tangents of freedom which stand in direct relation to eternity."[11] That the meaning of history somehow emerges from this intertwining of fact and norm, of the phenomena and the noumena which together constitute the history of man, is further made clear by the statement that "history as such, represents a total realm of coherence which requires comprehension from the standpoint of its ultimate *telos*." But a shift occurs when Niebuhr implies that somehow the meaning is immanent in the process itself as he writes: "In so far as every act and event, every personality and historical construction is immersed in an historical continuum, it takes its meaning from the whole process." Such a view is decidedly at variance with Kant's view which throughout maintains that the norm which gives meaning is superimposed by the higher reason of freedom.

Kant's essay, *Idea for a Universal History*,[12] not only is central to his philosophy of peace and war, but in a very real sense

---

[9] *Einführung in die Geisteswissenschaften* (1883), i, 89ff. Dilthey's contribution is not mentioned in Karl Löwith's thoughtful article, "The Theological Background of the Philosophy of History," *Social Research,* xiii, 51ff. Cf. also Vladimir G. Simkovich, "Approaches to History," *Political Science Quarterly,* vols. xliv and xlv (1929-30).

[10] I suspect that this omission is in part due to Niebuhr's too-great reliance upon Troeltsch and Brunner, especially in his treatment of Luther in his seventh chapter. See for this aspect of the matter Chapter IV below.

[11] *Human Destiny,* p. 300. The next two quotations are from p. 313 and p. 301.

[12] This essay, entitled *Idee zu einer allgemeinen Geschichte in weltbürgerlicher Absicht* (1784), *Werke,* iv, 151ff, first appeared in *Berlinische Monatsschrift,* iv (1784), 395-411.

represents a novel departure. The theme is announced in the first sentence: "Whatever conception one may form of freedom of the will in a metaphysical respect: the phenomena resulting from it [the will], the human actions, are determined by general laws of nature like every other event in nature." [13] To make that theme probable, Kant refers to marriage and birth statistics which show great regularity, though marriage be influenced greatly by a free decision of will. This reference to statistical data is, of course, in line with modern sociological approaches.

On the basis of this general premise, that there must be laws of nature operative in history, Kant constructs his theory of history as a development through which man's moral destiny unfolds itself, in spite of his failure to will it, because nature knows how to employ his evil as well as his good propensities to bring this progress about. He thus transcends both the optimism of those who had argued the inevitability of progress as a result of man's fancied goodness and the pessimism of a Hobbes, who could not assume anything but a static coercive scheme because of Man's apparent propensity to evil, or selfishness.

It is customary to refer to this aspect of the political philosophy of Hobbes, Machiavelli, and others as "pessimistic." This expression is misleading. In most cases, the critic wishes to say that the particular view of human nature in question offends his moral sensibilities (that is, is contrary to his preconceived notions), in depicting men as "bad." In other words, he regards it as a misanthropic view. Considered functionally, and in terms of the question as to whether there is hope that men can succeed in constructing a working political order, both the

---

[13] That this assumption of laws permeating all nature is in a strict sense hypothetical is repeatedly acknowledged by Kant, and the assertions quoted above (p. 52) made by Dewey and others are in my opinion incorrect. Cf. also John Dewey's essay specially devoted to Kant in *Characters and Events* (1929), I, 63-68. For the hypothetical nature of Kant's basic order concept, see Ernst Cassirer, *Leben und Lehre* (1923), *Werke,* XI, 123ff.

critic and the criticized here are "optimists," since each believes that all that is required for the establishment of such an order is an adoption of his particular program of action. They are unconscious rationalists, in terms of the instrumentalities of power, who believe that the scientific delineation of a program of action requires only its rational demonstration as a sure road to its adoption. This "instrumentalist optimism" of the great theorists of "power" has its modern counterpart in the theories of both Communist and Fascist elite theorists which are inspired by a fanatical belief in the "future" that is theirs. Genuine pessimism of the Buddhist type is a bird of a very different feather.[14]

As Hobbes had argued that man's state of nature was a state of constant war, so Kant argues that man's state of nature was a state, if not of actual, then at any rate of potential, war. This state of potential war is a state of actual fear which engenders a powerful desire for security which in turn leads to a social contract. This line of reasoning was, of course, familiar in the literature of natural law. Since Pufendorf, writers on natural law had been seeking to combine Hobbes with Grotius.[15] Kant proceeded to argue that this same process applied to states, and that they would be propelled toward a general treaty or *foedus* which would establish lasting peace. But Kant buttressed both ideas by a concept wholly alien to Hobbes and his school: that it was the end and purpose of human existence to achieve moral autonomy and freedom, that such freedom was possible only under laws adopted with the participation of all—that is to say, self-imposed laws—and that, therefore, only a universal reign of law under a world-wide popular constitution could

[14] See Arthur Koestler's suggestive treatment of this problem in *The Yogi and the Comissar* (1945).

[15] For further detail, see Chapters IV and V, below. Kant generally inclined toward legal terminology and definitions. In the *Critique of Pure Reason,* for example, the discussion of the antinomies is put in the form of a case before a court. Cf. Josef Heller, *Kant's Persönlichkeit und Leben* (1924), p. 20.

satisfy the moral destiny of man. For that reason, he argued that it was the moral duty of man to work for the establishment of eternal peace, even though the laws of nature the great artificer were inevitably bringing on this reign of peace. It is very clear that this way of putting the matter raises the problem of freedom and necessity most sharply, and we shall turn to that issue in the next chapter. It may, however, be well first to state more explicitly and in positive form the view of war previously alluded to.

It is easy to misread the foregoing propositions as a concealed approval of war as the "father of all things." The famous alliterative phrase of Heraclitus, *Polemos pater panton*, does not necessarily mean that *war* is the father of all things, as has been customarily assumed. Apart from the poetry of the alliteration, which must have been a well-nigh irresistible temptation for the great Ionian philosopher, the word *polemos* means strife, struggle as well as war. That strife and struggle are closely associated with creation is much more universally true than that war is, and it would probably be more true, as well as more literal, to say that conflict is the father of all things.[16]

In point of fact, Kant is most explicit in condemning war as incompatible with the moral nature of man, because "victory never settles who is right." War is merely the payoff for the moral depravity of man, who will not do freely what is right and hence must be compelled by nature. *Fata Volentem ducunt, nolentem trahunt.* The terrible ordeal of war is the road toward a universal constitution for mankind.[17] The sequence of Kant's

---

[16] This is the form Werner Jaeger gives to the idea when he shows how it is linked with Heraclitus' general philosophy of *logos* and universal law. Cf. *Paideia: The Ideals of Greek Culture,* I (1939), 177ff, especially p. 181: "Only in conflict could *dike* establish herself."

[17] It has been customary in Germany to use this issue for the purpose of proving that Kant was favorable to war after all. The most extreme of these interpretations I find, curiously enough, is an essay by the German philosopher Paul Natorp, a supposed progressive and pacifist, in his *Kant ueber Krieg und Frieden* (1924). Similar views are set forth in Dr. Willy Moog's *Kant's*

argument in his essay on universal history is very straight, and while only a reading of the full text will give a thorough grasp of his idea, a brief outline of the development of the argument may be useful. First, all natural aptitudes of a creature are destined to unfold themselves completely and purposefully. Second, as for man (the only rational creature on earth), those natural aptitudes which are directed toward his use of his reason will develop fully in the species, but not in the individual. Third, nature has willed that man should develop completely by himself everything which goes beyond the mechanical ordering of his animal existence, and that he should not partake of any happiness or perfection except such as he has secured by and for himself through his own reason, independent of instinct. Fourth, the means which nature employs to produce the development of all man's aptitudes is the antagonism in society, since this antagonism becomes in the end the cause of a lawful order of society. Fifth, the greatest problem for the species man, the solution of which nature forces upon him, is the establishment of a civil society which generally administers the law. Sixth, this problem is mankind's most difficult problem and will be the last solved by the species. Seventh, the problem of the establishment of a perfect civil constitution is dependent upon a lawful external relation between states and cannot be solved without it. Eighth, it is possible to look upon the history of the human species in the large as the execution of a hidden plan of nature—to bring about a constitution which is perfect internally, and for this purpose also externally—because this is the only state in which nature can develop all aptitudes of mankind fully. Ninth, a philosophical attempt to treat general world history according to a plan of nature which aims at the

---

Ansichten über Krieg und Frieden (1917). The speech by O. Pfleiderer, *Die Idee des Ewigen Friedens* (1895), is more accurate in that it attacks Kant for not holding such views. English and American writers have always been more nearly sound. Cf., in lieu of many, William Ernest Hocking, "Immanuel Kant and International Policies" (1924), a reprint from *Advocate of Peace*, July 1924.

perfect civil association of the human species must be considered possible and as itself promoting this purpose of nature.

It is obvious that this train of reasoning rests upon several unexplained major premises: the assumption of an end or *telos,* the assumption that "nature" is somehow concerned with such ends, the assumption that law is valuable, because it provides the condition for freedom, the assumption that history constitutes an ordered whole, and finally the assumption that there is a destiny related to the end of a being. All these assumptions are deeply rooted in Kant's whole system of philosophy, and find expression in the essay *Eternal Peace,* just as much as in the *Idea for a Universal History;* they recur frequently in other parts of Kant's systematic works, more especially in the *Critique of Judgment.*[18]

This teleological realm of being which is implied in Kant's view of history superimposes an ordering, albeit hypothetical, general concept of progress toward fulfillment. It produces a basically unilinear conception of history, even though the end be conceived as an "infinite" one toward which mankind marches by slow degrees. For such a view rejects all types of interpretation of history and government which see development

---

[18] *Kritik der Urtheilskraft* (1790), *Werke,* v, 176-568. The second part of this work is devoted to what Kant calls "critique of teleological judgment." He starts with a discussion of the "objective fitness [*Zweckmässigkeit*] of nature." On page 453 occurs the striking sentence: "To speak exactly, the organization of nature has nothing analogous with any causality we know." How John Dewey could write of Kant that he expounded "a system of belief which would give mechanical science, conceived after the Newtonian pattern, complete sway in all matters of fact, in all matters where thinking has a claim to intervene," seems difficult to explain, even if one conceded, as Kant would not, that the moral realm was not "a matter of fact," or "a matter where thinking has a claim to intervene." See John Dewey, *Characters and Events* (1929), I, 65. Cf. also Chapter VI, below. There is no doubt in my mind that Dewey's conception of Kant's philosophy is wrong. Not only does he fail to grasp the Kantian approach to causation and experiment, but he entirely neglects Kant's recognition of the organic in nature and history, and he finally invests Kant's moral philosophy with an uncritical fundamentalism which it does not possess.

in the form of recurrent cycles. This "cyclical" theory had for long ages been in vogue; it is familiar to even the casual student of Plato and Aristotle, of Polybius and Machiavelli. The work of the great Vico as well as the writings of Montesquieu were inspired by such a cyclical view. Whether the organic analogies of birth, youth, aging, and death are explicitly employed or not, there is always somewhere implied a vitalist position in which life and death are ultimate standards and values.

In our time such views have reappeared with increasing frequency and insistence. Oswald Spengler's is perhaps the most dramatic and soul-searing of these works,[19] but there are quite a few others which, while stating their position more guardedly, are basically conceived in terms of cycles. Thus Eugen Rosenstock-Hüssy's great interpretation of the European revolutions treats European history in terms of cultural cycles culminating in revolutionary rebirths of the spirit.[20] P. A. Sorokin's approach to the entirety of history likewise leans toward a cyclical interpretation, although his conception of sensate culture and its opposite rather ranges him with those who incline to interpret

---

[19] Oswald Spengler, *Der Untergang des Abendlandes* (1919). The English edition appeared under the misleading title *The Decline of the West* (1926), misleading because *Untergang* means collapse, decay, in fact literally sinking, and means definitely the end.

[20] *Die Europäischen Revolutionen* (1931), English edition under the title *Out of Revolution* (1938), interestingly enough suggests a transcending underlying trend; but this phase of Rosenstock's philosophy of history represents a significant return to Christian universalism. Rosenstock's work, incidentally, was implicitly a reply to Spengler's corroding skepticism, and has not had the appreciation which it deserves. Such comments as that of Crane Brinton in the bibliographical notes to his *Anatomy of Revolution* (1938), suggesting that Rosenstock's work is "something in the tradition of Spengler," "the German cloud-cuckoo land of beautiful and inexact ideas, choosing convenient and rejecting inconvenient facts," are regrettable to say the least. If there can be a philosophically conceived world history which does not choose and reject facts as they fit the general conception, I should like to know of it. Germans, while perhaps rich in ideas, have no monopoly on the procedures Brinton ridicules.

history in polar terms as an oscillation between two extremes.[21] An imposing effort to combine the cyclical with the unilinear view is Arnold J. Toynbee's portrayal, as yet incomplete, of the history of human culture in its entirety.[22] Toynbee himself states this when he writes: "In the view that has been put forward above, a Spenglerian belief in an element of recurrence in human affairs has been combined with an Einsteinian belief in an element of uniqueness and irreversibility in the movement of the stars." And more explicitly: "If any inference at all can be drawn legitimately from these minor movements [the rise and decline of civilizations] we may rather infer that the major movement which they bear along upon their monotonously rising and falling wings is of diverse order, or, in other words, that *it is not recurrent but is progressive.*"[23] In short, there is a one-directional movement of the whole of mankind which defies "the incubus of the predestinarian creed," and this movement, in the view of Toynbee, is linked with the creative capacity in man. In a moving and poetic figure, Toynbee says that the divine spark of creative power is instinct in ourselves; and if we have the grace to kindle it into flame, then the stars in

[21] Pitirim A. Sorokin, *Fluctuations of Social Relationships, War and Revolutions* (1937), is vol. III of his *Social and Cultural Dynamics.* Polar interpretations are subject to the danger of all either–or propositions: verbalism. Another example is Saint-Simon, who suggested that history consists of organic and critical periods.

[22] *A Study of History* (1934-   ). Cf. also W. Gurian's significant review of the work in the *Review of Politics,* IV, 508 (October 1942). The monumental learning of this challenging work is a clear indication that the Germans have no monopoly on either broad ideological ideas ("beautiful and inexact") nor on the learning required to implement them and mold them into a universal history. Incidentally, it may be worth mentioning here that Toynbee cites Empedocles along with Saint-Simon as a philosopher of the polar or rhythmic approach to history, in his case "love" and "hate" being the two poles (see vol. I, pp. 200ff). He remarks that Saint-Simon adopted his position in order to combine the undeniable "up-and-down" in history with the conception of unilinear progress. These two poles Toynbee in turn links with the Chinese *Yin* and *Yang* and with Goethe's *Faust.*

[23] *A Study of History,* IV, 37. The remarks are a sequel to a sharp and explicit repudiation of Spengler's views, on pp. 10ff.

their courses cannot defeat our efforts to attain the goal of human endeavors.[24] The very expression "goal of human endeavors" suggests the kinship with Kant's view of the "objective fitness" of nature and its inherent natural goals or ends (*Naturzweck*). Man, Kant thinks, we may consider hypothetically the ultimate or final goal (*letzten Zweck*) of nature; not just as he is, however, but in his potential and gradual perfection as a civilized being. The creation of the fitness of a reasonable being as a free being is the essence of culture.

We find only one kind of being in this world whose causality is teleological, i.e. directed toward ends, and yet at the same time is structured in such wise that the law in accordance with which they have to determine their goals or ends is perceived [*Vorgestellt*] by them as unconditioned and independent of natural conditions, yet as intrinsically necessary. This being is man . . . ; the only natural being in which we can recognize [*erkennen*] a supersensual [supernatural, *übernatürlich*] capacity: freedom . . ."[25]

It is not difficult to envision the relationship between such a view and the general conception of history which Toynbee favors and which he puts forward in the words of Lord Acton: "By Universal History I understand that which is distinct from the combined history of all countries, which is not a rope of sand, but a continuous development . . ." It is obviously the conception underlying Kant's *Idea for an Universal History*.

The issue involved in this question, then, is whether man's history is or at any rate contains an unilinear pattern and therefore can be conceived as moving toward an intrinsic end, or whether it is cyclical and characterized by recurrencies. This question arose in Kant's own time between himself and Johann Gottfried Herder (1744-1803). Indeed, we have from Kant's

---

[24] In a magnificent metaphor reminiscent of Plato's image of the cave, Toynbee likens mankind's story to the ascent of a mountain, a view closely akin to the view Kant expounds in his *Idea for a Universal History*.

[25] *Critique of Judgment* (*Werke*, v, 515).

own pen a critical review of Herder's main work, *Ideas for a Philosophy of the History of Mankind*.[26] He criticizes Herder for the vagueness of his concepts, especially that of humanity; for his vitalist (as we would now characterize it) derivation of man's reasoning faculty from a physiological fact, man's erect posture; and finally for his failure to recognize that civilization is something which only the species and not the individual can realize. Kant puts it positively by insisting that it is the destiny of human kind steadily to progress. He adds that the fulfillment of this destiny is merely an idea, but a very useful one toward which we have to direct our efforts. Herder replied in two long and bitter essays[27] which fail to set the issue straight. The real objective of Herder's reflections upon history appears quite similar to Kant's. Both men seek to find within the vast array of human deeds and human suffering a "plan" of a meaningful development, of a "purpose of providence." But whereas Kant's, in keeping with his critical position, maintains that such a universal end cannot be "discovered" empirically because our finite minds cannot be expected to handle the totality of all that has happened and will happen, Herder seeks to find this "idea" by intuitive interpretation of a mass of concrete data. As one student puts it, Herder believed that "the wise and benevolent creator of the universe must have put a wise and benevolent

---

[26] *Ideen zur Philosophie der Geschichte der Menschheit* (1784-85). Kant's reviews are to be found in *Werke*, IV, 179-200. Cf., for Herder's political views, Reinhold Aris, *A History of Political Thought in Germany from 1789 to 1815* (1936), pp. 234-249. The relationship of Kant and Herder has been subjected to a detailed analysis by Theodor Litt, *Kant und Herder* (1930), chapters xix-xxiv being especially devoted to their philosophy of history. In keeping with his general philosophy as expounded in *Individuum und Gemeinschaft* (1926), Litt interprets Herder as an expounder of the sharply organicist conception which Litt himself professes, while contrasting Kant's conception as rigidly rationalistic, even mechanistic. Both interpretations are strained, to say the least.

[27] *Metakritik* (1799) and *Kalligone* (1800), in *Saemtliche Werke* (ed. Suphan), vols. XXI and XXII.

plan into the destiny and organization of mankind . . ."[28]
Herder, like Kant, detested war, but when it came to determining how to eliminate it, he became confused and uncertain.
His passionate interest in the historical individuality of groups
and cultures clashed with his conception of a universal history
of man. But his Rousseauistic belief in the goodness of man and
in the creative potentialities of the felt community left him
without any definite notions as to how order and peace are to
be organized and maintained. Without ever clarifying his ideas
on the role of government in history, he protested sharply
against Kant's idea that natural man needed a master, misin-
terpreting it as applying to the whole man, when in fact Kant
sees man's development in terms of the progressive perfecting
of a constitution which takes full account of human rights.[29]
This may be a relatively rationalistic end or *telos* of man's history, but it certainly provides a firm basis for the elimination of
war and the building of peace.

Kant's clash with Herder was a foretaste of what was to come.
For post-Kantian philosophy, although claiming to accept Kant's
critiques of the rational faculty, proceeded forthwith to cast
aside the quintessence of his critical philosophy with its dual
worlds of determinism and freedom and to proclaim a new
metaphysical synthesis. Fichte opted for freedom, Schopenhauer for will, Hegel for reason, to name only three. Of these,
Hegel is at once the most ambitious and the least Kantian. The
pompous grandeur of his dialectic would surely have been casti-
gated by the "old man of the king's mountain" more caustically

---

[28] R. Haym, *Herder, nach seinem Leben und seinen Werken* (1880), ii, 194,
quoted by Aris, p. 240. Similarly Litt, p. 225.

[29] This side of the matter can be clearly seen in Kant's review (*Werke*, iv,
199). Aris is quite wrong when he writes that "Kant had considered man as
an animal which needed a master" (p. 248). Kant could readily have agreed
with Herder's antithesis that "the man who needs a master is an animal; as
soon as he becomes a human being, he needs a proper master no longer"
(*ibid.*).

than Herder's *Ideas,* for Hegel undertook to do precisely what Kant had labored so diligently to prove impossible. Hegel's famous definition of world history as "the description of the spirit and how it labors to arrive at the knowledge of what it is in itself"[30] would no doubt have scandalized Kant.

This is not the place to attempt a thorough examination of Hegel's philosophy of history.[31] As Morris Cohen has pointed out somewhere, Hegel may be said to have helped to introduce the organic and historical method into the social sciences and the method of abstract ideology into history. The famous dialectic is, of course, part of the second enterprise, describing as it does according to Hegel the unfolding of reason in history. In this connection, Hegel assigns specific roles to specific peoples who come to the forefront to fulfill their particular assigned roles in carrying forward this process through its necessary stages of thesis, antithesis, and synthesis. In this connection, Hegel assigns primary value to the state as the "form of freedom" to the point where he glorifies the national state.[32]

This sanctification of the role of the national state in history as the carrier of the leading ideas, and thus as the preordained carrier-out of the destiny that is man's, culminated for Hegel

[30] "Die Darstellung des Geistes sei, wie er zum Wissen dessen zu kommen sich erarbeitet, was er an sich ist." Cf. *Die Vernunft in der Geschichte,* II, i, c. See also the following section (d) for more of this sort of thing: "Der Volksgeist ist als Gattung für sich existierend; hierin liegt die Moeglichkeit, dass in diesem Existierenden das Allgemeine, das in ihm ist, als das Entgegengesetzte erscheint . . . ," etc., etc.

[31] Perhaps the most thoughtful German effort to date is F. Rosenzweig, *Hegel und der Staat* (1920). Paul Barth, *Die Geschichtsphilosophie Hegels und der Hegelianer* (2nd ed., 1925), is also important. For Hegel's philosophy of history within the setting of his general philosophy, see Nicolai Hartman, *Die Philosophie des Deutschen Idealismus,* vol. II (1929), and Edward Caird, *Hegel* (1883).

[32] Attention deserves to be drawn to Toynbee's sharp rejection of this aspect of the Hegelian position when he denies that the history of national states constitutes an "intelligible field of study," and specifically asserts that "English history does not become intelligible until we view it as the history of a wider society of which Great Britain is a member . . ." (*A Study of History,* I, 23; cf. the entire section, pp. 22-26).

in the famous dictum that world history is the world court (*Die Weltgeschichte ist das Weltgerichte*). What this means is, of course, that the value of ideas, movements, states, nations is revealed by their success. It is another way of proclaiming that the actual is an embodiment of historical reason, and that "whatever is, is right." [33] Whether Hegel's view be accepted or rejected, it is necessary not to misinterpret it, as has been common, by interpreting his "actuality" as mere phenomena. On the contrary, throwing aside all that Kant's critical reëvaluation of reason and the rational faculties had attempted, Hegel in his position as an absolute idealist insisted that his dialectic method represented the divine plan of creation in its entirety, and was, therefore, the a priori pattern of all reality. While Hegel himself drew strictly conservative conclusions from this premise, it was not necessary to do so. Not only Marx[34] but bourgeois philosophers of the liberal era derived a potent challenge to existing institutions from this premise by declaring that the Prussian state was not rational, and hence not real in the sense of genuinely actual.

In any case, this idealization of actuality in terms of preconceived notions of right profoundly affects Hegel's concept of the state. Without entering here upon the complex issues involved in definitions of the state, it is clear that the Hegelian concept is closely akin to the *polis* concept of classical antiquity, especially as set forth by Plato and Aristotle. When Aristotle defines the *polis* as the highest community and hence organized for the highest good, he has in mind a political community built

[33] This line from Alexander Pope not only suggests that strong roots run from Hegel's rationalization of the actual to eighteenth-century rationalism and enlightenment, but also that the Germans have no monopoly on that sort of glorification of success. War in all such views must appear as a positive good which must be understood to be appreciated. How readily such views provide an underpinning for an opposition to political reform appears from Pope's other couplet in *Of Man:* "O'er forms of government let fools contest; that which is best administered is best."

[34] See Chapter VIII, below, for a discussion of the "materialist" version of Hegel's rationalization of history and its consequences.

upon the principle of group solidarity, in matters not only of politics and economics, but of religion, art, and all the numerous manifestations of the ritual of everyday life. *Polis,* therefore, designates both state and church rolled into one. Hegel's concept, while not identical with this view (any more than was Rousseau's), is nevertheless akin to it, in that the state is all-engulfing, the totality of values being in a sense comprised by it. It is not primarily the government, as is traditionally assumed by Englishmen and Americans, but the organized nation in all its manifestations.[35] In spite of such reinterpretations, the purely instrumental aspect of power and control has remained dominant in the concept of the state, and all cultural and national broadening of this concept served merely to adorn and glorify the coercive apparatus which a growing centralized bureaucracy with a standing army back of it wielded in pursuit of the relentless Hobbesian "search for power after power unto death." Hence it is not surprising to find Hegel and his followers indifferent, if not hostile, to the Kantian cosmopolitan ideal of eternal peace founded upon a world federation of constitutional governments. The inexorable forward march of the dialectic of ideas is realized through wars and battles deciding the fate of nations.

Like Darwin's survival of the fittest and the Spencerian evolutionary theme, the Hegelian philosophy of history does not know a separate and wholly autonomous realm of freedom and moral obligation which binds men to the pursuit of what to them appears right regardless of their estimate of its probable success. Hegel's philosophy is an implicit and explicit rejection, not only of the *Critique of Pure Reason,* whose mocking analysis was directed against Hegel's predecessors of the "whatever is, is right" school, but also of the *Critique of Practical Reason,* with

[35] The Hegelian school in England, men like Bosanquet, Green, and the rest, have introduced this approach into a great deal of English writing, and a similar development has more recently occurred in America in the wake of the writings of Hegelians of a variety of schools. Cf. *The New Belief in the Common Man* (1942), ch. ii, and the literature cited there.

its insistence upon the autonomy of free men to will that which they should want to will. It is finally a rejection likewise of the *Critique of Judgment,* with its clear recognition of the *telos,* or end, as something which judgment must seek to distill from "the actions of men" by careful observations and an evaluation of the intrinsic evidence.

The penetrating subtlety of Kant's position has precluded its general acceptance. Indeed, in large part, the nineteenth century was dominated by divergent systems of thought of which the Hegelian and Marxian are only prominent examples. Against these, the critical analysis of Kant has from time to time been reasserted. Wilhelm Dilthey subjected the Hegelian type of philosophy of history, and the corresponding systems of general sociology *à la* Comte to a searching critique. After examining the several special sciences or fields of study concerned with man and society, Dilthey raised the question: "Is there a science [*Wissenschaft*] which . . . can comprehend the relations which exist between historical fact, law, and the rule of guiding judgment?" This clearly Kantian triad Dilthey had previously defined as the threefold connection of every special inquiry with the whole of historical and social reality and knowledge: connection with the concrete causal nexus of all facts and changes of reality (*Wirklichkeit*), with the general laws which govern this reality, and with the system of values and standards.[36] Dilthey's answer is to deny the claim of both philosophy of history and sociology to fulfill this need. He argues persuasively that the problem is insoluble, that the methods of both are wrong, that they fail to understand the relation of the study of history to the social sciences, that the rise and decline of metaphysics raises the problem of a methodological foundation for the special fields in the humanities.

---

[36] Wilhelm Dilthey, *Einführung in die Geisteswissenschaften,* I, 89ff. What follows is a general indication of the position taken by Dilthey in the same work, pp. 93-120.

A sharp and explicit rejection of all philosophies of history was also offered by Jakob Burckhardt.[37] Burckhardt rejects the ideas of progress and providence as unhistorical, and restricts himself to the idea of continuity. This continuity is more than mere sequence; it is a sense of the past, a historical consciousness. It is a strictly subjective phenomenon, in Burckhardt's view, and we cannot know whether it has any corresponding basis in fact or whether a divine mind similarly conceives of history. Hence all judgments of right and wrong, of what is "fortunate" or "unfortunate," are relative to the observer, and cannot be considered conclusive beyond this subjective realm. As a recent writer has put it: "How different is this modern wisdom of Burckhardt's from all those philosophies of history—from Hegel to Augustine—which definitely knew or professed to know, the true desirability of historical events and successions!" [38] How different, also, from Kant's normative evaluation in terms of a non-historical realm of freedom.

Reason of state, so intimately linked to Machiavellian trends in the modern world, emerges from this Hegelian conception of history as an inescapable concomitant. Once the proposition is granted that the state is the carrier of the particular idea expressed in a national spirit in its ascendancy, and hence the essential instrumentality of the highest value, all that is required for completing the fateful doctrine is the further proposition that the building and maintaining of this state, pragmatically considered, requires the discarding of operationally irrelevant considerations. Such considerations may spring from a psychic or moral source of high and compelling import; they cannot significantly alter the course of action required of the servant of

---

[37] See *Weltgeschichtliche Betrachtungen* (1918). These have lately been published in an English version with a penetrating introduction by James Hastings Nichols, under the title *Force and Freedom—Reflections on History* (1943). See also the analysis by Karl Löwith in "The Theological Background of the Philosophy of History," *Social Research*, xiii (1946), 52-63.

[38] Löwith, p. 63.

the state, since all his actions are *infused* with the highest value—permeated by it, as it were. This frightful and fateful doctrine, often falsely and tritely stated as the doctrine of justifying the means by the end, has been gaining ground steadily in our own time.[39] While its prevalence is most marked in Fascist and Communist thought, the idea is by no means limited to totalitarian ranks. Not only were many similar arguments advanced by those who would subordinate "victory" to all other considerations in the late war, but even the building of a permanent peace has been advocated in corresponding terms. Thus Mr. Justice Jackson has repeatedly defended his position of the trial of war criminals on such grounds;[40] and courses of action are advocated for our relations with the Soviet Union on grounds of survival, against the Soviets' own unqualified adoption of a doctrine of reason of state in terms of their Marxist-Hegelian position. Marx, having substituted the class for the nation as the carrier of historical necessity, and having placed the dictatorship of the proletariat in the position occupied by the state in the Hegelian philosophy of history, provides as completely unqualified a value in the proletariat's historical mission of establishing a universal brotherhood of material well-being. The notorious amoral conduct of every little Communist functionary, so brilliantly portrayed by writers in our time, is nothing but the local and specific manifestation of a philosophy of history which infuses with superior value any action contributing to the success of the Soviet Union—that body politic which has come to occupy the

[39] The historical development of the idea of a reason of state was brilliantly traced by Friedrich Meinecke in *Die Idee der Staatsräson in der Neueren Geschichte* (1925); its philosophical limitations were sketched in my critical review of this volume in *American Political Science Review*, November 1926, p. 1064.

[40] Having discarded arguments drawn from natural law and having insisted on a positivist basis of existing law such as the Kellogg Pact, the American prosecutor was obliged to insist that it was justifiable to disregard such a basic norm as that no one should be punished for *ex post facto* crimes when it would have been better and wiser to argue that the crimes were recognized in natural law.

place of the state in the Hegelian epic of unfolding world history. To argue from the conduct of these petty commissars that a corresponding pattern of action and behavior is required of us is natural. But such a contention is likely to be rationalized by some kind of assertion that the American state is the savior and fulfillment of world history, or at any rate its next phase. "The American Century," expounded as a rallying cry by a leading American publisher, is a groping attempt to supply such a Hegelian basis of action. Within such a context, all kinds of amoral actions, including war, become infused with the higher value which they serve. That they may also become contributory elements in an emerging American Fascism few will deny who understand the deep relationship which exists between the Hegelian and neo-Hegelian philosophy of history and the Fascist glorification of the nation, its spirit and its state. The fact that the neo-Hegelian adoration of the British Empire which permeated the Oxford school did not carry them to the extremes of brutality and rascality distinguishing their latter-day brethren on the Continent proves little more than that its expounders occupied a more favored position. No believer in the doctrine of the reason of state is advocating violence for its own sake, but he readily condones it.

No such position can ever be developed from the Kantian premises. In terms of these, one would reject Mr. Justice Jackson's sophistical argument, that the end of peace justified the violation of the moral law, just as readily as he would reject the totalitarian doctrines which attribute absolute value to some kind of body politic as the supreme arm of destiny. Kant's critical approach to the problems of history enables him to project an end beyond all past experience: a universal reign of peace under law. But this end is not a "conclusion" drawn from phenomena, from the course of history as we know it, but is projected from the realm of freedom which contains the norms for all human conduct. It cannot therefore be made the ground for violating the fundamental law of this realm, which is the categorical imperative. Kant cannot, like Hegel and Marx, be brought to glorify war.[41] The moral law, the challenge of creative freedom, the *telos* of man, transcend all empirical data and cannot be derived from them.

In this chapter I have tried to show how the idea of a universal peace is linked to Kant's philosophy of history. It could not be otherwise. The destiny of man must be faced by him who would build a lasting peace. It is Kant's unique contribution to have shown in his philosophy of history that such an enterprise is not precluded by the actual and foreseeable course of history. But how it is derived from the higher reason which constitutes the realm of freedom needs further and fuller exploration. That the problem is not the afterthought of an old man, but central to Kant's philosophizing, can be seen from the fact that both the *Critique of Pure Reason* and the *Critique of Practical Reason* address themselves to the problem at a crucial point.[42] Without a more complete analysis of this foundation it will not be possible to grasp the full meaning of his approach to peace—nor ours.

[41] In the case of Marx it is, of course, the class war.
[42] See *Critique of Pure Reason,* part ii, section 2 (*Werke,* iii, 347ff), and *Critique of Practical Reason* (*Werke,* v, 48ff).

❧ III ❧

FREEDOM AND NECESSITY
IN THEIR RELATION
TO THE PHILOSOPHY OF PEACE

A pragmatic age is prone to forget that most political thought rests upon philosophical premises. The rival thought patterns of Communism, Fascism, and democracy are built upon assumptions which none of them undertake to prove, all of them take for granted. So general has become the acceptance of naturalistic, materialistic science that all social phenomena are, rightly or wrongly, interpreted in deterministic terms. Value judgments, normative appraisals, imperatives of any kind are considered suitable for the preacher's pulpit, the political orator's platform, or the propagandist's effusions, especially in war time. But the same man in a workaday mood, the tool-conscious toiler and the efficiency engineer, as well as the men-of-the-mind who emulate them, avoid all such "nonsense" and proceed to go about their business without further ado. In doing so, these "realists" forget that the tools of their minds were fashioned for them by men with more subtle imaginations. Such more imaginative folk have a more self-reflective appreciation of the words by which the goals and ends of all the businesses and machines are designated. Five-year plans, four-year plans, three-year plans, get-ready-for-war plans and get-ready-for-peace plans—they all turn upon words which embody ideas shaped by the minds who entertain them. These minds are as much a part of the whole situation as the material facts and the naturalistic fancies which the realists behold.

Our political ideas, whatever they may be, are sired by men of comprehensive, even if mistaken, views. Machiavelli and Hobbes, Spinoza and Locke, Rousseau and Kant—these names conjure up the key concepts of modern political thought. In saying this, we by no means necessarily embrace the belief that their ideas are causes or determinants of institutional configurations or patterns of behavior. They are antecedents in the realm of thought resembling the mother tree scattering its seedlings all about. And it is one very striking characteristic of these powerful shapers of thought that they were by no means all determinists. In fact, those among them whom the democracies would more readily acknowledge as their inspiration—Locke, Rousseau and Kant—are voluntarists, that is they believe in the reality of freedom and the operative causal impact of freely willing persons. The determinists—among them Machiavelli, Hobbes and Spinoza—are glorifiers of power and have delivered some of the intellectual armor of the Fascist creed.

One of the most important questions of political theory in historical perspective is why democratic ideology, the philosophy of the coöperative commonwealth, should be thus associated with a philosophical outlook which the climate of opinion in our time does not favor. For if the connection between voluntarism, the metaphysics of the free will, and constitutionalism and democracy is inherently necessary, it augurs ill for the future of our scheme of things—unless the climate of opinion changes and the deterministic position is abandoned. This problem is as central to the issue of a lasting peace as it is to the future of democratic constitutionalism. For peace can be lasting only on one or the other of the two opposed assumptions, *either* by voluntary agreement between free peoples or by involuntary subjection of all powers under one. The first of these assumptions obviously underlies the San Francisco Charter, the second constitutes the totalitarian approach. The world being what it is, the second alternative cannot be realized except by a series of further wars in the course of which the weaker would be subjected by the stronger.

But can there be voluntary agreement? Is there any ground for assuming that men are free to will their future? Kant would not have been the profound thinker that he was had he not faced this issue squarely. And he answers: Yes, there can be voluntary agreement; men can will their future. But does Kant therefore deny the unbroken chain of natural causation? Does he deny determinism? By no means. Having shown, in the *Critique of Pure Reason,* that the category of cause was a "necessary form" of the speculative reason—that is to say, i.e. the observing mind —he was bound to state the determinist position uncompromisingly, and he does so in the following passage:

All actions of man as they appear to the senses are determined by his empirical character and by the other concomitant causes according to the order of nature; and if we could investigate all the phenomena of his will to the bottom, there would not be a single human action which we could not predict and which we could not recognize as necessitated by its preceding conditions. In regard to this empirical character there does not exist any freedom, and it is only thus that we can consider man when we merely *observe*.[1]

It would be hard to state the deterministic position more radically. This statement would satisfy a Hobbes, according to whom "man is but a machine" [2] and all his actions subject to mechanical laws. And yet there are some important qualifications. It is merely the *empirical* character for which this statement holds, and only the actions as they appear to the senses, the actions as phenomena, for which the argument is advanced. What is the

[1] *Critique of Pure Reason* (*Werke,* iii, 430). Italics Kant's.
[2] *Leviathan,* Introduction and Book I. For further elaboration of the Hobbesian position see Chapter IV, below.

opposite of the empirical character? And what other aspect of the actions is reserved which does *not* appear to the senses? It is the aspect of the actions which appears when we consider them in relation to reason, says Kant, not speculative reason which explains, but practical reason which itself creates the actions themselves. We enter upon an entirely different level of discourse, says Kant, an entirely different order from the order of nature. For when so considered, the action *should* perhaps not have happened at all, although it obviously did happen and according to the course of nature inevitably had to happen. This "antinomy," as Kant calls it, is central to human thought, because "one can think only of two kinds of causality for whatever happens, namely either that of nature or that of freedom." Pointing this moral at our present problem of war and peace, one may show that the war had to happen, that Hitler who declared it, and all the Nazi generals who waged it in accordance with his command, were mere pawns in the hand of nature which predetermined all these actions as they appeared by natural and inescapable causes; and yet—we hold him and his camp-followers responsible, because Hitler was nevertheless free not to act thus, since he possessed reason and "decided" to act as he did.[3] In other words, Kant recognizes two realms, the realm of nature and the realm of freedom, the one governed by the laws of nature and the other by the moral law. They are both equally given in the mind of man, and neither one of them can be proved to be "the thing in itself" which is behind the curtain of the *phenomena* and below the sky of the *noumena*. This thing in itself, or *Ding an sich*, we can never know.

These expressions, which frequently recur in the Kantian discussion of these problems, are of course two further ways of indicating the basic dualism of nature and freedom, of observa-

[3] For an elaboration of the problems of war guilt and its punishment see Chapter VII, below.

tion and action, of the pure reason and the practical reason, and so forth. The literature on Kant's philosophy cited in the bibliography is full of discussions on this subject.[4]

Before we consider the problem of this dualism, it will be best to explore fully the meaning of the realm of freedom.[5] For it obviously "exists" in a very peculiar way. Toward the end of the discussion which we have quoted from the *Critique of Pure Reason,* Kant explicitly states that his argument does not pretend to demonstrate the existential reality (*Wirklichkeit*) of freedom. Nor does it even demonstrate the *possibility* of freedom. He merely shows freedom to be what he calls a transcendental idea. It is important to recall that according to Kant ideas are "necessary," not arbitrary or fictitious conceptions, in that they derive from the very nature of reason. Nothing in nature corresponds to them exactly. He illustrates this approach with the basic ideas of the Euclidean geometry. It has been held by many that the rise of non-Euclidean geometry destroys Kant's approach. This is incorrect; for Kant treats these ideas as hypothetical, even though "necessary" and subject to evolution as reason develops. A transcendental idea is an idea which defines the conditions of potential experience. It provides the necessary form, or channel, or mold for experience without which no experience can be had or even thought of.[6] The Kantian idea of freedom unfolds slowly, but the wonder at the complete dichotomy between "the starred heavens above"

[4] Cf., for example, Kuno Fisher, *A Critique of Kant,* trans. by W. S. Hough (1888); Friedrich Paulsen, *Immanuel Kant, His Life and Doctrine* (1916).

[5] The problem of causation and the laws of nature will be more fully considered in Chapter IV, below.

[6] The attempt of W. T. Jones's *Morality and Freedom in the Philosophy of Immanuel Kant* (1940) to reinterpret the Kantian moral philosophy in monistic terms, though searching, cannot be accepted. It is to be regretted that Kant's ideas are treated without adequate attention to their evolution, with the result that Jones believes "consistency" to be "hardly a Kantian virtue." Kant is consistent enough, if his basic dualism is accepted and his thought of different periods is not treated as homologous, which it patently is not, any more than that of Plato, Aristotle, or Hobbes.

and "the moral law within" persists. These are the data to which reason brings the unifying ideas of causality and freedom for purposes of giving meaning and thus providing understanding.

The quintessence of the transcendental idea of freedom is this: it enables reason to think of that which is not conditioned by anything in the world of the senses as commencing the sequence of conditions as they appear to the senses. But as it stands, this idea of freedom involves reason in an antinomy with itself as it speculates upon the course of nature, since such speculation requires bringing in the ordering principle or idea of causality. Hence there are two ways of looking at such situations, two grounds upon which to consider them: the causality of nature, and the causality of freedom. The necessity of the first rests upon the law of nature, the necessity of the latter upon the moral law. Unless this dualism is comprehended, no sense can be made of either the natural or the moral world. The prime datum of "experience" in the latter is the moral law, the recognition of the "ought." But this is not sense experience, but the experience of willing. Thus the moral law is the *causa cognoscendi* of freedom; we discover freedom through experiencing the compulsion of the moral law. Freedom, on the other hand, is the *causa essendi* of the moral law, because without freedom there could not even be the thought of a moral law.[7]

This way of putting the matter raises clearly the problem of causation. Within the context of Western thought no problem has been more central to all scientific inquiry. The study of politics and history has been no exception to the rule. It is well known, of course, that one of the primary objectives of the Kantian *Critique of Pure Reason* was to refute the skeptical position of Hume which insisted that causal relationships were not observed in nature, but were imputed to things whose sequence was observed recurrently in time. Without going into

[7] *Werke*, iii, 422-441.

the philosophy of Hume at length here,[8] we must note that Hume utilized his rejection of cause as a "law of nature" for a purely hedonistic theory of volition. "By the will," he said, "I mean nothing but the internal impression we feel, and are conscious of, when we consciously give rise to any new motion of our body, or new perception of our mind." That this definition is subject to criticism on various grounds is obvious. But since the law of causation, so called, means nothing more than that our impressions of phenomena follow a certain regularity and order of succession, we are justified in applying that same fictitious law of causation to internal impressions, if our experience suggests an orderly succession of them. Deeply convinced, as Hume was, of the essential likeness of all men, he therefore looked to history as the field of knowledge from which to gather the necessary insight into what he termed "the constant and universal principles of human nature." He insisted that the men whom Aristotle, Polybius, and Tacitus dealt with are as like to ourselves as the earth, air, and water of Attica now and then. Therefore he could argue that "the chief use of history" is the discovery of these universal principles. History shows men in all kinds of circumstances and conditions, and through its study we become familiar with "the regular springs of human action and behavior." This rigid and unbroken determinism is most strikingly expressed by Hume's definition of liberty: "a power of acting or not acting, according to the determinations of the will." [9] These determinations follow regularities which make men "universally acknowledge a uniformity in human motives and actions as well as in the operations of the body." Hume's

[8] See for further detail Chapter V, below, p. 151, and Chapter VII, p. 188. Cf. also Thomas H. Huxley, *Hume* (1896), especially ch. x, where Hume's doctrine of volition, liberty, and necessity is summed up. The basic source is, of course, Book II, Part III, Section 1 of Hume's *A Treatise of Human Nature* (1739-40).

[9] The preceding quotations are from Section VIII, entitled "Of Liberty and Necessity" in *An Enquiry Concerning Human Understanding* (1777).

skepticism regarding causation and his skepticism concerning
absolute norms are both born of his general skepticism about
the human mind and reason.

Hume's proposition was not frontally attacked by Kant, but
was put into a different perspective by Kant's accepting Hume's
view that causation cannot be derived from experience, but then
insisting that causation is itself the premise upon which all
experience rests, since without it no experience is possible to
the speculative reason. It is the form, the mold, the tool of the
mind as it observes the things as they appear. This position
is the terminal point in a development which for its starting
point goes back to Aristotle. The Aristotelian doctrine of the
four causes underwent a steady transformation as Western
science developed. In retrospect, and looking at this development in terms of the meaning with which the term "cause"
has come to be indentified, we find the Aristotelian doctrine
"difficult to understand" in that neither the formal, nor the
material, nor the final cause are causes in the modern sense.
Only the efficient cause has remained as the essence of the idea
of causation. This difficulty can easily be reduced, however, if
we recall that the Greek word *aitia,* as well as the Latin *causa,*
is derived from court proceedings, and originally means the
ground upon which an action is pleaded. Looked at in this perspective, the Aristotelian doctrine is in point of fact not a doctrine of causation at all, but merely a doctrine as to the frames
of reference in terms of which any given thing or phenomenon
may be considered. Either its matter, its form, its end, or its
"cause" may be the basis for discussing it. Leaving aside the
issues connected with the first two as not relevant to the present
issue,[10] there still remain two frames of reference: end and cause.

[10] It is encouraging to find these views supported in a recent study of the
problems of the Aristotelian doctrine of causation: Richard McKeon, "Aristotle's Conception of Moral and Political Philosophy," *Ethics,* April 1941, pp.
253ff.

These are "grounds" upon which to consider a phenomenon,[11] and it is in terms of these "grounds for being" (*Seinsgründe*) that Kant states his doctrine of a dual causality, the causality of freedom and the causality of nature.

But how can freedom "cause" anything? The question sounds absurd, but this paradoxicality is deceptive, since the word cause is not used in the sense of an efficient cause by Kant when he puts this question. The efficient causes belong to the realm of nature, and their nexus is complete and unbreakable. What then is "grounded" in freedom? What exists because freedom exists? Kant answers, a man's way of thinking, his *Denkungsart*. But in putting it thus Kant means this pattern of thinking interpreted not as part of the realm of nature as psychology would interpret it, but as a purely normative scheme. The moral law which each and all acknowledge is the idea that a man *ought to do something*, whatever it is, because it is right. What is right is strictly *noumenal* and cannot be determined by anyone but the man himself. That is the reason why no might ever makes right, since no conclusions can be drawn from what happens in the realm of nature regarding what ought to happen in the realm of freedom.

A full comprehension of this strictly dualistic position is essential for an appreciation of Kant's position with regard to peace and war. War is a phenomenon of nature which has its causes and which can be avoided, by men who understand these causes, through the manipulation of nature. But the reason men should avoid war, and the "ground" upon which they must act in their efforts to achieve peace, are normative and belong to the realm of freedom. Hence they will feel compelled to act even against overwhelming odds. It is their reason which shows them that this is the end and fulfillment of mankind. Why?

[11] The discussion of this problem in English is more difficult than in Greek, Latin, or German, because the word *Grund*, like *aitia* and *causa*, is associated with the concept of "pleading." Cf., however, the searching modern treatment of the problem by Robert M. MacIver, *Social Causation* (1942).

Kant does not explicitly answer this question in *Eternal Peace,* although he repeatedly states that peace is a "duty" which reason discovers in the moral law,[12] and war a "scourge of mankind." In fact, he refers his reader, toward the end of the essay, to a forthcoming work in which he intends to deal with this question. This work is the *Theory of Law (Rechtslehre)* which appeared in 1798 as part of *Die Metaphysik der Sitten.* In its conclusion it states Kant's position with great emphasis: Eternal peace is the highest political good. The duty of striving for its achievement is in no wise determined by the chances of its realization: "It is our duty to act according to the idea of such an end (which reason commands) even if there is not the least probability that it can be achieved, provided its impossibility cannot be demonstrated." This last proviso is made by Kant because, according to his moral philosophy, nothing which can be shown to be impossible can be morally obligatory.[13] Kant is confident that such a demonstration is entirely out of the question, as he had indeed shown to the contrary both in his *Eternal Peace* and in his *Idea for a General History* that a workable order for the maintenance of peace was probable in the light of past human history, and had reinforced that demonstration by showing in *The Argument of the Faculties* that progress in the moral sense of a spread of civilization is the probable pattern of human history.[14]

But why does reason command peace? Kant speaks of the

---

[12] Karl Vorländer has brought together the different passages in Kant's works dealing with peace in his special edition of Kant's *Zum Ewigen Frieden* (Leipzig: Feliz Meiner, 1919), and has dealt with the problem at some length in his valuable introduction. See esp. p. xxiii.

[13] This position is one of the important links between the realm of nature and the realm of freedom, and will be more fully discussed in Chapter VI. Obviously, the impossible is incompatible with the categorical imperative. See below, p. 175.

[14] *Der Streit der Fakultäten (Werke,* vii, 391ff). This curious work contains a most vigorous denunciation of war, quoting Hume's view that a war between nations resembles a row between drunkards. Here Kant calls war "the greatest hindrance to morality."

"absolute veto of practical reason": *there shall be no war,*
neither between individuals nor between states. "For this is not
the way in which one should seek one's right." In other words,
the idea of peace flows from the idea of right. "One may say
that the general and continuous establishment of peace constitutes not only a part, but the entire end and purpose of a theory
of right within the limits of pure reason; for the state of peace
is the only state in which what is mine and what is thine are
secure *under laws* among a multitude of neighboring men" (the
italics are Kant's). Such a multitude of neighbors living under
laws are hence together under a constitution. "The provisions
[*Regel*] of such a constitution are not, however, derived from
the experience of those who have been best off under it to date,
but are deduced by reason a priori from the ideal of a rightful
[*rechtlich*] association of men under public [constitutional]
law." [15] "All examples, because they illustrate but do not prove
anything, are treacherous and require a metaphysics . . ."

One can not but feel that Kant's answer is somewhat inadequate and abstract. To argue the moral necessity of peace solely
upon the basis of the security of the mine and thine under laws
may be very persuasive to a bourgeois society (even if the expression "mine and thine" is not taken in the narrow sense of
mere material property), but it certainly lacks universal significance.[16] This universal significance is there, nevertheless. But

---

[15] *Die Metaphysik der Sitten, Werke,* vii, 160-162. It may be worth noting
here that Kant by implication rejects the position of Edmund Burke and his romantic followers and predecessors in Germany, men like Justus Moeser and
Gentz, who stressed tradition and "right by prescription." Kant, in keeping
with the ideas of the French Revolution, thinks in terms of universal and abstract right. See below, Chapter V.

[16] Kant's stress on property is brought out by Reinhold Aris in his *History
of Political Thought in Germany from 1789 to 1815,* pp. 96ff, but Aris overstates
his point and consistently overlooks the Kantian affinity with socialism which
Karl Vorländer has analyzed in a number of works. Cf., for example, Vorländer's *Kant und Marx* (1911), to which we find no reference in Aris. Aris,
however, quotes some of the most relevant passages in Kant's work which
contradict his own position. Cf. also Chapter VIII, below.

the absolute veto which reason opposes to war was so self-evident
to Kant, it seems, that he never fully stated the answer which his
own ethical philosophy provides. We might start with a famous
statement in which Kant vindicates the idea that consent is essential to true law. "Nobody can compel me to be happy in
some way which he believes to be the good life for other people;
rather may everybody seek his happiness in the fashion which
seems good to him, if only he does not reduce the freedom of
others to seek a similar end . . ." [17] Reason commands, in other
words, that rights must be compatible, and it is inconceivable
that under law two persons have a right to the same thing. They
may have such a right in fact under an empirical system of law;
but that merely proves that there is a defect in the empirical
system.[18] "Right—law—is the restriction of the freedom of
everybody so that it accords with the freedom of everybody else,
in so far as this is possible according to a general law." [19] These
phrases are clearly akin to the "freedom from fear" and the
"freedom under law" which have been written on the banner
of the United Nations. They are common to the French and
English revolutions and are deeply embedded in the key efforts
of thinkers during the latter struggle.[20] If, therefore, Kant's
contribution stopped here, one would be justified in considering
him rather unoriginal. But against these views in their simple
form as just stated formidable critics had arisen, who, like
Hobbes and Hume, had argued that no right could be imagined
except that which the sovereign, whoever he might be, had

[17] This phrasing occurs in *Theory and Practice* (1793). The parallelism to
the famous sentence of Frederick the Great quoted above (Chapter II, footnote 15) is striking.

[18] Hence Kant's observation that no true theory of law or right can be derived from empirical observation of actual systems of law. See *Theory of Law*
(1797), *Werke*, v, 317ff.

[19] *Theory and Practice*, II, second paragraph.

[20] Cf. G. P. Gooch, *English Democratic Ideas in the XVII Century* (2nd ed.,
1927), and Charles H. McIlwain, *Constitutionalism, Ancient and Modern*
(1940).

willed. It should be remembered that Kant's second chapter in *Theory and Practice* is specifically directed against Hobbes. In alleging that these propositions flow directly from human reason a priori and without any reference whatsoever to any empirical ends such as are usually comprehended under the general term of happiness, Kant reclaimed an absolute validity for "right" and "rights" which from his standpoint was unchallengeable.

This standpoint is, as pointed out before, that of a sharp differentiation of the realm of nature and the realm of freedom, of laws of nature and moral law. If this dualism is neglected, the Kantian position becomes incomprehensible. Now the basic law (*Grundgesetz*) of the realm of freedom, the law which formulates in categorical terms the command which flows from the definition of freedom under law, is the famous "categorical imperative" which Kant had deduced in the *Critique of Practical Reason* and which is assumed to be familiar to readers of *Eternal Peace* and *Theory of Law*. The pure, practical reason is legislating directly here, Kant tells us. "Act in such a way that the maxim of your will could at all times be valid as a principle of universal legislation." [21] To attack Kant for the formalism of this basic law is to miss his central achievement, which lay precisely in this reduction of the idea of law to its formal aspect.[22] He is fully aware of the fact that he has excluded all "material" ethics, all specific rules and definite content. He has done so because these specifications do not belong to the world of reason and of the *noumena* but to the world of empirical observation and of *phenomena*. "The will is here thought of as independent of empirical conditions, that is to say as pure will determined

---

[21] *Werke,* v, 141. This basic law has repeatedly been the subject of searching criticism, from Schopenhauer to the present, especially on the score of its formalism. The most comprehensive and uncompromising recent analysis is Max Scheler's *Der Formalismus in der Ethik und die materiale Wertethik* (1921).

[22] Kant occupies a middle position concerning the important distinction of an ethics based on law as contrasted with one based on virtue. See H. Spiegelberg, *Gesetz und Sitten-Gesetz* (1935) and my review in *Isis,* October 1936.

solely by the form of the law, and this determining ground considered as the highest condition of all maxims" (the italics are Kant's).

From this basic position, Kant's argument proceeds to set forth that any freedom other than that which is compatible with the freedom of others is self-contradictory and hence can not be made the principle of universal legislation. It does not take any great amount of logic to derive from this set of propositions the absolute veto against war; for peace is essentially nothing else than the state of constitutional order where general laws consented to by all prevent raw license from striving after that which is also sought by others without regard for the other's right.

It is clear that self-realization in the Kantian philosophy is not so much a psychological phenomenon belonging to the realm of nature as it is a moral phenomenon belonging to the realm of freedom. And yet there must be somewhere a connection between the two realms. This connection Kant does not explicitly concern himself with in the *Critique of Judgment,* where the teleological position is strikingly revealed, but it obviously is the mind in which, and through which, the transcendental ideas a priori operate in enabling man to relate himself to others and to the world.[23] It is the mind which relates values or norms, the realm of freedom, of *noumena,* to the realm of sensory experience, the realm of the observation, of *phenomena.*

How vital the mind's function is in this task of relating the two spheres, the problem of peace demonstrates with striking impressiveness. As we have seen, Kant is not satisfied with demonstrating a conclusion in favor of peace with reference to only one of these two realms. In Chapter II, we have shown that his teleological judgment and his philosophy of history both support the possibility—nay, the probability—of universal peace. Such a

[23] Kant's is neither an ethics merely of law nor one purely of virtue. See below, Chapter VI.

demonstration is decidedly relevant to the moral problem of peace as a duty, as an emanation and manifestation of the categorical imperative. "There shall be no war" is a moral law which would be invalid if the impossibility of its realization could be demonstrated. No one can be obliged to strive for the impossible, as we have seen. But the impossibility of universal peace can *not* be demonstrated. That there always have been wars constitutes no rational proof of their continuing necessity. Freedom and its realm of moral laws is, therefore, linked to cause and its realm of natural sequences, of determinism and necessity, by the fact that the free man is also the natural man, that it is his duty to realize the potentialities of his self, but that it cannot be his duty to do more than is possible and attempt to realize what is beyond his potentialities.

Thus freedom becomes the one and only inborn and imperishable human right. "Freedom, that is, independence from the arbitrary compulsion of another, is the sole, original right which belongs to each human being by virtue of his humanity, in so far as such freedom can coexist with the freedom of all other human beings according to universal law." [24] Here we have the core of the idea of freedom and self-realization as the essence of a philosophy of peace according to critical rationalism. It is a manly and unsentimental doctrine which need not fear the militarist's familiar attack upon pacifism as soft and unrealistic. Cassirer is right when he comments upon the often-heard critics of Kant's severity by stressing the liberating and revitalizing effect of his rigorous doctrine of universal freedom under law. Unfortunately, we cannot follow him when he expresses the view that this aspect of Kant's moral teaching affected the nation and the age, and gave it a new direction. On the contrary, we feel that the quintessence of Kant's doctrine of freedom and self-realization through the establishment of a reign of universal peace was largely missed by German, and even European, think-

---

[24] *Die Metaphysik der Sitten* (*Werke,* vii, 39). See also Chapter V, below.

ers and poets. His views struck a more sympathetic chord among the radical elements in England and America. The kinship of his basic premises with certain Christian, and more especially Puritan, beliefs helped to crystallize efforts to bring about what Kant had taught to be the natural end and inherent duty of mankind. But even today the world is far from a realization of the full significance of this doctrine of universal freedom under law.

PEACE AND NATURAL LAW
AS DIVINELY ORDAINED ORDER:
THE CHRISTIAN TRADITION

The ejection of God from nature and its laws had been pretty well completed by the time Kant conceived his philosophy. The heavenly city of the eighteenth-century philosophers—the city of reason and enlightenment—had been erected[1] and Kant was to complete it by bringing it down to earth. In the process of doing so he badly jolted the structure, so that one of his fellow philosophers, Moses Mendelsohn, called him the "crusher of everything" (*Alleszermalmer*). But, as Kant in criticizing Mendelsohn's pessimism concerning man points out, moral progress and eternal peace are realizable because they are rational, because they are appropriate practical ends, and because they are right in theory.[2] In other words, the law of nature which consists of "the dictates of right reason" and the laws of nature

---

[1] Carl Becker, in *The Heavenly City of the Eighteenth-Century Philosophers* (1933), implied by this phrase—and made the idea explicit in his treatment—that the faith of the eighteenth-century philosophers in reason was essentially parallel to the faith of an earlier age in the *Civitas Dei*. I am afraid that I cannot agree. The faith of the Christian in his heavenly city was supernatural and based upon revelation, whereas the faith of the eighteenth century was natural and based upon reason itself. To be sure, this faith has a metaphysical root, but I would stress that a metaphysics which is based upon ratiocination can be equated with a metaphysics founded upon revelation only from the standpoint of a complete agnostic or skeptic. That position, however, is the most difficult of all, because of the paradox involved in reasoning against reason.

[2] "Concerning the Common Saying: That may be true in theory, but does not apply to practice," an article which appeared in *Berlinische Monatsschrift* (1793), cited as *Theory and Practice* (*Werke*, vi, 355ff).

which are "generalizations concerning established matters of fact" are joined together in the concept of a "destiny of humanity" and the progress which leads to it.

Kant's moral and political writings, especially the essay concerning eternal peace, are plainly in the tradition of the natural law and natural rights, and he made every effort to make his doctrine compatible with his critical approach to reason.[3] Yet the dualism of the realm of nature and the realm of freedom which has been analyzed in Chapters II and III posed problems of peculiar difficulty in the field of natural-law doctrine—difficulties which were not new, but have a long history of their own. Indeed, the extended process of transformation by which medieval natural law became the rationalist doctrine of eighteenth-century absolutism was filled with precisely this issue of the relationship between the realm of nature and the realm of reason.[4]

To look upon nature and reason as antithetical to each other is an ever recurring tendency of human thought. It dominates the great metaphysical speculations of the Middle Ages. But on the other hand, it is well known that modern natural science is founded upon the contrary belief that nature is governed by laws, and that it is the task of man to discover this rationality, to find the laws which govern nature and thus to depict nature

---

[3] We know Kant's views on natural law both from his systematic *Rechtslehre* and from a number of small special works, particularly his reviews of Hufeland. There is a slow evolution to be noted from the traditional rationalist position, through the Rousseauistic phase in which reason becomes "will" as general "will," to the final "critical" conclusion of the *Critique of Practical Reason* and the *Rechtslehre*. It is not admissible, as is habitual with many authors, to quote passages from Kant's works as if they were all written at the same time and from the same point of view.

[4] In my *Johannes Althusius' Politica Methodice Digesta* (1932), ch. iv, paragraphs 1 and 2, I stated this problem in its relation to Calvinist theology. The position I took was critically examined by A. Passerin d'Entrèves in "Giovanni Althusio e el Problema methodologico nella storia della filosofia politica e giuridica," *Rivista Internazionale di Filosofia del Diritto,* Anno xv, Fasc. iv-v (1935), to which I replied in the same issue in an article entitled "Diritto naturale e leggi di natura."

as the rational cosmos God has willed it to be. To meet this challenge, natural science has developed since the sixteenth century a set of distinctive methods for the study of nature, of which observation, measurement, experimentation, and generalization based upon observed matter of fact are outstanding features.

Such empiricism raises peculiar difficulties, however, when thought turns to law and government. For when the focus of interest becomes man, the issue of the laws of his nature cannot be as simply resolved as the "scientific" method implies. Though it is readily seen that the "ought" perennially clashes with what "is," the belief in norms and values is as readily observed in men as is their inclination to act contrary to their beliefs. We cannot escape from this dilemma by having recourse to the usual appeal to laws of nature, because the "laws of human nature"— valid generalizations based upon observed behavior and conduct —leave the realm of reason as one of the facets of human nature to be observed, analyzed, and generalized about. That, as we have seen, was precisely at the center of Kant's philosophical speculation. In order fully to appreciate his contribution to modern political thought, we shall have to explore the evolution of the law of nature from the end of the Middle Ages to the time of Kant.

A detailed and documented history of the law of nature is one of the most imposing and as yet unfulfilled tasks in the field of the history of ideas.[5] All we propose to do here is to sketch this history from one particular standpoint, the secularization of natural law. By this we mean the slow process extending from the sixteenth to the eighteenth century, in the course of which "God was ejected from natural law." This process had a dual aspect, depending on whether the idea of *law* or the idea of *na-*

---

[5] A very valuable beginning was made by Otto von Gierke in his *Natural Law and the Theory of Society 1500-1800,* translated with an introduction by Ernest Barker (1934).

ture was being stressed. We must therefore trace the interrelation of two ideas: one, the idea of a law of nature consisting of rules of "right reason," and the other, the contrasting idea of laws of nature which though beyond the finite reason of man are presumed to underly nature. Further to limit the task, we shall, after a brief discussion of Luther's own position, select for analysis a few outstanding representatives whose thought is vitally related to the prevailing theologies of the period.[6] Melanchthon and Oldendorp for orthodox Lutheranism, Hooker for Anglicanism, Althusius for Calvinism, and Suarez for Catholicism when taken together should give a fair idea of how the doctrine of the law of nature was developing after the Reformation, in the view of the several dominant trends of Christian faith. Grotius will next be considered, because he attempted to transcend the several different theologies in terms of a natural religion and a "right reason" which harked back to the Stoics. Finally, we shall treat a series of philosophers who undertook to construct a law of nature without the benefit of clergy. From Catholicism stemmed Descartes, from Calvinism Hobbes and indirectly Spinoza, from Lutheranism Pufendorf, and from Anglicanism Locke. The welter of eighteenth-century systems, such as those of Wolff, Thomasius, and Vattel, though they are increasingly readable and clear, consist of little more than so many restatements of the positions arrived at in the great seventeenth century. Rather than deal with these, we shall conclude with an analysis of Hume's and Kant's positions relative to the law of nature in view of Hume's trenchant critique. Kant's view has been called unoriginal, but when seen within the con-

---

[6] Ernst Troeltsch, "Das stoisch-christliche und das moderne profane Naturrecht," *Historische Zeitschrift*, 106:237ff (February 1911). Troeltsch later referred to this topic in a lecture entitled "Ideas of Natural Law and Humanity," reprinted in translation by Ernest Barker in the Gierke volume cited above. This is a very unfortunate sketch of the problem—preoccupied as the author seems to be with ephemeral political controversy.

text of his general jurisprudence, it is anything but that. However, we are anticipating.

In English-speaking countries, the problem of the "law of nature" has been complicated by a linguistic difficulty. The word "law" has to serve for both *jus* and *lex*. Thus the "law of nature" may refer, as we already have said, to two very different referents, namely (1) to a legal or moral standard based on reason, and (2) to a generalization believed to be valid because based upon established matter of fact.[7] Of course, in so far as reason or reasoning itself is believed to constitute "established matter of fact," the two approaches imperceptibly merge into one another. And yet, a rather striking difference in emphasis remains. This is especially true as long as standards and norms are believed to be traceable to divine revelation so that "reason" is "revealed" in these "commandments of God." The formula of laws derived from such a source is an "ought" which man is called upon to obey. "Do unto others as you would have others do unto you." The scientific inquirer, on the other hand, would put the question: "Do men do unto others as they would have others do unto them?" He would then consult experience and would finally return with the answer: "Men do not do unto others as they would have them do unto them." The "scientific" laws of nature are likely to deviate from the "normative" laws of nature.

The naturalism of the Renaissance found its most poignant expression, as far as politics is concerned, in the writings of Niccolo Machiavelli.[8] Although himself deeply inspired by the

[7] For what follows, cf. my article "Diritto naturale e leggi di natura," in *Rivista Internazionale di Filosofia del Diritto,* 1935. In this connection also see Giorgio del Vecchio, *Il Concette della natura ed il principio del diritto* (1908; 2nd ed., 1922), or, in translation, *The Formal Bases of Law* based on the first edition.

[8] English and American thought, and more especially political thought, has to this day resisted the "Machiavellian" approach to government. Hence we do not have a single first-class treatment of the great Florentine in English. An article by R. N. Carew in the *Hibbert Journal,* October 1928, brought out

classical ideal of the warrior hero and his virtue, he shocked the age by blandly stating as observed matter of fact what most practical men knew to be the actual practice in government and politics. Everyone read Machiavelli, but few acknowledged the truth of his assertions. Machiavelli was not a systematic thinker, and he did not undertake to formulate his observations in scientific form. Yet throughout his writings there runs like a red thread the passion for looking at political behavior as it actually is. This passion is nourished by Machiavelli's conviction that the greatest work of art is an organized community, or state, and that the greatest artist is the builder and organizer of a *civitas,* or state. It is in keeping with the characteristic approach of the Italian Renaissance to conceive the state as a work of art. Its "climate of opinion" was predominantly aesthetic.[9] Once the state is seen as a work of art, it becomes of paramount importance to grasp fully the nature of the materials with which the statesman-artist has to work. In Machiavelli's approach there pulsates the passion for superb workmanship which had led the Florentine painters and sculptors to the peak of creative achievement. To understand the laws of human nature appeared a task comparable to that of understanding the laws of perspective or gravitation, or the nature of various materials and colors. Even the most shocking phrases in *The Prince* are thus related to the task in hand, and Machiavelli's misfortune was lack of adequate information. This led him to generalize from observing the political practices of Renaissance courts, which represented a low ebb in political conduct not reached again until our own time.

---

the importance of the *virtù* ideal. George H. Sabine in his *History of Political Theory* (1937) has given a reasonably good sketch, but the lack of a comprehensive treatment is deeply felt. The history of the impact of Machiavellian thought on European political theory is superbly treated by Friedrich Meinecke in his *Die Idee der Staaträson in der Neueren Geschichte* (1925). For an examination of this book, see my review in *American Political Science Review,* xxv, 1064ff (November 1931).

[9] For this aspect of the matter cf. Jakob Burckhardt's *The Civilization of the Period of the Renaissance in Italy* (15th ed., 1929), especially part i, chapter i.

It stands to reason that so complete a break with the Christian tradition should elicit vigorous reactions. There is a vital relation between Machiavellian thought and the corrupt practices of the papal court which so outraged the monk from Wittenberg, and one is led to suspect that his trumpet call for reform of the Christian Church was bound to lead to a revival of the normative approach to natural law. Luther himself has little to contribute to this problem. His whole mode of thought was at the opposite pole from jurisprudential rigor. In his famous anti-humanist tract *De Servo Arbitrio* or *The Servant's Choice* he denounced all thought of a free will or free choice and asserted that a true Christian's faith made him the willing servant of God's will. The freedom of the faithful consists, according to Luther, in doing what God has ordained and commanded him to do, including obeying the established governmental authorities. This was not, as propagandists have since repeatedly alleged,[10] a matter of servile acceptance of the government, but rather a near-anarchist refusal to take government seriously. Like Saint Augustine, Luther considered government "a gang of robbers," a sorry affair at best which was necessitated by man's utter corruption. It was only his profound hostility toward the Roman Church that pushed him, as a matter of practical politics, toward the state, whose princes he looked upon as potential protectors of "true religion." Luther's one and only real interest was religion—the salvation of man's immortal soul through faith. He was motivated by an extreme pessimism concerning this world and hence could write that "the temporal power can do no harm."

In spite of this hostility to secular power and government, Luther was emphatic in rejecting the monkish life as ungodly. Everyone, he held, must strive to do his best in a "calling" which contributes to the common life. "Inner-wordly sanctification"

---

[10] Cf. in lieu of many, William M. McGovern, *From Luther to Hitler* (1941), pp. 30ff.

is as much a doctrine of Luther as it is of Calvin.[11] This doctrine of the calling implied Luther's demand that each member of the government should, in his proper sphere, consider himself responsible for the rule of law. In discussing the right of resistance in the Empire, he stated: "The law is above a lord and tyrant, even more [*sic*]; for they are unshakeable, and at all times certain and steady, while a man is unsteady and follows his lust when he is not restrained; therefore one is more due and obliged to follow the law [*Recht*] and the laws [*Gesetzen*] than a tyrant." [12]

In his *Von Weltlicher Obrigkeit* (1535) Luther had already stated this position thus: "If the prince were outside the law, is his people obliged to follow him? Answer: no. For no one is obliged to act against the law or what is right; rather one must obey God (who wants law [*Recht*] more than man." [13] It can be seen clearly that the right of resistance has become a duty of resistance on behalf of the commonwealth. With regard to certain outrages, Luther would even go so far as to concede to the people the right to murder a tyrant.

[11] See, for example, Luther's *Von Weltlicher Obrigkeit* in *Ausgewählte Werke,* ed. by H. H. Borcherdt and Georg Menz (1934-1938), v, 14. See also Max Weber, *The Protestant Ethic and the Spirit of Capitalism,* ed. T. Parsons (1930); E. Troeltsch, *The Social Teachings of the Christian Churches,* tr. by Olive Wyon (1931); and Talcott Parsons' keen comments on the frequent misinterpretations of Weber's views in *The Structure of Social Action* (1937), pp. 516ff and pp. 573ff. The more widely read and accepted discussion of the problem by R. H. Tawney, *Religion and the Rise of Capitalism* (1926), while in some respects superior to Weber's theory, lacks the trenchancy and acumen of the latter's analysis.

[12] This passage, contained in his *Tischreden,* in *Ausgewählte Werke* (Borcherdt and Menz) vii, 206, is one of a number which show that the recurrent allegation that Luther was an unqualified authoritarian is onesided and superficial. Cf., for example, McGovern, *From Luther to Hitler,* pp. 30ff, and Lewis Mumford, *The Condition of Man* (1944), pp. 184ff. The conflict in Luther's position is discussed in George H. Sabine, *History of Political Theory,* pp. 358ff.

[13] For Luther's Table Talks we now have a most thorough critical edition by E. Kröker, *Tischreden in der Mathesischen Sammlung, aus einer Handschrift der Leipziger Stadtbibliothek,* in six volumes (1903).

It does not become a private and common man who occupies no public office or command [to kill a tyrant who acts against law and equity] even if he can do it; for the fifth commandment forbids it: Thou shalt not kill. But if I caught someone, even though he be no tyrant, with my wife or daughter, I might kill him. *Item:* If he took this man's wife, that man's daughter, the third man's land and estate by force, and the citizens and subjects gathered together, and could not bear nor endure his violence and tyranny, they may kill him, like a murderer and gangster." [14]

The reason for such a view is to be found in Luther's contention that "when an overlord acts tyrannically, against the law, he becomes equal to the others; for he abandons the person of an overlord [*Obersten*] and therefore he loses his right against the subject." [15] This is precisely the doctrine which prevailed

---

[14] Luther (Borcherdt ed.), V, 213. The Lutheran doctrine of right and law above government, and of the duty of officials to enforce the law even against their superiors, is interestingly reflected in the German military code which holds inferiors responsible for illegal acts. The most detailed application to the constitutional law of the Empire was attempted in *De Jure Magistratuum in subditos et officio subditorum erga magistratus* (1578). This work, while generally attributed to Theodorus Beza (de Bèze) is, judging from internal evidence, much more likely to be the work of a German lawyer of Lutheran propensities.

[15] These strong statements are not adequately considered by Kurt Wolzendorf, *Staatsrecht und Naturrecht in der Lehre vom Widerstandsrecht des Volkes* (1916), pp. 95ff, nor by J. W. Allen, *Political Thought in the Sixteenth Century* (1928). Indeed the entire literature tends to overplay Luther's role in the Peasants' War; the reason is that these writers, in keeping with our modern political perspectives, give inadequate attention to the lawless violence of the peasants themselves, a violence which no man seriously concerned with the rule of law could possibly accept even though he might sympathize with the peasants in the sufferings which brought them to violence. For Luther the situation was aggravated by the fact that Thomas Münzer, the leader of the peasants, was to him a misguided extremist, of whom he said: "When Thomas Münzer opposed me, as if to help things [I think Luther means the reformation by "things"], I had to resist him; but I did not like to do it, yet was forced to by great emergency; God helped me in his grace" (Borcherdt ed., v, 146). Luther's view regarding the right of resistance is difficult to state, because it underwent a continuous evolution. A recent evaluation of the new evidence is offered by Karl Müller in "Luther's Aeusserungen über das Recht des be-

among the English revolutionaries in the age of Cromwell. It is the recurrent idea that law and only law confers real authority and a governmental office becomes such only through the law, so that the person occupying it reverts to a private status if he acts *ultra vires*.

From such a standpoint, it becomes, of course, of the greatest importance to determine whether there is a higher law over and above the positive law. Luther himself is quite explicit about it, and in many different writings at different periods he accepts the medieval canonist doctrine of such a higher law. What is more, he interprets this law as a law of reason. At the end of his famous tract *Of Secular Authority and How Far One Owes It Obedience* (1523), he roundly states: "Therefore one should place written laws under reason out of which they have flowed as out of a fountain of law—and not bind the fountain by its brooks and capture reason within literal constructions [*Buchstaben*]."[16] This idea of a higher law conceived of as the dictates of reason dominates the thinking on jurisprudence of the entire Reformation. But, as stated by Luther, it leaves open the vital question as to who decides, or at least determines, what this reason may be. Medieval Christianity could always have recourse to the ecclesiastical authorities. But where were men to turn now?

The universities, repositories of the search for truth, offered

---

waffneten Widerstands gegen den Kaiser," in *Sitzungsberichte der bayrischen Akademie der Wissenschaften*, Phil. hist. Klasse, 1915, and by F. Kern, "Luther und das Widerstandsrecht," *Zeitschrift der Savignistiftung für Rechtsgeschichte*, vol. 37, Kanon. Abt. 6 (1916). Müller does not interpret the evidence correctly, in my opinion. Instead, he tries to make Luther an opponent, and since the evidence is against him, he questions the text when it does not fit his assumptions, draws artificial distinctions such as that between *Hausrecht* and other *Recht* which have no foundation in law or theory, and imputes "meaning" to Luther which he does not clearly state and even contradicts elsewhere. Consult also E. Troeltsch, *Die Soziallehren der Christlichen Kirchen* (1912), which is often quoted in this connection in spite of its lack of precision and its failure to grasp the theoretical issues involved.

[16] Cf. Borcherdt ed., v, 44 and 35ff.

one possible answer.[17] The role of professors, and more especially professors of law and philosophy, was greatly enhanced
as humanism and reformation combined to celebrate the independent mind in its effort to develop the use of reason apart
from authoritarian tradition. Philip Melanchthon (1497-1568),
humanist and scholar that he was, pointed the way by his assimi-
lation of Aristotelianism to Protestantism. Natural law was a
significant feature of his political thought. Developing Luther's
insistent emphasis on the feeling for law and right as specifically
human, he taught that the Decalogue in its explicit form and
political authority is specifically entrusted with the task of
guarding natural law.[18] He went beyond Luther in maintaining
a right of resistance, and adduced both the Roman law and the
constitutional law of the empire and kingdoms of Europe in
support of his position. This "positivist" turn of Melanchthon's
doctrine of natural law, treating it as embedded in actual legal
institutions, meant that jurists—and more especially professors

[17] Characteristically, Thomas Hobbes in his radical secularism turned to
the universities. See *Leviathan* (1651), ch. xlvi.
[18] See *Commentarii in aliquot politicos libros Aristotelis,* in *Corpus Re-
formatorum,* xvi, 416-451. Troeltsch, *Die Soziallehren der Christlichen Kirchen,*
pp. 54ff, as well as the whole treatment of Lutheran natural law (*ibid.,* pp.
532ff), markedly differs from the position taken here by stressing too much the
authoritarian aspect of Lutheran natural-law doctrines, interpreting the few
contrary views he cites as "aberrations" and "concessions," whereas the am-
bivalence in the approach of Luther and Melanchthon to the problems of natural law is characteristic for their outlook. Troeltsch's views are too much
influenced by his concern with modern political party issues and his justified
annoyance with the Prussian conservatives who, following the authority of
F. J. Stahl and his legal philosophy, had appropriated Luther and Lutheranism.
Troeltsch bases his discussion on a number of studies by men who all more or
less followed the same tradition of authoritarian interpretation: K. Köhler,
Luther und die Juristen (1873); Erich Brandenburg, *Martin Luther's An-
schauung vom Staate und der Gesellschaft* (1901); G. Müller, *Luther's Stellung zum Rechte* (1906); L. Cardauns, *Die Lehre vom Widerstandsrecht im
Luthertum und Calvinismus* (1903); S. Lommatzsch, *Luthers Lehre vom
ethischreligiösen Standpunkt aus, mit besonderer Berücksichtigung seiner
Theorie vom Gesetz* (1879); K. Eger, *Die Anschauungen Luthers vom Beruf*
(1900); R. Hupfeld, *Die Ethik Joh. Gerhards, Ein Beitrag zum Verständnis
der Lutherischen Ethik* (1908).

of law—were needed to give an authoritative interpretation of reason as revealed in the law.[19]

Of these men, Johann Oldendorp (1480-1567) is perhaps the outstanding figure and may serve as a representative thinker.[20] Having adopted Cicero's definition of natural law, "It is the highest reason implanted in nature which commands what is to be done, and forbids the opposite," [21] he rejects the Roman-law doctrine of Ulpian that the law of nature is the law common to all animals, on the ground, traditional since the Middle Ages, that animals who do not possess reason cannot have a law. This clearly puts him into the company of those who think in terms of a law of nature defined as the dictates of right reason before.

Oldendorp then proceeds to show how the Decalogue is embodied in the civil law, and suggests that the Decalogue is the source of the twelve tables of the ancient law of Rome, because the Romans derived their law from the Greeks and these from the Hebrews.[22] He then in turn shows how the law of the

[19] This legal "positivism" is made the central issue in Kurt Wolzendorf's important history of the doctrine of the right of resistance, cited above, footnote 15.

[20] Concerning him, see R. Stintzing, *Geschichte der deutschen Rechtswissenschaft*, I, 311ff (1880); Carl von Kaltenborn (und Stachau), *Die Vorläufer des Hugo Grotius auf dem Gebiete des Jus naturale et gentium so wie der Politik im Reformationszeitalter* (1848). The latter contains some extracts from Oldendorp's *Eisagoge juris naturalis sive elementaria introductio juris naturae gentium et civilis* (1539)—the main contribution of Oldendorp to the problem here under consideration.

[21] "Est ratio summa insita in natura, quae jubet ea quae facienda sunt, prohibetque contraria." This statement is found in *De Legibus*, I.vi.18. The doctrine is further developed by Cicero in *De Republica*, III. For a modern translation see George Sabine and Stanley Barney Smith's translation, *On the Commonwealth* (1929). See also their introduction, p. 48. Why they should translate *summa* as "transcendent" in the passage given above I do not profess to know. The passage of Ulpian is found in *Corpus Juris Civilis, Inst.* I.ii.1, and begins: "Jus naturale est, quod natura omnia animalia docuit, nam jus istud non humani generis proprium est, sed omnium animalium . . ."

[22] This passage is cited by Troeltsch (*Die Soziallehren der Christliche Kirchen*, p. 545n) as offering an insight into ancient Lutheran thought. It offers such an insight, but not in the sense meant by Troeltsch, who, incidentally, misquotes Stintzing and gives the page as 371, when it is actually 327.

twelve tables is to be understood in the light of natural law. He does this in a pithy and dogmatic manner. This attempt to derive the positive law from natural law was highly original, but it is essential to keep in mind that the natural law itself is not derived from reason but seen to consist in the revealed Decalogue, reinforced by the authority of the Roman law and Cicero.[23] Oldendorp thus carried out Melanchthon's suggestion that natural is embedded in positive law, and that both have their ultimate sanction in revelation.[24]

A distinctive version of the Lutheran position was developed in England by the Anglicans. It is generally recognized that this development had its roots in part at least in the divergent political, governmental, and legal traditions of the island kingdom. Remote from the Pope and Empire, English lawyers had steered clear of Roman law to a much greater extent than their brethren on the continent, and while the common law contained traces, it was on the whole the slow product of national consolidation.[25]

Richard Hooker's *The Laws of Ecclesiastical Polity*, while explicitly written to defend the Elizabethan settlement,[26] is at the same time a comprehensive statement of the Anglican doctrine of natural law. A more extreme authoritarian position was later developed by James I and Francis Bacon with their radical in-

---

[23] It is difficult to understand why Stintzing should deny the originality of Oldendorp, in view of his own statement that the comparison between Decalogue and Roman law is peculiar to Oldendorp and represents a first attempt in this field. Cf. Stintzing, I, 328.

[24] See Melanchthon's *Epitome Philosophiae Moralis*. Cf. also Albert Hänel, "Melanchthon der Jurist," *Zeitschrift für Rechtsgeschichte*, VIII (1869), 249ff.

[25] See especially Charles H. McIlwain's magistral *The High Court of Parliament and Its Supremacy* (1910), and the papers by Plunkett cited in note 28, below.

[26] The ablest recent treatment of Hooker's views is by A. Passerin d'Entrèves, in *The Medieval Contribution to Political Thought—Thomas Aquinas, Marsilius of Padua, Richard Hooker* (1939), which is based on his earlier *Ricardo Hooker, Contributo alla teoria e alla storia del diritto naturale* (1932) and the preceding study, *La teoria del diritto e della politica in Inghilterra all'inizio dell' era moderna* (1929).

sistence upon the law of reason as above the law of the realm.[27] This view clashed with the common-law tradition represented by Sir Edward Coke, although the latter's notions regarding the relation between the higher law and parliamentary statutes underwent a gradual evolution toward a recognition of the supremacy of parliament.[28] Ever since Dean Church made the point, it has been a commonplace that Hooker's doctrine of natural law closely follows that of Thomas Aquinas.[29] It should be noted, however, that no man ever took a more comprehensive and enthusiastic view of law in general than Hooker. Indeed, he may be said to have been intoxicated with his admiration for the idea of law as such. At the end of the first book, which deals with "laws and their several kinds in general," Hooker says:

Of law there can be no less acknowledged, than that her seat is the bosom of God, her voice the harmony of the world; all things in heaven and earth do her homage, the very least as feeling her care, and the greatest as not exempted from her power; both Angels and men and creatures of what condition soever, though each in a different sort and manner, yet all with uniform consent, admiring her as the mother of their peace and joy.[30]

Among these laws, the approach of Hooker distinguishes between the laws of nature which he also calls the law which natu-

---

[27] For this entire controversy see Charles H. McIlwain, *The Political Works of James I* (1918), Introduction, esp. pp. xxxviiiff.

[28] See Roscoe Pound, *The Spirit of the Common Law* (1921), p. 61 and elsewhere. T. F. T. Plunkett, "The Place of the Legal Profession in the History of English Law," *Law Quarterly Review*, 48:328ff (1932) contains an authoritative account of its topic. For further bibliography see my *Constitutional Government and Democracy*, pp. 607ff.

[29] See, besides A. Passerin d'Entrèves cited above, F. Paget, *Introduction to Book V of the Ecclesiastical Polity* (2nd ed., 1908); J. N. Figgis, *From Gerson to Grotius, 1414-1625* (1916); and the introduction by R. W. Church to his and Paget's three-volume revision of the *Ecclesiastical Polity* (1888). D'Entrèves has, however, rightly emphasized that the Thomistic doctrine of natural law "underwent subtle modification" at the hand of Hooker.

[30] *The Laws of Ecclesiastical Polity*, Bk. I, sec. x, art. 8.

ral agents observe and the laws of human nature which he calls the laws of reason. In the great humanist tradition, Hooker exalts reason as an antidote to the literalism of the Bible-quoting Puritans like Cartwright. Hooker takes them severely to task for their "disparagement of reason." He in many ways resembles Melanchthon, as he turns to Aristotle and the Thomist tradition for guidance in defending the Elizabethan church settlement and Tudor government in general against the onslaught of radicals, who under the guise of expounding the Bible attacked tradition and the aristocratic *status quo.* The traditionalist and authoritarian element in Hooker's reasoning is strong; for the sign and token of reason according to him is tradition and the general persuasion of mankind.[31] His awareness of the limits of reason is strikingly illustrated in his approval of a sentence from Theophrastus' *Metaphysics:* "They that seek a reason of all things do utterly overthrow reason."

Yet Hooker goes further than the thinkers discussed so far in separating natural law from revelation. He states explicitly that the laws of reason are "investigable by Reason, without the help of Revelation supernatural and divine." Therefore the world has always been acquainted with these laws of reason, and they are agreed to by all.[32] This "law is such that being proposed no man can reject it as unreasonable and unjust." What then, is this law of Reason? This law "comprehends all those things which men by the light of their natural understanding evidently know, or at leastwise may know, to be beseeming or unbeseeming, virtuous or vicious, good or evil for them to do." He adds: "we restrain it to those only duties, which all men by force of natural wit either do or might understand to be such

---

[31] *Ecclesiastical Polity,* I, vii, 3. "The general and perpetual voice of men as the sentence of God itself."

[32] *Ecclesiastical Polity,* I, viii, 9. The complete discussion is contained in chapters v-ix of the first book. It seems to me that d'Entrèves (p. 119) stresses the traditional and revealed aspect of Hooker's concept of the law of nature a bit too much.

duties as concern all men." Specifically referring to Saint Augustine, he repeats that in the law of Reason there are "some things which stand as principles universally agreed upon." What is commonly called the Law of Nature is therefore the "Law rational" meaning "the Law which human Nature knoweth itself in reason universally bound onto."

This strong insistence upon reason is founded upon a strictly rational doctrine of the will. Expounding a doctrine of rational freedom, Hooker states: "To chose is to will one thing before another. And to will is to bend our souls to the having or doing of that which they see to be good. Goodness is seen with the eye of the understanding. And the light of that eye, is reason." [33] He insists that "evil as evil cannot be desired," and again, "Goodness does not move by being, but by being apparent." Therefore, "the laws of well-doing are the dictates of right Reason." It is this capacity to will that which is in accordance with reason which links man to God, his Maker. This light of reason, resulting from education, study, and natural aptitude, is much stronger in some men than in others—a fact which justifies the established order and utterly denies any right of resistance and rebellion. Hooker here is the unqualified heir of the humanist tradition which followed Plato in its aristocratic slant. His view is diametrically opposed, indeed, to the Calvinist belief in the common churchman, if not the common man. To this approach we now turn.

The position which Hooker had expounded in clear and open opposition to the Puritans' "disparagement of reason" resembled, as we have seen, like Melanchthon's if not Luther's view, the Thomist philosophy. It later seemed to John Locke a "judicious" compromise, but it failed to deal with the most burning problem: was the law of nature, when seen as the dictates of a higher reason, really valid when tested by the actual conduct of government? Did it, in other words, contain the laws of nature as

[33] *Ecclesiastical Polity*, I, VII, 2. Cf. the discussion above, Chapter III.

displayed by man when acting politically? Or, on the contrary, was Machiavelli right in asserting that he who would run a government, who would build a state, had better make use of the passions of men, the irrational drives of fear, hate, love, and the lust for power? Hooker failed to deal with man as "a natural agent." The Calvinist emphasis upon God as the giver of laws, whose inexorable will had created the universe and thus predestined its course, obliged the orthodox Calvinist to try to discover this rational plan, since it is the revelation of God's majestic will. This view is palpably related to the framework of modern science; it is based upon the belief that there is an order in the universe, that this order is expressed in laws which can be found by observing the regularities which occur in nature, including human nature.[34] "Biological naturalism and determinism root in the Calvinist conception of God."[35] While this need not be a mechanistic theory of nature, it may readily turn into one, as it did in the philosophy of Thomas Hobbes. In any case, it is only a step from such a naturalist determinism to seeking to discover the "laws" of social life. For an order of nature comprises man. No one among the orthodox Calvinists made a more searching and determined effort to discover and systematize these laws of social life than Johannes Althusius.[36]

In a sense, it is an attempt to treat the commands of God as the revealed norms that they are, and yet to show that social life is in fact lived in accordance with them. This *tour de force* seeks to resolve the dualism of norm and fact. It is a recurrent aspect of philosophies conceived in the Calvinist tradition,

[34] Alfred N. Whitehead, *Science and the Modern World* (1926), p. 5, has popularized this idea, but it is familiar to all readers of Kant. Cf. also W. Dilthey.

[35] From introduction to *Johannes Althusius' Politica Methodice Digesta* (1932), p. lxxiii. At the time of writing this introduction, I was not so familiar with earlier Protestant thought.

[36] For Althusius see my introduction to his *Politica,* and O. von Gierke, *Johannes Althusius und die Entwicklung der naturrechtlichen Staatstheorien* (1880), translated by Bernard Freyd as *The Development of Political Theory* (1939), especially the first part, which deals with Althusius proper.

Hobbes, Spinoza, Bentham, and Marx. Might, in this view, does not make right, but "the righteous prevail," and success suggests, if it does not prove, that you are on the side of the godly. The hypocrisy and cant for which the Anglo-Saxon is so heartily disliked by other nations is a spiritual derivative of the Calvinist doctrine of predestination, according to which man may discover whether he is likely to be among the select by the success he has in his calling.[37] In Marx this idea reappears in the form of the inevitable revolution of the emergent proletariat and its preordained victory to which they are led by the "elect" among them, the Communists. "Freedom flowers in necessity" is a phrase which provides a clue to this approach, in which normative and existential judgments are made to coincide in a willed and hence predetermined order, wherein obedience to the divine prescription is the condition of eventual success.

Within this working pattern, a thinker like Johannes Althusius could criticize Machiavelli not only because he was morally wrong, but also because he was scientifically unsound. He could transcend the ideas of Bodin, the Machiavellian, for similar reasons and in the same spirit.[38] Since Bodin had raised the ques-

---

[37] See the literature cited above, note 11, especially Weber, pp. 98ff; and Troeltsch, pp. 615ff. A balanced appraisal of the various criticisms may be found in A. Fanfani, *Catholicism, Protestantism and Capitalism* (1935). However, Fanfani lacks the precision of T. Parsons' appraisal of Weber's view in the latter's edition of Weber's *The Protestant Ethic and the Spirit of Capitalism*.

[38] The strictly Machiavellian impetus in Bodin's work is often overlooked, especially by those who are overimpressed by the concessions to medieval traditions in Bodin—for example, M. A. Shepard in his admirable article "Sovereignty at the Crossroads—A Study of Bodin," *Political Science Quarterly*, 45: 580 (December 1930), or J. A. Allen in his chapter dealing with Bodin in *Political Thought in the Sixteenth Century* (1928). It is skillfully brought out by Friedrich Meinecke, in *Die Idee der Staatsräson in der neueren Geschichte* (1925), ch. ii, who shows that, in his very attempt to combat Machiavelli, Bodin became the expounder of his views. Bodin attempts to legalize Machiavelli through his doctrine of sovereignty, and his acceptance of a law of nature and of God as limiting the sovereign. Bodin's idea that nothing is shameful that is related to the welfare of the state, while reminiscent of today's totalitarian doctrine, turns upon the question of what constitutes the welfare of the state.

tion of the highest power, Althusius pushes the issue beyond the existing government and its organization and asks: Where does the final power to decide about the organization of the community rest? This leads him to the discovery of the constitution-making power, as contrasted with the Bodinian sovereign. It is "the people or the united members of the state." [39] But Althusius does not say "the ought is addressed to the beholder and reads like this: you *ought* to recognize that the people are the final power—because if you do not, you will fail."

As a consequence, Althusius is at length concerned with various *rationes* or rational ways of seeing and operating different social institutions. These *rationes* are based upon laws of "natural ought." The *ratio status* or *ratio administrationis* is such a concept. It is compounded of the general principles of good administration and an understanding of the particular necessities of the particular association. By transforming the *ratio status* into the *ratio administrationis* and the *ratio officii*, Althusius shows that he appreciated reason of state to be a special case of a general principle: conduct which is directed toward achieving group ends is shaped by the facts of the situation into a rational pattern in which means are selected in accordance with their likelihood to produce success. Laws of nature, an order of nature, and more especially the laws of human nature, are the only safe guide for such rationalized conduct.

It is evident that such a viewpoint must affect the idea of the law of nature. Whereas, in Hooker's treatment, reason is the capacity to discover the good and thus to provide the will with moral guidance, reason in Althusius is the capacity to study nature and to discover its laws as revealed in the functioning of human society. In Kantian terms, Althusius is focusing atten-

---

[39] This is not the place to enter into these questions. For a more detailed discussion see my Introduction to *Johannes Althusius' Politica*, pp. lxxxivff.

tion upon the realm of nature, whereas Hooker is preoccupied with the realm of freedom. But both of them are far from the strictly secular outlook of the age of Kant, since they both struggle to relate their view of the law of nature to theology— Althusius by his Calvinist insistence upon the majesty of God who in his Decalogue has offered to man the working hypotheses of a descriptive science of society and government, Hooker by exalting reason through his humanist and Anglican insistence that the primary commandment of God to man is to follow his higher moral reason. According to Althusius, the law of nature is not a separate body of law, but implicit in all legislation. No legislation, in other words, can be made without taking the laws of nature, of human nature, into account. In other words, the law of nature does not consist of separate and distinct rules of the higher reason, but permeates all rule-making for the community.[40] That is the reason why you cannot say that the prince is *legibus solutus* bound by no laws except the law of nature. Nor does this mean that the law of nature is obscure or impalpable (*unbegreiflich*); quite the contrary. In keeping with the formalism and legalism of orthodox Calvinism, Althusius insists that they are explicit *rules*. Identifying *lex* and *jus*, Althusius, like Reformed Protestantism generally, says that the law of nature is contained in the sentence that you do unto others as you would have others do unto you,[41] from which flow the last six commandments which constitute the second table of the Decalogue. For these are the quintessence of Christian ethics, and upon them a Christian commonwealth rests. Althusius, like other Calvinists, treats these commandments as metarational and given by the inscrutable will of God. They are as much a part

[40] The same view is expounded by Oldendorp and others. See O. von Gierke, *Johannes Althusius* (3rd ed., 1913), pp. 297-298, footnote 82.
[41] See *Politica*, ch. x, paragraph 7. For the whole matter, cf. Ernst Troeltsch, *Die Soziallehren der Christlichen Kirchen*, pp. 493ff, and my introduction, pp. xcivff. See below, Chapter V, p. 122.

of the world in which we live as physical and material circumstances.

From the foregoing it is clear that Althusius, for all his scientific ardor and search of empirical evidence, is firmly rooted in the Calvinist faith. We are face to face with an ultimate religious foundation. It is not the belief in reason, but the faith that man, God's creature, cannot succeed unless he follows God's commands, his inner predetermined laws of human nature. These laws may be summed up in saying that man is naturally sociable. God's commandments are striking confirmation of this sociability. It is readily granted that men may violate and often do violate these commandments. But if they do, they will ultimately be punished by their failure as men and as peoples. There is a transcendent faith in the pre-ordained order of things.

The view of the law of nature which we find in Counter-Reformation Catholicism diverges as sharply from this pattern as does the Anglicanism represented by Hooker. Their most searching and profound representative is unquestionably Francisco Suarez. In his *De Lego ac Deo Legislatore* (1612) we have a striking attempt to reassert the ancient positions of the Thomist philosophy against all comers.[42] Once again: God is the law-

---

[42] Cf. James Brown Scott, *The Spanish Conception of International Law and of Sanctions* (1934), esp. pp. 52-111. Scott's estimate of the relative merit of Suarez and Vittoria is warped by his preoccupation with the growth of international law. Suarez was incomparably the deeper legal philosopher. His *Disputationes Metaphysicae* (1605) are the last great contribution to scholastic philosophy. For Suarez' political and juristic thought, see Heinrich Rommen, *Die Staatslehre des Franz Suarez* (1926), a careful descriptive account from the standpoint of a devout Catholic with Thomist sympathies; Josef Kohler, "Die Spanischen Naturrechtsleherer des 16. und 17. Jahrhunderts," *Archiv für Rechts- und Wirtschaftsphilosophie*, x, 235ff (1917); Adolphe Franck, "Les Publicistes du XVII siècle," *Comptes rendus de l'Académie des Sciences Politiques et Morales* (1860), pp. 13-51; Raoul de Scoraille, *François Suarez* (1913), vol. iii; K. Werner, *Franz Suarez*, vol. ii (1861). The remarks in W. A. Dunning's *A History of Political Theories from Luther to Montesquieu* (1905), pp. 135ff, while brief, are the most straightforward statements of Suarez' position in English. Cf. also J. N. Figgis, *Studies in Political Thought from Gerson to Grotius, 1414-1625* (1907); and an article by A. L. Lilley on Suarez in F. J. C. Hearnshaw, ed., *The Social and Political Ideas of Some Great Thinkers of the 16. and 17. Century* (1926).

giver and the laws he gives are addressed to reason and the higher moral aspirations of man. Once more, we revert to a clear dualism of body and soul. Suarez defines natural (as distinguished from positive, including international) law as "that which dwells within the human mind for distinguishing the upright from the base." Natural law, in other words, is the moral propensity in man. But it is not only that. It is also willed by God, and in this sense it is law in the true sense. Natural law is the mirror of divine law. Through it men participate in divine law. Natural law, therefore, is a judgment of right reason which represents actions as either commanded or forbidden by God, the creator and guide of rational nature. This judgment of right reason which is implanted in man by nature is a sufficient sign of a divine will which obliges fully and does not require any further promulgation. Right reason by itself is not enough. We must perceive that it corresponds to the will of God.[43]

It is clear from even these brief statements that Suarez, like Thomas Aquinas, takes a position midway between a strict rationalism and an unqualified voluntarism. "An act of will is essential, though a dictate of right reason is no less indispensable." The law of nature is not merely indicative, but also imperative (Dunning). Suarez thus arrives at a comprehensive doctrine of natural law which comprises three classes of commands, the broad and self-evident principles of right conduct such as the Decalogue and the Golden Rule; the somewhat less certain, but still very general rules, such as "Justice must be

[43] "Lumen naturale intellectus repraesentans voluntatem Dei auctoris naturae, et supremi Domini gubernatoris ejusdem naturae, obligantem homines ad servandum, quod recta ratio dictat" (*De legibus,* Book ii, chs. v and vi; Rommen, *Die Staatslehre des Franz Suarez,* p. 69). This doctrine of the willed quality of natural law was developed against Francis Vasquez, another Spanish Jesuit, who had maintained that natural law flows directly from the nature of man, just as divine law flows directly from the nature of God. The doctrine of Vasquez anticipates Grotius, see below, Chapter V. For this controversy see *Jahrbuch der Görresgesellschaft,* 1888, pp. 421ff, and Scott, *The Spanish Conception of International Law and of Sanctions,* passim.

served" (*justitia est servanda*); and finally, more definite rules of conduct which can be deduced from the general principles by logical reasoning, such as that stealing or adultery are bad. All these are part of an immutable code which no human power can alter. The resulting rigidity is, however, modified by Suarez' doctrine of the "circumstances," which may alter what Suarez calls the *materia* or material situation so that the immutable rule does not apply. As Dunning, following Franck, rightly observes: "The distinctions and qualifications . . . bring the moral code into practical harmony with those systems which assume an origin not in the will of an omniscient and all-wise supernatural being, but merely in the conclusions of human reason." [44]

The foregoing should suffice to show that Suarez' close kinship to Thomas Aquinas also puts him near the thought of Hooker. The middle ground between rationalism and voluntarism which they both occupy is built up from a rational doctrine of will. Reason is throughout superior to will, guides and directs it. At the same time, they share the distrust of the common man which an exalting of the rational faculty carries with it. They both feel that it takes a superior mind to trace out the application of reason to concrete situations. They both stress the weight and importance of tradition and agreement among the learned. Yet, because of the profound difference in their views of church government (church and state), Hooker's reason has a secular and humanist cast, and an individualist potential. At the same time, his resulting authoritarianism in matters of secular government leads him to deny, as we saw, the right (and duty) of resistance, whereas Suarez, in true medieval fashion, asserts it. To assert, as a consequence, that Suarez is a step in the direction of Rousseau's (and Althusius') doctrine of popular sovereignty, as Gierke, and following him, Scott,

---

[44] *A History of Political Theories from Luther to Montesquieu*, p. 140. See also Rommen, p. 73, and Scoraille, *François Suarez*, ii, 155ff.

do, is very misleading indeed. There is no doctrine of sovereignty involved here, but a doctrine of collective power to act in accordance with what the ecclesiastical authorities have declared to be right.[45]

Looking back to our original question, we can conclude that Suarez sees law as dictates of right reason, but these are tied to the Catholic theology, because they possess no force and lack the "obligation" of being obeyed, unless they are conceived as reinforced by the commands and will of God. Nature, accordingly, is not the manifold of regularities which manifest themselves in man's irrational drives, passions, and other elements of behavior, but is an ordered whole whose principle of order is the *summum bonum* of man, the salvation of his eternal soul.

If we look over the range of ideas which the foregoing analysis has brought into view, we find that they are all groping toward a view of the law of nature independent of theology and ecclesiastical doctrine, but that each of the writers in turn hesitates to take the plunge, and links the theory once more to his particular religious views. Why should the two generations between 1555 and 1618 be so bent on finding a *secular* and rational basis for natural law? I believe it is clear that the urgency is twofold, at least. The passing of the pre-Reformation unity of *credo* and hence of moral authority made it appear essential to all reformers to discover a separate basis of political obligation. The absolutist and despotic possibilities of vesting authority in the secular authorities demanded a counterweight. This might be found in an insistence that these secular authorities accept standards of extraneous rationality, such as those contained in the Roman law, or it might be found in an insistence that estates and other official bodies act as guardians of the law on their own responsibility. Against these Protestant and humanist methods it was only natural that Catholic writers

---

[45] See Gierke, *Johannes Althusius,* p. 67; Suarez, Bk. iii, chs. i-iv.

should return to the medieval constitutionalist position which "separated" power between secular and ecclesiastical authorities and assigned to the latter an independent sphere. Indeed, writers like Suarez and Bellarmin sharpened medieval doctrine by claiming direct divine sanction for the church authorities, and treating the secular authority as partly derived from "the people." They added further to the contrast by developing the doctrine of papal "infallibility" in matters of faith, and thus, after linking the law of nature and reason to divine law as its partly corrupted emanation, claimed final authority in matters of reason for the papal office.[46]

But none of these several attempts could possibly be satisfactory as a universal solution to the urgent task which the disappearance of medieval unity had posited. The problem of

[46] See for the linkage of medieval and modern constitutionalism my *Constitutional Government and Democracy* (1942), ch. i, and Charles H. McIlwain's *Constitutionalism, Ancient and Modern* (1940), chs. iv, v, vi. The latter stresses "constitutional limitations," through all its phases; thus McIlwain writes: "Constitutionalism has one essential quality; it is a legal limitation on government; it is the antithesis of arbitrary rule; its opposite is despotic government, the government of will instead of law." This enumeration covers up more complexities than it clarifies, because the four criteria all differ from each other, and they do not correspond to each other. Government of will may be government of law, if law is interpreted as will. This issue in turn relates to the problem of the relation of will and reason, so keenly debated in the Middle Ages and in neoscholasticism, no less than in the type of controversy epitomized by the names of Hegel and Schopenhauer. Again, not all nonconstitutional government is despotic. Finally, and most significantly, such a statement avoids facing the most decisive issue, namely how a "legal" limitation on government can be conceived, once all "law" is conceived of as manmade, that is to say, government-made, government being, above all, the process of rulemaking, that is to say, lawmaking. I tried to cope with these difficulties and to construct a theory of constitutionalism which would not be subject to these objections in *Constitutional Government and Politics* (1937), ch. viii. After a brief survey of five different classes of definitions of a constitution—the philosophical, the governmental, the legalistic, the documentarian, and the procedural—a "political definition" was offered: a government is constitutional when it contains effective regularized restraints upon political and more especially governmental action." It is a question of fact whether such restraints exist and to what extent. Regularized restraints may be extra legal, as are many of the restraints characteristic of the British constitution.

the restraint of power, either domestically or internationally, called for a solution which was entirely independent of any sort of dogmatic interpretation, requiring in turn the acceptance of a particular ecclesiastical authority. Instead, there was wanted an approach which effectively "bracketed out" the theological bases of reason and rationality, and provided a common ground for all. It was Grotius' great achievement to accomplish this feat for the relations between the powers, called states after the religious wars.

To assert, as James Brown Scott has done, that Grotius is a popularizer, albeit an excellent one, of the views of the "Spanish School," and that he had nothing to contribute beyond what they had taught is completely to overlook the philosophical and theoretical foundations of his juridical teachings. It is difficult to see how Scott, who delved deeply into the philosophical background of men like Suarez,[47] could have failed to see this sharp and abiding difference between a view such as Suarez', which is built upon an independent ecclesiastical authority which exists *de jure divino* and is the ultimate arbiter of what the *recta ratio dictat,* and the view of Grotius, which asserts an all-inclusive secular sovereignty vested in the *civitas* (or state) and makes reason a function of the individual mind.[48] Gierke denied that Grotius conceived the "state" as sovereign, and interpolated that he meant the "people" when he says "civitas," but this conclusion derives from Gierke's own concept of the "state" as an "organic whole." This involves him in serious verbal difficulties, since Grotius explicitly denied sovereignty to the people. But whatever the merits of this controversy, there can be no doubt that Grotius attributed to the sovereign "civitas" and its ruler, whoever he might be, power

---

[47] See above, footnote 42.
[48] Cf. Otto von Gierke, *Johannes Althusius,* p. 175ff. (English translation by Bernard Freyd, p. 167ff.)

over all lesser associations, and hence denied, with Gallicanism, all independent power to the church.[49] Ever since Grotius wrote, natural law has been predominantly a secular affair. How it lived and how it died, it is the purpose of the next chapter to show.

[49] See Figgis, *Studies in Political Thought from Gerson to Grotius.* That Grotius was aware of the contrast is clear from his comment on Francisco de Victoria, *Prolegomena,* paragraph 37, where he criticizes him for confusing the law of nature, divine law, and the positive law.

~V~

SECULAR NATURAL LAW:
FROM HUGO GROTIUS TO HUME AND KANT

Grotius is now mainly remembered for his great work in international law, *De jure belli ac pacis* (1625). But to his contemporaries, Grotius was at least as important as a philosopher
and a theologian, and the catastrophe of his early manhood
which deprived him of his fatherland was in no small measure
bound up with his religious convictions: he was a member of
the party of Oldenbarnevelt which incurred the wrath of
orthodox Calvinists by its espousal of Arminianism.[1] One need
only read the passionate declarations of Althusius concerning
Grotius' religious views to sense the atmosphere aroused by this
controversy.[2] It has been said that the man in the street in the
Netherlands at that time was more concerned with predestination than with anything else. To soften the severity of the doctrine of predestination the Arminians argued that God had
foreseen the sins of men. They also asserted that the civil authorities had a right to arbitrate in theological controversies in

---

[1] The vast Grotius literature is listed in the careful bibliography of Jacob Ter
Meulen, *Concise Bibliography of Hugo Grotius* (1925), and in the publications
of the Dutch Vereeniging voor de uitgave van Grotius (1928-). Cf. also
W. S. M. Knight, *The Life and Works of Hugo Grotius* (1925); the great
English-Latin edition published by the Carnegie Foundation in 1925 of *De jure
belli ac pacis;* and J. Huizinga, *Hugo de Groot* (1925).

[2] Letter from Althusius to Sibrandus Lubertus, November 20, 1614. Lubertus
had written a reply to Grotius' *Pietas*. This reply had been banned, and Althusius assures his friend that he had expounded orthodox doctrine, and that
Grotius' *Pietas* should rather be called *impietas*. Cf. my Introduction to *Johannes Althusius' Politica* (1932), pp. xli and cxxix. Cf. also Erik Wolf, *Grotius,
Pufendorf, Thomasius* (1927), p. 17ff.

order to maintain the peace. This, of course, was a recurrent theme of moderates of the time, the *Politiques* in France, the Erastians in England, and others who desired to avoid civil war resulting from religious dissensions.

It is important to keep this setting clearly in mind, because Grotius' doctrine of natural law is fully comprehensible only in its contrast to preceding views, if his acceptance of the sovereign, omnicompetent state is clearly grasped. Of the thinkers we have examined in the last chapter, Richard Hooker is undoubtedly nearest to Grotius' position in the sense that he holds the law of nature to be the law of reason, and that this reason is primarily to be looked for among the elite groups which constitute the government of state and church seen as an integral whole. But he goes well beyond Hooker in abandoning the basis of divine law for both reason and natural law. This does not mean that he abandons God altogether; far from it. Grotius acknowledges divine authority in moving sentences.[3] Nevertheless, natural law is so firmly rooted in natural reason that it "would have a degree of validity even if we should concede . . . that there is no God."

The thought of the Prolegomena is broadened in the first book, where Grotius put it thus: "Natural law is so immutable that it cannot be altered even by God. For although God's power is immense, some statements can be made to which it does not extend . . . thus that twice two does not make four cannot be effected even by God, nor that what is intrinsically bad, be not bad."[4] What this amounts to is the assertion of an

---

[3] Prolegomena to *De jure belli ac pacis,* paragraphs 11-13. See also his great treatise *De veritate religionis Christianae* (1627), more celebrated than *De jure belli ac pacis* among his contemporaries as an attempt to find common ground among all Christians, and especially all Protestants.

[4] Prolegomena to *De jure belli ac pacis,* I, i, x: "Est autem jus naturale adeo immutabile, ut ne a Deo quidem mutari queat. Quanquam enim immensa est Dei potentia, dici tamen quaedam possunt ad quae se illa non extendit . . . Sicut ergo ut bis duo non sint quatuor ne a Deo potest effici, ita ne hoc quidem, ut quod intrinseca ratione malum est, non malum sit."

autonomous reason, on the strength of the inherent logic of the rule of the excluded third. This "proof" is obviously inconclusive on one of two grounds: if the statements contained in natural law are merely definitions of words or signs, they have neither legal nor moral significance; if they are more than definitions and contain normative judgments, the fact that definitions are *qua* definitions unrelated to the power of God, if such there be, has no bearing upon the question as to whether such normative judgments are or are not subject to the will of God. It was precisely this problem which had been central for Thomas Aquinas, the reformers, and Suarez. The relevance of theology for the determination of what is just was argued on the ground that the fundamental normative judgments were in some way or other related to and emanated from the divine will. The basic rules of natural law may indeed be self-evident to natural reason, but the argument of Grotius here offered does not suffice to establish the fact.

We have already made mention of the fact that Suarez became engaged in a bitter controversy with Fernando Vázquez Menchaca (Vasquius) on the subject of the relation of will and reason in law, divine, natural, and human.[5] This is not the place even to trace this searching controversy. Its echo in the Kantian *Critique of Practical Reason* has already occupied us.[6] Suffice it here to point out that Grotius, like Suarez and Vittoria, stresses the role of reason in the determination of the law of nature and of nations. This being recognized, Grotius appeals to the enlightened monarch and his enlightened advisers to

[5] See above, p. 113. Vázquez Menchaca was a Spanish jurist (1512-1569) whose most important work is *Illustrium controversiarum aliarumque usu frequentium, libri sex* (1564).

[6] See above, Chapter III where the problem of the freedom of the will is analyzed. It is very unfortunate that these interrelationships have not been thoroughly explored in their bearing upon political philosophy. Cf., however, Max Scheler, *Der Formalismus in der Ethik und die materiale Wertethik* (1913-16), and Herbert Spiegelberg, *Gesetz und Sittengesetz* (1935), as well as my review article in *Isis,* October 1936.

follow reason in the conduct of government, both in war and peace.

What is the content of natural law as derived from reason by Grotius? "Natural law [right] is a dictate of right reason which indicates that moral turpitude or moral necessity inheres in a certain act, because of its conformity with or divergence from this selfsame rational nature." [7] If we ask further what it is precisely that this rational nature asks of us, we get from Grotius the answer that it consists in those fundamental rules of law which the maintenance (*custodia*) of society calls for. Grotius enumerates these fundamental rules or standards as follows: (1) abstaining from (taking) what belongs to another, (2) restitution of whatever we possess that belongs to another, (3) the obligation to fulfill our promises, (4) the reparation of damage caused, and finally (5) the imposition of penalties upon those who deserve them. [8] But Grotius remains very vague as to just why human beings follow these fundamental rules, or what are the grounds for their validity, except simply that they are rational. Curiously enough, it was precisely this vagueness which greatly contributed to Grotius' success as a writer on law, as it did to his success as a theologian. Grotius has often been criticized for his lack of philosophical depth and of theological acumen, and not without reason. But in an age when men were increasingly weary of theological controversy and hence desperately anxious to ground law—and more especially the law of nations—upon secular rather than ecclesiastic authority, Grotius' humanist inspiration of founding as the Stoics had done the law of nature upon a propelling rational impulse in men received very wide acclaim. To the skeptics who would maintain that all human conduct was founded upon the pursuit of self-

---

[7] *De jure belli ac pacis,* Bk. I, ch. i, sec. x,1. "Jus naturale est dictum rectae rationis indicans, actui alicui, ex ejus convenientia aut disconvenientia cum ipsa natura rationali, inesse moralem turpitudinem aut necessitatem moralem . . ."

[8] Prolegomena to *De jure belli ac pacis,* section viii.

interest[9] Grotius replied, as Cicero had done before him, that man is governed by a desire for society, or sociableness.

This argument of Grotius against Carneades is not sufficient, because society itself may readily be admitted to be one of those interests and pleasures and that hence sociableness is nothing but a response to that interest and utility.[10] We have dealt in Chapter III with the Kantian line of reasoning which is to anchor the autonomy of the "ought" in man's nature.

That Grotius' answer is scarcely an adequate reply to the will-interest theory of law and legal obligation would have been readily apparent to a more philosophical mind. But so bent were Grotius and his contemporaries upon the task of separating the law of nature from theology that they were satisfied with this manner of proof. As long as the law of nature was grounded in dictates of right reason which were human in origin, the humanist passion for secularizing the law of nature was satisfied. If the idea could be further buttressed by extensive reference to history and the letters of classical antiquity, the desire of the age for verisimilitude was satisfied. It is indeed striking to examine the footnotes Grotius adduces in support of the proposition that natural law consists in the dictates of right reason. He cites Philo (30 B.C.–A.D. 45), whose Stoic doctrine of the *logos* as a universal power emanating from God led him to the proposition that "law is nothing else but divine reason [*logos*], prescribing what is right and forbidding what is wrong." Grotius specifically adduces a passage in which Philo refers to the law which forbids lying, a law "which is not mortal [coming from] this or that mortal, which is not lifeless [engraved upon] lifeless charters or columns, but cannot be destroyed, because it is engraved upon the immortal mind

---

[9] For the corresponding controversy between Hume, the Utilitarian, and Kant see Chapter VII.

[10] Sabine, in his Introduction to Cicero's *On the Commonwealth,* cited below, note 13, notes that the ancients seem to have been similarly dissatisfied with Laelius' reply (which Grotius adopts) to Philus.

[*intellectus*] by immortal nature."[11] He next cites Tertullian
(*c.* 160–*c.* 220), the legal-minded church father, whose thought
was profoundly influenced by the natural-law doctrine of the
Roman jurists[12] as suggesting that we look for God's law in
"natural tables." He next turns to the genuine Stoics, Marcus
Aurelius, and Cicero. Of the former, he especially notes the
statement that the end (*telos*) of beings using reason is to follow the law, while of Cicero he adduces the famous passage we
owe to Lactantius which constitutes chapter xxii of Book III
of *De Republica*[13] and which begins: "There is in fact, a true
law—namely right reason—which is in accordance with nature,
applies to all men, and is unchangeable and eternal." He rounds
out this galaxy of stars by reference to another church father,
Saint Chrysostom, also a Stoic, as well as to Saint Thomas and
Duns Scotus. But while it is very important to be fully aware
of the fact that Grotius thus ranges himself with the ancient
tradition of rationalism and nominalism, it is by no means certain that he fully grasped the philosophical implications of this
position, and more especially the Stoic doctrine of universal reason (*logos*) and the concept of innate ideas associated with it.

In any case, it is hardly justifiable in the light of these authorities for Rousseau to exclaim that Grotius supports his
doctrine by quotations from the poets.[14] Is it any more true

[11] For this and the following see *De jure belli ac pacis*, Bk. I, ch. i, section x.
Is it a coincidence merely that Kant should have singled out the problem of
lying as a particularly striking instance of the moral law as manifest in the
categorical imperative? Not only does he return time and again to lying as an
illustration, but he dealt with it specifically in "Ueber ein vermeintes Recht,
aus Menschenliebe zu lügen," *Berlinische Blätter, 1797*, in which he insisted
that veracity (truth telling) is an absolute or unconditional duty which admits
of no exceptions. For Philo see Franz Geiger, *Philo von Alexandria* (1932).
[12] See Edgar Salin, *Civitas Dei* (1926), pp. 98-141, and Alexander Beck,
Römisches Recht bei Tertullian und Cyprian (1930).
[13] For this work see the carefully edited translation by George H. Sabine and
Stanley B. Smith, *On the Commonwealth* (1929), pp. 215-216. For the general
background of doctrine in the Stoa, see Sabine's introduction, e.g., pp. 12 and
48, where it is shown that this definition of true law is a Stoic commonplace.
[14] *Emile*, Bk. v, at the beginning of the discussion of public law. Cf. C. E.
Vaughan, *The Political Writings of Jean-Jacques Rousseau* (1915), II, 30.

that their principles are exactly the same, as Rousseau likewise asserts, and that they differ only in their expression?[15] What Rousseau of course is primarily concerned with here is the two philosophers' views on state and sovereignty, seeing they are both "absolutists." But what about their respective doctrines of natural law? What does Hobbes expound, and on what ground does he claim natural law as obliging men to act in accordance with it? Does natural law possess a universal validity independent of the state, or is positive legislation needed to give it effect? In attempting to answer these questions we shall find ourselves in the very center of the Hobbesian philosophy and confronted with elaborate and explicit statements, for, unlike Grotius, Hobbes developed a detailed doctrine of natural law. And since he explicitly rejected the notion of innate ideas,[16] the doctrine must rest upon some novel philosophical foundation.

Hobbes believed that he had put political and moral science, including natural law, upon an entirely new basis. In his introduction to the *Leviathan* he proudly proclaims this new science, the science of reading mankind in himself. To read in himself "not this or that particular man, but Man-kind" is

[15] *Emile,* Bk. v. "Grotius n'est qu'un enfant, et, qui pis est, un enfant de mauvaise foi. Quand j'entends élever Grotius jusqu'aux nues, et couvrir Hobbes d'exécration, je vois combiens d'hommes sensés lisent ou comprennent ces deux auteurs." Kant shared Rousseau's dislike for Grotius, of whom he speaks in *Zum Ewigen Frieden (Werke,* vi, 440) as "a miserable comforter," who talked about "laws of war" even though his code does not have the least legal validity.

[16] The most penetrating and learned exposition of Hobbes's doctrines is found in Ferdinand Tönnies, *Thomas Hobbes—Leben und Lehre* (1925). A genetic analysis of its beginnings is contained in Leo Strauss's able study, *The Political Philosophy of Hobbes—Its Basis and Its Genesis* (1936). The mechanical aspect of his philosophy is fully developed in Frithiof Brandt, *Thomas Hobbes' Mechanical Conception of Nature* (1928; translated from the Danish). F. J. C. Hearnshaw, *The Social and Political Ideas of Some Great Thinkers of the Sixteenth and Seventeenth Centuries* (1926) contains a chapter by E. L. Woodward on Hobbes which may be compared with A. D. Lindsay's penetrating introductory essay to the Everyman's edition of the *Leviathan.* Leslie Stephen's and George C. Robertson's works are, of course, the classics on Hobbes, but their perspective is out of focus for us. Cf. John Laird's *Hobbes* (1934).

"hard to do, harder than to learn any language, or Science"; but Hobbes feels that he has done the job, and all that is left for others is to apply his findings, after testing them by introspection: "Yet, when I shall have set down my own reading orderly, and perspicuously, the pains left another, will be onely to consider, if he also find not the same in himself."

Reversing the ancient organismic analogy, Hobbes proclaims all life to be but an automaton. "What is the *Heart*, but a *Spring;* and the Nerves, but so many *Strings;* and the Joynts, but so many *Wheeles*, giving motion to the whole Body . . . ?" he exclaims. And a commonwealth or state, the great Leviathan, is "but an Artificiall Man," whose sovereignty, magistrates, and the rest are analogous to various parts and characteristics of the human body—but one must not forget that it is the human body seen as a machine whose life is but *motion of the limbs.* To understand this great machine, we must look into ourselves: "Whosoever looketh into himself, and considereth what he doth, when he does *think, opine, hope, feare,* etc., and upon what grounds; he shall thereby read and know, what are the thoughts, and Passions of all other men, upon the like occasions." [17]

It is upon this foundation of a strictly mechanistic conception of man, a conception which is in line with the new view of nature as employed by Galileo and the rest,[18] that Hobbes bases his interpretation of man as primarily driven on by "the fear of violent death." [19] It is this primordial and all-engulfing fear

[17] This and the preceding quotations are from the Introduction to the *Leviathan*—a much neglected bit which provides the key to the whole work, as one might suspect in dealing with as systematic a thinker as Hobbes.

[18] See Morris Cohen's discussion on mechanism in *Reason and Nature* (1931), and especially his remark on p. 211: "The remarkable rapidity with which this doctrine was at once adopted from Galileo by men like Kepler, Descartes and Hobbes, shows what a fundamental need of the time it met." The doctrine referred to is that "only extension and motion are truly existent in nature."

[19] That it is the fear of *violent* death, and not merely the fear of death, is cogently stressed by Strauss, esp. p. 111ff. Fear is the passion which enlightens man, Strauss writes, and he shows how in his opinion this makes Hobbes the philosopher of bourgeois, as contrasted with aristocratic, virtue. Here is the

that forces him to think; makes him self-conscious about himself and the dangers which surround him; focuses his attention
upon the task of self-preservation, compels him to seek power
after power unto death,[20] so as to protect himself against his
fellow men; plunges him into continuous warfare in an effort
to anticipate attack from a more powerful neighbor; and finally
persuades him to try and escape from such a miserable life by
entering into a compact with as many men as will join him to
subject themselves to a common superior and sovereign who
will be empowered to do all that is needful to their common
protection. In this wise that great "Artificiall Man," that Leviathan we call a state or commonwealth comes into being. It
provides men, fearful, desperate men, with an escape from a life
that was "solitary, poore, nasty, brutish, and short." [21] Fear
it is which inclines men to peace, and driven by this fear men
are led to consult their reason which "suggests convenient
Articles of Peace . . . These Articles, are they, which otherwise
are called the Lawes of Nature . . ." From this thumbnail
sketch it is evident that Hobbes diverges from Grotius essentially
in this, that he stresses fear, and more especially the fear of
violent death, as the emotional basis of what reasoning he does,
whereas Grotius laid emphasis, as had the Stoics and their Christian followers, upon sociableness—a desire for living together.
Like Aristotle's political being, an animal which likes to live in

---

unbridgeable gulf between Hobbes and Machiavelli, whose *virtù* ideal is strictly
aristocratic, centered as it is in the virtues of the warrior, which include more
especially courage and *grandezza dell'animo*. For this see Friedrich Meinecke,
Die Idee der Staatsräson (1925) and my review article in *American Political
Science Review*, November 1926.
[20] The word "power" has a very general meaning in Hobbes's political philosophy, comprising virtually all means available to realize any end. He defines
power thus: "The power of a Man is his present means to obtain some future
apparent Good." For a critical evaluation of Hobbes's concept of power, see my
Constitutional Government and Democracy (1942), chs. i and xxv, as well as
the literature cited there. Divergent concepts of power are there shown to
account for a good measure of persistent basic disagreements in political theory.
[21] *Leviathan*, ch. xiii.

towns (*polis*), Grotius' man was sociable, moved by sympathetic emotions. Hobbes, looking into himself, found no such propensity for sociableness, no natural enjoyment of the society of others; but he did find fear. The soundness of his analysis stands and falls with the universal soundness of his view of human nature. This is not the place to analyze this viewpoint in further detail. It must suffice to observe that Hobbes has been both violently denounced and enthusiastically acclaimed for his view of man, which his admirers have called realistic while his adversaries have denounced it as "pessimistic." [22]

In any case, Hobbes develops an elaborate doctrine of natural law upon this basis which is in his view a description of what men will naturally be inclined to do. "These dictates of Reason, men use to call by the name of Laws; but improperly: for they are but Conclusions, or Theorems concerning what conduces to the conservation and defence of themselves; whereas Law, properly is the word of him, that by right has command over others." [23] In other words, these natural-law propositions are not "laws" in any juridical sense, unless and until they become embedded in positive law, but are mere "patterns of behavior" of individual human beings, impelled as they are by fear of violent death into using their reason. This is true, even though Hobbes adds the after-thought to the sentence just quoted that "if we consider the same Theoremes, as delivered in the word of God, that by right commandeth all things; then are they properly called Lawes." [24]

---

[22] Modern psychology does not support Hobbes's view, of course, but some schools have taken an analogous position.

[23] *Leviathan,* ch. xv, end. The kinship between this view and that expounded by Althusius (and other Calvinists) was stressed in my Introduction to *Johannes Althusius' Politica Methodice Digesta* (1932), p. lxviiiff. See Chapter IV, above, footnote 4.

[24] This phrasing is reminiscent of the Protestant and more especially Calvinist efforts to show natural law to be nothing but an elaboration of the Decalogue. Cf. Chapter IV, above.

These theorems, or behavioristic hypotheses, as we might call them, are fully developed in chapters xiv and xv of the *Leviathan*. Hobbes differentiates at the outset the *jus naturale* from the *lex naturalis* in terms of right and law. The right of nature, he holds, is the liberty to use one's power for self-preservation. It is an unlimited right to do "anything which in his own Judgment, and Reason, he shall conceive to be the aptest means thereunto." [25] It is clear from this sentence that Hobbes thinks of reason as an instrument for the purpose of determining which *means* are useful for the given end of self-preservation. This *instrumental* view of reason needs to be sharply distinguished from all normative views of a higher reason which perceives *ends*. Kant restated this ancient contrast by opposing *Vernunft* (pure practical reason) and *Verstand* (prudence, intellect). It is a dichotomy which has played an enormous role in speculative philosophy ever since the Greek classical tradition had differentiated between technics (science) and wisdom. Teleological and instrumental reason are continuously in danger of being confused, especially in such terms as "rationalism" and "rationalization." The decline of a belief in the higher teleological reason in our time is well illustrated in the tendency to imply that all rationalizations, except those which increase the effectiveness of organizations and machines, are pure figments of the imagination. "This is merely a rationalization," is the reply which modern man makes to all arguments derived from higher normative reasoning. It is also the reply of Hobbes, who sees only one function of reason, which is to determine what is useful and contributes to self-preservation. Hence "a Law of Nature (*Lex Naturalis*) is a Precept, or generall Rule, found out by Reason, by which a man is forbidden to do, that, which is destructive of his life, or taketh away the means of

---

[25] *Leviathan,* ch. xiv, beginning. The quotations which follow are from this chapter and ch. xv.

preserving the same." It is, in short, a technical norm of prudent conduct. Such laws, which determine and bind to a certain course of action, should therefore not be confused with the right of nature, which is the liberty to do or to forbear doing.

It is upon this view of natural law as a body of behavioristic hypotheses which constitute norms of prudence that Hobbes develops his doctrine. It consists of fifteen laws, or hypotheses, of which the first is called the "Fundamentall Law of Nature." It is this: "That every man, ought to endeavour Peace, as farre as he has hope of obtaining it; and when he cannot obtain it, that he may seek, and use, all helps and advantages of Warre." Now it is clear that this first and fundamental law is nothing but the direct derivative, in normative form, of Hobbes's view of man. For if fear of violent death is the prime and central motivation of man, he must evidently by all means seek to escape from this fear. So Hobbes immediately proceeds to state the second law, to be derived from the first: "That a man be willing, when others are so too, as farre-forth, as for Peace, and defence of himselfe he shall think it necessary, to lay down this right to all things; and be contented with so much liberty against other men, as he would allow other men against himself." This very general second law Hobbes points out to be identical with the teaching of the Gospel: "Therefore all things whatsoever ye would that men should do to you, do ye even so to them." To seek peace and follow it, and by all means we can to defend ourselves—these are the basic rules, comprised in the first and fundamental law from which all the others follow as derivations.

This basic position of Hobbes has often been criticized, and from varying viewpoints. From Kant's standpoint, which grounds all moral laws in the higher practical reason, Hobbes's approach is completely false. For the concept of law and lawful obligation (right) has nothing to do, as we saw, with the purpose all men have naturally, the purpose of happiness and of the means to achieve it. Law (*Recht*) is the restricting of the freedom of every man so that it will harmonize with the freedom of every other man in so far as this is possible according to a general law. And this is so because reason wills it so—the pure reason which gives a priori laws and does not have regard for any empirical purposes such as are comprised under the term happiness. Kant rules out all such considerations, because men have most divergent ideas as to what constitutes happiness, and one can therefore never arrive at general laws in that way.[26]

Hobbes would answer that you cannot arrive at general laws through Kant's reasoning either. For surely men are as much in disagreement as to what are the dictates of right reason in the higher teleological sense as they are in disagreement as to what constitutes happiness. The Hobbesian assumption of one central, all-engulfing passion is an artificial simplification of human nature; but so is the assumption of self-evident conclusions of one higher reason. Hobbes, like Carneades and Philus, argues that the only road to determining what is in accordance with natural law is to consult men's interest. Kant's answer, like the answers of Grotius and Laelius, is not to consult their interest at all. Both positions seem to do violence to man's nature, compounded as it is of material and ideal ends, or, as the Freudians would say, of an ego and a superego. It is a curious and yet highly significant fact that these two positions, so sharply divergent on general grounds, converge so closely when it comes to the detailed working out of these positions. For what Kant and other believers in an autonomous moral law derive from such general formula as the categorical imperative or the golden rule, and declare to be self-evident derivations from this basic a priori formula, Hobbes with equal assurance derives from his basic and fundamental law of expedient and prudent conduct

[26] See for this discussion Kant's own criticism of Hobbes's doctrine in *Theory and Practice*, Part II (*Werke*, VI, 373ff). Cf. also Chapter III above.

as the rational conclusions, theorems, or, as we have said, be-havioristic hypotheses.

For what does the Hobbesian catalogue of such natural laws reveal? Here is the list of the remaining thirteen theorems: (1) covenants should be kept; (2) men should be grateful; (3) men should be accommodating; (4) men should be willing to pardon offenses; (5) in retribution, men should regard the future good rather than the past evil; (6) men should not show hatred or contempt; (7) men should regard each other as equals; (8) men should not seek special privileges; (9) in judging, men should treat fellow men as equals; (10) men should share what they cannot divide; (11) what they can neither share nor divide, they should distribute by lot; (12) all men that mediate peace should be allowed safe conduct; (13) controversies should be submitted to arbitration. It is clear that these rules or theorems are very similar to the basic positions of the Judæo-Christian code of ethics, and the only feature which differentiates Hobbes's treatment—and it is an important one—is that he argues that the true ground of their obliging men to follow them is their utility in achieving peace. He argues thus all the way through the discussion, and shows in each case how the breach of the particular rule would be the cause of war. To illustrate: the second of these rules, commanding gratitude, rests on the consideration that "no man giveth, but with intention of Good to himself; because Gift is voluntary"; hence if men discover that they do not get anything in return for what they have done, there will be "no beginning of benevolence, nor consequently of mutuall help; nor of reconciliation of one man to another; and therefore they are still to remain in the condition of War . . ." This is Hobbes's central theme, to which he returns time and again.[27]

---

[27] I have not given the thirteen laws of nature in their exact and often cumbrous wording, for which chapters xiv and xv in the *Leviathan* should be consulted, as well as the corresponding sections in *De cive*. See William Moles-

Would Hobbes deny, then, that these laws are absolutely binding? Are they "laws of nature" in that rigid sense in which the law of gravitation is? They are and they are not. As Hobbes puts it: "These are the Laws of Nature, dictating Peace, for a means of the conservation of men in multitudes . . ." He undoubtedly would argue in general, as he does in each particular case, that their violation is conducive to war, and weakens the peace and order of society. They are immutable and eternal according to Hobbes. Yet, "The Lawes of Nature oblige *in foro interno.*" What this means is that each man is himself the judge as to how far they contribute toward his self-preservation, so that under adverse conditions he may discard them. Such laws, Hobbes remarks, are easily observed, because they only oblige us to *endeavor* to fulfill them. Therefore, as long as we try to perform them, we fulfill them, "and he that fulfilleth the Law, is Just."

To make absolutely sure that no misunderstanding arises in the mind of the reader concerning the strictly hypothetical nature of these "laws" which are truly mere "theoremes," Hobbes adds the following uncompromising statement:

And the Science of them, is the true and onely Moral Philosophy. For Moral Philosophy is nothing else but the Science of what is *Good* and *Evill*, in the conversation, and Society of Mankind. *Good*, and *Evill*, are names that signifie our Appetites, and Aversions; which in different tempers, customes, and doctrines of man are different: And divers men, differ not onely in their Judgement, on the senses of what is pleasant, and unpleasant to the taste, smell, hearing, touch, and sight; but also of what is conformable, or disagreeable to Reason, in the actions of common life.

The only escape from the ensuing conflicts is provided by their common agreement "that Peace is Good," and "therefore also the way, or means of Peace . . . the Lawes of Nature." The only

worth's edition of *The English Works of Thomas Hobbes* (1839-45), vol. III and elsewhere.

trouble with Hobbes's argument, its real Achillean heel, is the psychology of fear upon which it all rests. You could either attack this psychology, as did Locke and others, or you could attack the underlying idea that considerations of utility are the true ground of moral and political obligation. This is the line of argument which Pufendorf, anticipating Kant, adopted.[28]

It is a commonplace of the history of political thought that Samuel Pufendorf (1632-1694) made an attempt to combine the approach of Grotius with that of Hobbes in developing his theory of natural law, and that whatever his originality or the lack of it, he exerted a greater influence on succeeding generations of writers in natural law than either of his illustrious predecessors.[29] Did he merely modify and attenuate their radically

---

[28] How binding these laws of nature are believed to be for Hobbes has been the occasion for extended controversy. Otto von Gierke stated the extreme view in his *Johannes Althusius* (1880): "The first effort to defeat natural law on its own ground and with its own weapons was made by Hobbes. He reduced the natural law which antedates the state to a 'jus inutile,' which contains not even the germ of a true Law; he made the State, by whose command and force law is created, absorb all rights which it does not itself create; he rejected all notions of a legal restraint of the State and its sovereign power of deciding as to right and the lack of it." (My translation; see translation by Bernard Freyd, *The Development of Political Theory*, 1939, p. 319.) Tönnies protested part of this interpretation when he wrote (*Thomas Hobbes—Leben und Lehre*, p. 202): "It is true that Hobbes denies all thought of a legal restraint on the state's power; not quite true, however, that he [Hobbes] allows every right not created by the state to be absorbed by the state." We agree with Tönnies that Hobbes did recognize a natural law, but it is not the "natural law" which Gierke himself recognized as such, and therefore he, too, was right. What Gierke has in mind is the very point which Kant protests in *Theory and Practice*, p. 388, namely, that Hobbes will not admit the natural law as a standard for evaluating the laws (statutes), that the sovereign cannot do anything which the subject has a right to call illegal or *unrecht*. We shall show that this interpretation is not entirely accurate when we come to discuss the problem of resistance. Hobbes recognized a subject's right to resist actions of the sovereign which violate the fundamental right to preserve himself from death. The relationship between Kant and Hobbes is misinterpreted also by Kurt Börries (*Kant als Politiker*, 1928), who finds himself startled by their agreement but really does not seem to have grasped the basic point at issue between them, as stated above.

[29] Cf. Samuel Pufendorf, *The Law of Nature and Nations*, with introduction by W. Simons, in Classics of International Law, Carnegie Foundation Series

rationalist and meta-rationalist views of man? Or did he develop a new and distinctive approach? Gierke strongly emphasized Pufendorf's doctrine of the moral beings (*entia moralia*) which he invested with rights and duties of which the natural beings were devoid. This doctrine implies a dualistic construction of the world of actions which seems to anticipate Kant. But its metaphysical basis is uncritically formulated, and is set forth more or less as a matter of course. In discussing and rejecting the doctrine of the Roman law that natural law is what nature teaches all living beings, Pufendorf insists that the actions of man result from freedom, those of animals from natural causation.[30] The clear-cut Christian dualism which is here implied follows the earlier lead of Oldendorp, who also, as we have seen, took especial trouble to reject the Roman-law doctrine on this particular point, as had Christian thinkers before him.[31] Without being detained by the metaphysical difficulties of such a position, Pufendorf makes them the basis of his conception of legal personality. The world of law was to him a world of moral beings which in themselves are only attributes ascribed by rational beings to physical beings. These moral beings thus become the factors which shape human will, which being free is shaped by its own creations, these *entia moralia*. There are simple moral persons and composite moral persons. The simple persons are the individuals, the composite ones are the various associations and groups—families, corporations, churches, *civitates*, and the rest. A composite moral person comes into being

---

(vol. xvii, 1934). See also, in the same series, the introductions by W. Schücking and H. Wehberg to *De officio hominis ac civis* (vol. x, 1927) and *Elementarum jurisprudentiae universalis* (vol. xv, 1931); Otto von Gierke, *Natural Law and the Theory of Society*, translated with an Introduction by Ernest Barker (1934); Otto von Gierke, *The Development of Political Theory*, translated by Bernard Freyd (1939), pp. 172ff and elsewhere; Eric Wolf, *Grotius, Pufendorf, Thomasius* (1927); Friedrich Meinecke, *Die Idee der Staatsräson in der neueren Geschichte* (1925), pp. 279-303; Hans Welzel, *Die Naturrechtslehre des Samuel Pufendorf* (1928).

[30] *Elementarum jurisprudentiae universalis.*
[31] See above, Chapter IV.

when a single will is ascribed to a multitude of individuals duly
and properly united and therefore invested by others with legal
personality which is just as real as the legal personality of individuals, both beings resulting from attribution of personality
by the beholder.[32]

It is obvious that this doctrine is completely at variance with
the mechanistic naturalism of Hobbes. But even the state of
nature which precedes this world of law and of moral beings is,
in Pufendorf's view, a state of peace rather than war. For
Pufendorf, like Grotius and in opposition to Hobbes, believed
men to be motivated by sociability (*socialitas*) as well as the
instinct of self-preservation. The two basic propensities combine to persuade groups of superior men, men especially endowed
with the capacity to reason, to abandon this state of nature and
enter into a state of society. Pufendorf suggests that this process is composed of three steps: the social contract, the constitution, and the governmental contract. The first step consists
in a contract among the individuals to form a lasting society
whose constitution shall be determined by majority vote. The
second step is taken when the form of government is adopted
by majority vote, at which time those who do not like the decision may withdraw. Finally, a contract between those who
are to constitute the government and the citizenry at large
provides the third step. Pufendorf, in spite of the last step,
maintained that the personality of the people becomes entirely
absorbed by the personality of the ruler or rulers. Thus the community is denied any rights against the governor. This sounds
like Hobbes, but, in contrast to Hobbes, Pufendorf vindicates
rights of the individual citizen, even when these rights are only

[32] Cf. Gierke, *Natural Law*, i, 118-121. Our interpretation differs somewhat
from Gierke's, because we do not share Gierke's regret about Pufendorf's in-
dividualistic basis which prevented him from seeing these groups as natural
superentities. When Gierke writes that "a unity thus interpreted in terms of
the rights of individuals was in the last analysis only a deceptive sham . . . "
we feel that he is quite wrong.

imperfectly guaranteed.[33] It is this vindication of individual rights which constitutes the kinship between Pufendorf and Locke, and which so strongly appealed to John Wise. The latter, a radical New England clergyman, who in his *Vindication of the New England Churches* (1679) explicitly grounded his argument on Pufendorf's doctrine of natural rights,[34] clearly perceived that Pufendorf had undertaken to show that supreme authority was not necessarily unlimited.

It is even more important to realize that for Pufendorf, in spite of his insistence upon the moral being, natural law is not a God-ordained set of rules, but flows from the metarational natural propensities of man. He resembles Hobbes in his sovereign disregard for authority and his insistence upon the individual as the ultimate reality. He followed Hobbes in freeing natural law completely from theology; yet it is clear that his particular metaphysic bears as striking a resemblance to his Lutheran background and antecedents as Hobbes's does to Calvinism and Locke's to Anglicanism. The source from which the pure knowledge of natural law can and should be derived by Christians is the orthodox doctrine concerning the state of integrity when man had a picture of God in his heart. For natural law is among its relics.[35] But it would be a mistake, according to Pufendorf, to limit natural law to Christians. In order to be universal, natural law must be derived from a principle which is recognized by men as men. There is no more a

[33] Here again the analogy to Kant is striking, and again the argument turns upon the dualistic construction which requires that the individual retain his status as "moral person," since to admit his being deprived of this quality would destroy the whole argument. For this aspect of the matter, cf. Gierke, *Natural Law*, pp. 142-143, and Dunning, *Political Theories from Luther to Montesquieu*, p. 323. Pufendorf's doctrine is found in *De jure naturae*, VII. II.7 and elsewhere.

[34] See the discussion in V. L. Parrington, *Main Currents of American Thought* (1927-30), I, 118-125; B. F. Wright, Jr., *American Interpretations of Natural Law* (1931), p. 49ff.

[35] Cf. Welzel, *Des Naturrechtslehre des Samuel Pufendorf*, p. 3n. Cf. also pp. 2 and 5.

Christian natural law than a Christian arithmetic. This insistence upon the universality and transcendence of natural
law which goes back to Grotius and the Stoics was of vital importance to an age which struggled to free itself of the incubus
of religious intolerance and theological bellicosity. Pufendorf
dwells again and again upon the laws of nature as being rooted
in man's nature and embodying his objective moral values or
beliefs. Natural law is simply the totality of norms which have
the objective moral values of human life as their content.[36]

What is their content? Basically, there are two such norms.
Each man should protect body and life and maintain himself
and his own. No one should disturb human society. From these
two basic rules Pufendorf derives a catalogue which in most
respects resembles the familiar pattern. Pufendorf's discussion,
however, is vitiated by the same fundamental flaw which destroys the cogency of Hobbes's reasoning: existential and normative judgments are confused and the latter are derived somehow from the former. The critical standpoint which made Kant
insist that there is no possible transition from one of these realms
of judgment to the other had not yet been achieved.[37]

There remains one important point to be noted, before we
turn from Pufendorf to Locke. The three great writers whose
doctrine we have so far considered, Grotius, Hobbes, and Pufendorf, were all of them to some extent historians. This is
least true of Hobbes, but even he had devoted much time and

[36] Cf. the introductions by Wehberg, Schücking, and Simons cited in footnote
29, above.
[37] When, in this connection, Welzel insists (pp. 16-17) that *socialitas* does
not mean "sociability" but "the most general concept of the objective moral
values," and that "nature is a complex of norms," I am afraid that his attempt
to remove the difficulty stated in the text raises others which are even more
grave, since such an interpretation runs afoul of the basic distinction between
moral and natural beings. Pufendorf's well-known doctrine that international
law was derivable only from natural law, and could not be so derived from
treaties and customs (a view which he shares with Hobbes against Grotius)
also seems incompatible with such an interpretation.

thought to history when he undertook to translate Thucydides.[38]

No such historical interests are part of the abstract speculation of John Locke. For while Locke had many predecessors, the secular individualism which we have found at the heart of most thought on natural law in the seventeenth century found in him its most persuasive philosopher. In his skillful hands the traditional doctrine of natural law turned into a doctrine of natural rights—rights which the individual could claim as inalienable, because they were his as a man and prior to all government.[39] With Hooker, Locke maintains that a state of nature precedes the social state; with Hobbes he suggests that the objection, "Where are, or ever were, there any men in such a state of Nature?" can be met by the answer that all independent governments are in a state of nature; but against Hobbes he insists that this state of nature is a state of relative peace and mutual coöperation. He adduces the authority of Hooker at considerable length in support of "that obligation to mutual love amongst men on which he builds the duties they owe one another, and from whence he derives the great maxims of justice and charity" (Second Treatise, §5).

[38] The importance of Hobbes's work on Thucydides has been brought out with striking effect by Leo Strauss, *The Political Philosophy of Hobbes*, ch. vi, pp. 79-107. Studies such as this serve to correct the generalizations offered by Carl Becker in *The Heavenly City of the Eighteenth-Century Philosophers*, pp. 71ff. Cf. also Meinecke, *Die Idee der Staatsräson*, pp. 263-270.

[39] Locke's political philosophy is conveniently at hand in his *Two Treatises on Government* (1690). Their general tenor has become so familiar that it is difficult to appreciate their true originality. No one has ever especially addressed himself to the doctrine of natural law in Locke in its relation to earlier doctrines, especially that of Hooker, but Paschal Larkin's *Property in the Eighteenth Century, with Special Reference to England and Locke* (1930) is valuable, as is Walton Hamilton's article "Property—According to Locke" in *Yale Law Journal*, 41:864-880 (April 1932). A challenging chapter on the law of nature in its relation to majority rule is contained in Willmoore Kendall, *John Locke and the Doctrine of Majority Rule* (1941), ch. v. Besides the general works of Alexander, Fowler, and Fraser, we would draw special attention to the chapter on Locke in T. H. Green, *Lectures on the Principles of Political Obligation* (1895), pp. 68-79.

In the state of nature, the law of nature governs, for it is not a state of license. This law of nature is clearly equated with reason (§6) and Locke believes that "it teaches all mankind." It is all a matter of sweet reasonableness; for

everyone as he is bound to preserve himself, and not to quit his station wilfully, so by the like reason, when his own preservation comes not in competition, ought he as much as he can to preserve the rest of mankind, and not unless it be to do justice to an offender, take away or impair the life, or what tends to the preservation of the life, the liberty, health, limb, or goods of another. (§6)

But how is such a law to be enforced in the state of nature where everyone has a right to act with perfect freedom? Locke answers: "The execution of the law of nature is in that state put into every man's hands." Thus everyone has a right to punish the transgressors. For the complete equality in the state of nature precludes any special "superiority or jurisdiction." But is not this the war of all against all which so greatly disturbed Hobbes? Not at all, answers Locke; for this right to punish does extend only "to retribute to him so far as calm reason and conscience dictate." Man is not permitted to take revenge; all he is entitled to do is to punish the transgression sufficiently to serve for reparation and restraint.[40]

This extraordinary doctrine of the enforcement of natural law by everyone had, of course, a significant application to the relations between independent sovereigns, since it provided

[40] It is striking, indeed, how closely this reasoning and that which follows resembles the official American approach to the problem of the trial of war criminals. Indeed, the presentation of the case as given by Mr. Justice Jackson reads as if taken straight from Locke, and illustrates in an extraordinary way the dominance of these ideas in America—for admittedly Jackson's plea is "representative" of American sentiment, as was shown by the overwhelmingly favorable comment in newspapers and magazines. A very interesting recent discussion of related issues was offered by Erich Hula in "The Revival of the Idea of Punitive War," *Thought*, xxi (1946), 405ff.

demonstrable ground for making war one upon the other for the purpose of "preserving mankind." However, Locke stays with his hypothetical state of nature among individuals, and asserts everyone's right to kill a murderer—a criminal "who, having renounced reason, the common rule and measure God hath given to mankind, has, by the unjust violence and slaughter he hath committed upon one, declared war against all mankind." This type of reasoning clearly leads into the conception of a world organization for the punishment of aggression, and there is a peculiarly telling note in Locke's suggestion that such an aggressor "may be destroyed as a lion or tiger, one of those wild, savage beasts" (§11).

Locke is, on the whole, rather elusive concerning the actual content of this law of nature on the basis of which people in the state of nature may punish each other. He even tells us that it is beside his purpose to enter into its "particulars." Yet he states one great law of nature as "Whoso sheddeth man's blood, by man shall his blood be shed," and he cites the case of Cain, who cried out that anyone who found him should slay him as a clear indication that this great law is "writ plain in the hearts of all mankind." And because it is all so plain, and there is hence no need to go into it in any particular, Locke goes so far as to claim that the law of nature is more readily understood than municipal law. What is more, these municipal laws are right only in so far as they are founded on the law of nature. This idea is a familiar one; we noticed it in Althusius and other writers as a recurrent theme. But few, if any, had argued this proposition on the ground of the "comprehensibility" of the law of nature, although the bitter fight between Francis Bacon and Sir Edward Coke had partly turned on this issue. There seems to be a faint echo of this argument in Locke's animadversions upon "the fancies and intricate contrivances of men," when speaking of the laws which he says "follow con-

trary and hidden interests." In contrast to this "artificial reason of the law," [41] Locke not only feels that it is certain that
there is such a law (§12), but that it is "as intelligible and
plain to a rational creature" as municipal law ever was.

There is one final argument which Locke has to dispose of in
connection with his doctrine of the natural law enforced by all
men in the state of nature, and that is the argument that it is
"unreasonable for men to be judges in their own case." Locke
readily admits that the establishment of "civil government" is
the proper remedy, but until that happens he who judges amiss
"is answerable for it to the rest of mankind." That statement is
a most extraordinary one, if meant to apply to these men in the
state of nature. For they surely would not be deeply moved by
the disapprobation of so intangible a being as mankind would
be for them. What he presumably means is that any man could
hold the malefactor answerable. This interpretation is suggested
by Locke's drawing an analogy to the relation between states.
For it surely is a much more real sanction when fellow sovereigns are justified in resisting an aggressor like Louis XIV, who
might be tempted to fall upon their neighbors without provoca-
tion. It is not surprising, therefore, that Locke at this point
brings in these independent governments as showing that there
exist numerous men in the state of nature.

It is worth noting at this juncture that Locke expresses the
opinion that the world "never will be without numbers of men
in that state." This he said within three years of William
Penn's project of a league of nations as offered in *An Essay
Towards the Present and Future Peace of Europe* (1693), which
was inspired by the very ideas of toleration which stood at the
center of Locke's thinking. But since Locke's state of nature is
capable of being a state of peace and coöperation, the avoiding

[41] Sir Edward Coke's famous phrase coined in the fight against the inclination
of James I to urge the superior force of the natural law in typical absolutist
fashion. Cf. Roscoe Pound, *The Spirit of the Common Law* (1921), p. 61.

of war did not *necessarily* require establishing a government. The plain difference between the state of nature and the state of war is this: one is a state of peace, good will, mutual assistance, and preservation, the other is a state of enmity, malice, violence, and mutual destruction. They have in common that there exists no common superior.[42] It is evident that Locke believes in some kind of "moral law within," and his recurrent use of the expression "ought" as well as his appeals to key tenets of Christian ethics clearly reveals his attachment to a law of nature in terms of the higher reason.

But before Pufendorf and Locke attempted their modifications, a more radical and uncompromising statement of the natural law as mere power had been undertaken by Baruch Spinoza (1632-1677).[43] This thinker "drunk with God" carried the idea of a world permeated by laws to its penultimate conclusion. Nature and God are brought to coincide in an all-engulfing pantheism, a monistic, mathematically ordered cosmos which is God. This attempt at infusing every fragment of nature with God by treating it as an emanation of his being resulted in removing him as a molding, ordering, norm-creating factor from the realm of government and law. "The big fish devour the little fish by natural law [or right]"—this is the

[42] The close connection between these views and Locke's relational concept of power turns upon his conception of man as motivated by sympathy. See his moving passage in §87. Cf., for the relational power concept, my *Constitutional Government and Democracy* (1942) ch. i.

[43] Spinoza's views on peace and natural law have never been the subject of a special investigation, but the matter is usually discussed in the general treatises. Spinoza lays out his views very clearly, especially in the *Tractatus politicus,* which should be supplemented by *Tractatus theologico-politicus,* especially chs. xvi and xvii, and by the *Ethica.* I have used the Latin edition of his works, edited by J. van Sloten and J. P. N. Land, and published by M. Nijhoff (3rd ed., 1913). Bohn's Philosophical Library has a translation of Spinoza's chief works, edited and introduced by R. H. M. Elwes, which is sound. I would add the valuable discussion by A. Wolf in *Spinoza's Short Treatise on God, Man and His Wellbeing* (1910), and I should also like to draw attention to Leo Strauss's helpful discussion in *Die Religionskritik Spinoza's* (1930), pp. 217-236. H. A. Wolfson, *The Philosophy of Spinoza* (2 vols., 1934), is the most satisfactory general work.

formidable consequence of treating all law as power.[44] "By the law of nature [*jus naturae*] I understand the laws of nature or rules according to which every thing happens, that is nature's power itself." [45] The complete identification of *jus naturae* and *leges naturae* is the philosophical underpinning of Alexander Pope's famous words in the *Essay on Man*: "Whatever is, is right." It is not without interest in this connection to consider the whole context within which this statement occurs in Pope:

> All nature is but art, unknown to thee;
> All chance, direction, which thou canst not see;
> All discord, harmony not understood;
> All partial evil, universal good;
> And spite of pride, in erring reason's spite,
> One truth is clear, Whatever is, is right.[46]

For these lines reveal clearly the general rationalist inclination to rationalize the world as it is by vindicating its reality against criticisms derived from some norm-giving supernatural being or code. Neither Pope nor others, however, dared follow Spinoza to the final implication of identifying nature and God, even if they were ready to agree with him that these two expressions were "two sides of the same being." Thus Pope proclaimed: "All are but parts of one stupendous whole, whose body nature is, and God the soul." [47] For Spinoza this meant that the natural right (*jus naturale*) of this whole, and "consequently of each individual [being]," extends as far as its power does. He states

---

[44] *Tractatus theologico-politicus*, ch. xvi.

[45] *Tractatus theologico-politicus*, ch. ii, ¶ 4. In the preceding paragraph Spinoza explicitly states that "God's right is none other than God's power," and from this it follows "unamquamque rem naturalem tantum juris ex Natura habere, quantum potentiae habet ad existendum et operandum." Why does it follow? Because its inherent laws are the laws of nature and of nature's God.

[46] Epistle I, line 289.

[47] *Ibid.*, line 267.

flatly that "whatever a man does in accordance with the *laws* of his nature, he does by the highest *right* of Nature; for he has as much right as he has power." [48] It is small wonder that such a philosophy should have appealed to a Bismarck, as it did to Hegel. No wonder, either, that Spinoza should have expressed his high regard for "the keen-witted Florentine" Machiavelli.[49] It is an error, however, to assume that such a political philosophy necessarily means authoritarianism; for its ready acceptance of might as the basis of right applies as readily to a successful revolution as it does to a successful autocrat. Thus the right of resistance is clearly based on the might of resistance, and anyone will resist such power as he can.

What is more, Spinoza believes a democracy to be of all forms of government the most natural. In it, he feels, no one transfers his natural right so unconditionally that he has no further part in shaping the laws. This conclusion is bound up with Spinoza's idea of freedom as obedience to the laws of human nature: "He alone is free who lives with free consent under the entire guidance of reason." [50]

In all this reasoning we have a secularized form of Calvinist thinking. Predestination, the most "irrational" aspect of Calvinist orthodoxy, has its secular counterpart in Spinoza. Spinoza's conviction of man's complete dependence is, if anything, more uncompromising than Calvin's. All that man (or any other thing) does, he does with those powers in himself which are the emanation of God's power. Man is like clay in the hand of God. Spinoza saw himself as the fulfillment of the doctrine

---

[48] *Tractatus theologico-politicus,* ch. ii.
[49] *Ibid.,* v. 7.
[50] *Tractus theologico-politicus,* ch. xvi (Elwes edition, pp. 206-207). In view of this statement, it is much to be regretted that Spinoza was prevented by death from dealing with democracy in his *Tractatus politicus.* It is clear, however, that he intended to deal with direct democracy only, and not with the representative and constitutional democracies which developed later.

of predestination, completely opposed as he was to any kind of "justice through good works." [51]

The kinship between this kind of naturalism and the Calvinist setting in which it grew is well expressed in a remark William III is said to have made to a bishop as he stepped upon England's soil: "Do you now admit of predestination?" For William's Calvinism was "of the extremist kind." To him predestination was a reality, and he never doubted that he was an instrument of the divine will.[52] That this concept of predestination is intimately related to the idea of a cosmos ordered by laws unrelieved by any interference even from God has been shown in Chapter IV.

Although Spinoza mentions Hobbes only once,[53] and there to differentiate himself from the philosopher of Malmesbury, Spinoza's view of man's prime motivation is closely related to Hobbes's: self-preservation is the primary task. "Now it is the highest law of nature that every thing should attempt to continue in its state as much as it can . . ." "Nor do we recognize

---

[51] Cf., for all this, Leo Strauss, who brilliantly develops both the relation and the critical antitheses between Calvin and Spinoza (*Die Religionskritik Spinoza's*, pp. 182-206).

[52] Cf. G. J. Renier, *William of Orange* (1933), who does not, however, cite this remark. If the story is untrue, it is, as the Italians say, "ben' invenuto."

[53] This mention is in a note (27) to ch. xvi of *Tractatus theologico-politicus,* which insists that "reason is always on the side of peace, though Hobbes thinks otherwise." (This is footnote xxxiii in the Latin edition.) W. A. Dunning, *A History of Political Theories from Luther to Montesquieu,* p. 317, expresses the opinion that the view here attributed to Hobbes is "far from anything he ever expressed." In the *Leviathan* we read: "That every man ought to endeavour Peace, as farre as he has hope of obtaining it; and when he cannot obtain it, that he may seek, and use, all helps, and advantages of Warre." Cf. the clear analysis by Leo Strauss (*Die Religionskritik Spinoza's*, pp. 222-228), though the contrast is a bit overstated when he writes that the natural-law doctrines of Hobbes and Spinoza are "toto coelo verschieden." Strauss's statement that the two philosophers "mean something very different" when they speak of self-preservation is not adequately supported by his statement that Spinoza's idea of self-preservation leads to theory while according to Hobbes it obliges one to seek security, peace, and a commonwealth (*Staat*). Strauss himself correctly develops Spinoza's doctrine of self-preservation in terms comparable to those given in the text.

any difference between men and other of Nature's individuals; nor between men who are endowed with Reason, and others who do not know true Reason; nor between fools, madmen and sane men." [54] Why should this be? Why should Spinoza thus cast aside one of the most ancient traditions in the doctrine of natural law (although to be sure one strand of the Roman and Stoic tradition had done the same)? It is because men are motivated by passions, and if wise men have a right to be wise, fools have a right to be fools. "The ignorant and weak-minded has the highest right to all that his Appetite suggests and to live according to the laws of Appetite." It is, in other words, the self *as it is* that natural law lets a man preserve, and whatever suits that self and its inherent needs is lawful. The *Tractatus politicus* builds up to the triumphant challenge: "The affections by which we are afflicted the philosophers conceive to be vices from which men suffer by their own fault; therefore they deride, bewail and censure them, or execrate them, if they wish to seem more saintly." It culminates in the assertion that "they [other philosophers of natural law] have never conceived a theory of politics which could be turned to use." For these philosophers conceive of men "not as they are, but as they would like them to be." Spinoza believes that man, the emotional, irrational creature, must be studied like any other thing in nature, and his inherent laws discovered, if a genuinely scientific politics (and ethics) is to result.

In the sphere of the relations between sovereign commonwealths, this means that they are naturally enemies. What follows is ruthlessness unrestrained by anything but a shrewd appraisal of one's actual power. "If one commonwealth wishes to make war on another and employ extreme measures to make that other dependent, it may lawfully make the attempt . . ."

---

[54] *Tractatus theologico-politicus,* ch. xvi. The translation is my own, because Elwes introduces terms such as "sovereign" into the text which the Latin does not warrant.

Similarly, there is no real limit to treachery, such as that suggested by the rule of natural law that contracts must be served. "Every commonwealth has the right to break its contract, whenever it chooses, and cannot be said to act treacherously or perfidiously in breaking its word." [55] Neither reason nor scripture, Spinoza assures us, teaches one to keep one's word in every case. It is clear from these and numerous similar statements with which the work of Spinoza abounds that we have in him the most radical exponent of the doctrine that might makes right, the doctrine which in our time has found new believers in the various totalitarian creeds. Spinoza has completely transformed the law of nature conceived in terms of a higher reason into the laws of nature which he so aptly illustrates by his fishes, which are by nature conditioned for swimming, and the bigger for devouring the little ones. There is no difference between these and men; they all follow their natural laws, which is their right.

That such a doctrine should have shocked Spinoza's contemporaries can scarcely be wondered at. For such a statement of natural right and law, while preserving the traditional terms, did in fact use them in so different a connotation that the theory of Spinoza amounted to a complete destruction of the established doctrine.[56] At the same time, Spinoza made this

[55] *Tractatus politicus,* ch. iii, sections 14-15. With regard to Pearl Harbor Spinoza would have observed: "If then a commonwealth complains that it has been deceived, it cannot properly blame the bad faith of another contracting commonwealth, but only its own folly in having entrusted its own welfare to another party, that was independent, and had for its highest law the welfare of its own dominion."

[56] God and liberty suffered the same fate at Spinoza's hand, and it has been rightly observed that God and nature are the same looked at from two different sides. "Liberty," Spinoza insists time and again—that is, to be free—is to follow "the laws of human nature," and this does not mean obeying the commands of a higher reason. "Liberty does not take away the necessity of acting, but presupposes it." It will be clearly seen that this liberty which consists in employing the means requisite for a given end, e.g. self-preservation, is actually a rigid determinism. That this concept is completely at variance with Kant's concept of freedom is obvious. See Kant's discussion of Spinoza's attempt to eliminate the idea of *telos* (*Endursache*) in *Kritik der Urtheilskraft,* §73 (*Werke,* v, 471). Spinoza's argument is especially subject to the Kantian criti-

denial of the traditional rationalist interpretation of the dictates of right reason the basis of a most explicit and radical doctrine of peace. Not only do we owe to him the highly significant definition of peace as "virtue that springs from strength of mind," but he went further and insisted that the man of reason will always seek peace.[57] In other words, an ever more complete grasp of the laws of nature, including those of human nature, will produce an ever greater readiness to make allowance for human weakness, persistently seeing manifestations of the divine even in imperfect beings. Blessedness is freedom of mind, and virtue.

Thus Spinoza's radically monistic doctrine, completely identifying right, law, and power, still leaves room for a glorification of peace, purely as a matter of rational good sense. But at the same time it is clear that this doctrine constituted a complete perversion of the traditional doctrines of natural law and right. It is even excusable to ask whether there was anything left of the doctrine of natural right after Spinoza had thus interpreted it as natural power. The explicit rejection of natural law and right, however, was undertaken by David Hume. Writing in the Hobbesian tradition and carrying the psychological approach to understanding to its radical limit, Hume developed the utilitarian implications and at the same time destroyed the belief in the "higher reason." It is common knowledge that

---

cism of the equivocal meaning of *bonum* and *malum* as used by the schools, for which see *Kritik der Praktischen Vernunft*, I, 1, 2 (*Werke*, v, 66ff). Cf. also the *Ethica* of Spinoza, prop. xlviii and xlix, and the definition of good and evil at the beginning of Part iv and prop. lxv. Part iv is entitled "Of Human Bondage" and is juxtaposed to Part v, entitled "Of the Power of the Intellect or of Human Liberty." This juxtaposition shows that Spinoza believed liberty to result from the mind's grasping and accepting the laws of nature and of nature's God, i.e., from loving God-nature. Cf. Part v, prop. xxxvi.

[57] The statement occurs in *Tractatus politicus*, Part v, §4 and reads: "Pax enim non belli privatio, sed virtus est, quae ex animi fortitudine oritur." There are numerous passages in the two *Tractatus* and in the *Ethica* which state this view emphatically, e.g. *Ethica*, ch. iv, prop. xxxv. We have noted above, note 54, the disagreement between Spinoza and Hobbes on this point.

Hume attempted to apply the basic principles of experimental psychology to the construction of a theory of knowledge, and the experimental, or at any rate, observational method to all study and knowledge of human nature. This approach led Hume to deny that the "law of causation" had any basis in experience, and that it is impossible to demonstrate the existence of any fact. Experience of the kind which leads to knowledge— that is, experience that we are conscious of—gives us merely a succession of sense impressions of which ideas are fainter copies or reproductions. By associating these ideas we build these successions into patterns which we call facts and causes. Hume linked this thoroughly skeptical doctrine of cognition with the doctrine that all human motivation stems from a desire for pleasure (and an avoidance of pain). It takes no great ingenuity to conclude from these two starting points that the idea of a natural law as composed of the "dictates of right reason" is without validity or even meaning.[58]

In Section III of *An Enquiry concerning the Principles of Morals* (1751), Hume addresses himself specifically to the problem of Justice, and undertakes to show that "public utility is the sole origin of justice." He insists that justice is wholly related to the "condition" in which men find themselves, that a virtuous man in a society of ruffians must abandon his ideas of right and "make provision of all means of defense and security"; and that since his particular morals, like his regard for justice, are no longer of USE[59] to him, he must consider the requirements of self-preservation only. When such a view is applied to a topic like the law of war, which was a familiar concern of traditional natural law, we find Hume arguing a doctrine of *rebus sic stantibus.* "The laws of war . . . are rules calculated for the advantage and utility of that particular state [of war]."

---

[58] For a fuller discussion of the problems here involved, especially causation and utility, see Chapter VII, below.
[59] Hume himself capitalizes the word to emphasizes its significance.

His argument is simple: once you reverse the conditions under which justice is useful, you suspend its obligation. "By rendering justice totally *useless*, you . . . suspend its obligation upon mankind." These arguments may seem startling in the abstract, but who would deny their universal employment in the war just past? As Hume says very flatly: "And were a civilized nation engaged with barbarians, who observed no rules even of war, the former must also suspend their observance of them . . ." [60] Indeed, Hume is convinced that none of the writers on the law of nature has ever succeeded in offering any more convincing ground than the "convenience and necessities of mankind" as the ultimate reason for every rule which he establishes. And Hume adds, with some irony, that " a concession thus extorted, in opposition to systems, has more authority, than if it had been made in prosecution of them." Poor old Socrates! All his efforts were in vain. "Thus the rules of equity or justice depend entirely on the particular state or condition, in which men are placed, and owe their origin and existence to that Utility, which results to the public from their strict and regular observance."

What then is the ground of obligation of such rules as we do observe? What makes them binding upon us? According to Hume, it is all a matter of habit and convention. Such habit and convention are rooted in the "necessities of human society." If the necessities change, the habits and conventions change, and the moral norms which flow from them. The typical optimism of the Scotish enlightenment, with its touchingly reasonable view of human progress, is clearly part of this view and helps to make it compatible with elementary ethical sense. Thus Hume expects an enlargement of human sympathy through ever-widening contacts to bring about an eventual universal recognition of civilized conduct as conducive to happiness.

[60] All these quotations are from the *Enquiry* just cited, section III, entitled "Justice."

"History, experience, reason sufficiently instruct us in this natural progress of human sentiments, and in our gradual enlargement of our regards to justice, in proportion as we become acquainted with the extensive utility of that virtue." In the same breath Hume, the amiable and enlightened Tory, denounces the dangerous fanatics who sought to make equality the basis of justice. "Fanatics may suppose, that dominion is founded on grace, and that saints alone inherit the earth," but he is relieved to reflect that "the civil magistrate very justly puts these sublime theorists on the same footing with common robbers." What would Hume have thought of an age in which these "fanatics" dominate a large part of the earth's surface, and propose to take charge of the rest? Common sense, he thought, can readily teach us that these ideas of equality are not only impracticable but pernicious to human society. It remains to point out that such conclusions reveal Hume's thought to be dominated by "preconceived" ideas of what is right, as he undertook to rationalize the particular institutions of the society with which he was familiar. When he talks of the interest of mankind and the necessities of human society, he is as much engaged in abstract and doctrinaire rationalization as Grotius and the other natural-law writers ever were.

Any "conventionalist" doctrine of the "whatever is, is right" pattern will be especially unsatisfactory when the problem is that of war and peace, because the inclination will be to accept war as a part of "human nature." This was precisely Hume's position, when he agreed with Rousseau that the project of the good Abbé Saint-Pierre was hopelessly impractical and utopian.[61] Hume always stayed completely within the

[61] The stress which Hume was bound to lay on allegiance as a ground for obedience on the part of the common man in following the precepts of convention induced him to attribute much weight to war as the foundation of government. Cf. Bk. III, section viii of *A Treatise of Human Nature* (1739-40). This and the three sections following are of central importance for the subject we are considering. They all deal with different aspects of "allegiance."

framework of the traditional "law of nations," with its law of war, and in fact derived considerable gratification from the observation that his strictly conventional theory of moral obligation enabled him to treat the rules of justice between states as mere adaptations to a different set of conditions. Consequently, since war is a convention among the states, it is silly to question their right to engage in it. Kant's firm assertion that the "practical reason" could clearly show that "there shall be no war" runs counter to a basic tenet of Hume's philosophy: moral principles are not derived from reason.[62] But this contrast can be overdone; for Hume held that our morals were derived from a moral "sense," and this "sense" shows some striking resemblances to Kant's practical reason. When Hume uses the term "reason," he is concerned with what Kant called the "pure" or speculative reason, for it consists in discovering whether there is truth in a statement, that is, agreement to real relations of ideas, or to real existence and matter of fact. Kant goes along with Hume in thinking that this particular faculty of the mind is in no sense concerned in moral judgments; to that extent they are both opposed to the rationalism of traditional natural law. But the moral sense which Hume makes the basis of justice and other virtues is rooted in "impressions" which "are nothing but particular pains or pleasures." If we feel satisfaction in viewing a character, a sentiment, or an action, it is good; if we feel uneasiness, it is bad. It is certainly possible to condemn certain wars, from this standpoint. But counterbalancing considerations of self-preservation, patriotism, and allegiance may cause us likewise to view it with satisfaction, and hence consider it good.

It is at this point that the Kantian criticism protests. Kant is by no means the despiser of happiness he is often believed to be. He even goes so far as to assert that it is one's duty to secure

---

[62] *Treatise*, Bk. III, Part I, Sections i and ii.

one's happiness;[63] yet on the basis of his critical appreciation of the limits of human speculative reason he points out that "happiness" is so uncertain a concept that every man, although he wishes to achieve it, is unable to say definitely and unequivocally what it is that he desires and wants.[64] Man would have to be all-knowing in order to be able to say what would make him truly happy; for happiness is not a rational idea, but a creature of the imagination which rests upon empirical grounds. But there is something into which we may indeed inquire on a priori grounds, and that is the question of the *ought* as such, the normative or value judgment involved in all actions of the will when that will is taken in its primordial form of a free will such as we assume it to be when we speak of "willing" as a primary experience. It is this inquiry which led Kant to his formulation of the categorical imperative.[65] This imperative is nothing but the explication of the intrinsic meaning of the act of willing rationally, that is, what is implied in the concept of a pure will which Kant defined as "an ability [or faculty—*Vermögen*] to determine oneself to act in accordance with the notion of certain laws."

It is evident that this approach enabled Kant to "reformulate" the philosophical basis of natural law. His undertaking to do so has often been interpreted as a mere reiteration of accepted doctrine. Kant himself protests against the notion that what he has undertaken is essentially identical with traditional natural law, such for example as Christian Wolff's famous introduction to his *Philosophia moralis sive ethica* (1750-53), which he called a general practical wisdom. Kant naturally remarks that Wolff had neglected to consider the problem of "pure will" which may

---

[63] *Grundlegung zur Metaphysik der Sitten* (*Werke*, IV, 255). Cf. also, of course, *Critique of Practical Reason*, passim.

[64] *Grundlegung zur Metaphysik der Sitten*, p. 275. The succeeding statements are found on p. 276.

[65] For the categorical imperative see above, Chapter III.

be determined on the basis of principles a priori[66] and had thus failed to discover the metaphysical principle of morals (and of natural law) which resides in the idea of a norm as such.

Kant's specific treatment of the problems of natural law in the *Metaphysics of Morals*[67] reinterprets the famous Roman-law dictum in *Institutes,* I.l.3, *Juris praecepta sunt haec, honeste vivere, alterum non laedere, suum cuique tribuere,* in terms which suggest that they are emanations of the categorical imperative: jural duties (*Rechtspflichten*) which may be internal, external, or derived from both. Jural duties are those duties for which legislation is possible; they depend for their rationality upon the concept of freedom (see above, Chapter III), which itself constitutes the one and only natural and inborn right. The remarkable series of deductions by which all the basic principles of right and law are shown to be manifestations of this fundamental right possessed by all men and hence capable of being exercised only within the framework of general laws constitutes one of the most extraordinary feats in the history of general jurisprudence and the philosophy of law.

It is a curious and amusing commentary on the wayward development which goes under the name of the growth of thought and the history of ideas that the great Blackstone, oblivious of what Hume had done to natural law and incapable of what Kant was to attempt by way of a reformulation of the ancient "dictates of right reason," expounded in his celebrated *Commentaries on the Laws of England* (1765) the notion that these "first principles of the law of nature," while arrived at by "due exertion of right reason," depended for their attainment upon self-love and the search for happiness. The Creator, he taught, "has so intimately connected, so inseparably interwoven the laws

[66] *Grundlegung zur Metaphysik der Sitten* (*Werke,* IV, 246).
[67] *Die Metaphysik der Sitten* (1797), the first part of which is entitled "Metaphysische Anfangsgründe der Rechtslehre." This work (*Werke,* vol. VII) is not to be confused with *Grundlegung zur Metaphysik der Sitten* (*Werke,* vol. IV).

of eternal justice with the happiness of each individual, that the latter cannot be attained but by observing the former; and if the former be but punctually obeyed, it cannot but induce the latter." Blackstone thus stated once again the happy optimism of an age which believed in the preëstablished harmony of what Leibniz called this best of all possible worlds. Blackstone thus became the butt of Bentham's impassioned teaching to such an extent that we tend to forget that Hume and Kant between them had transcended both. For it is as curious that Bentham should have gone forward with his primitive utilitarian doctrine in the light of Kant's criticism as it is that Blackstone should have reiterated the traditional doctrine of natural law in the face of Hume's sweeping destruction of its underpinnings. But such is the course of the history of ideas. There is, indeed, no better statement with which to conclude this analysis of the natural-law doctrines which, critically refined, came to form the basis for Kant's philosophy of peace than that offered by Blackstone:

This law of nature, being coeval with mankind and dictated by God himself, is of course superior in obligation to any other. It is binding all over the globe, in all countries, and at all times: no human laws are of any validity, if contrary to this; and such of them as are valid derive all their force, and all their authority, mediately or immediately, from this original.[68]

We owe it to Kant's critical rationalism that what is contained of a priori truth in these statements remains philosophically sound to this day, and can still serve as a basis for universal peace.

[68] *Commentaries* (3rd ed., 1765), vol. i, sec. ii, p. 38.

❧ VI ❧

THE COMMON MAN,
THE GENERAL WILL, AND FREEDOM
UNDER LAW AS A FOUNDATION FOR
PEACE: KANT, ROUSSEAU, AND SAINT-PIERRE

The reconstruction of natural law on the basis of a recognition of the volitional, metarational basis of all normative judgments raised as many problems as it solved. Hume, Rousseau, Kant—they all were confronted with the problem of the source of authority—the ground of obligation, to use the words of T. H. Greene—in terms of which the binding nature of these normative judgments could be made convincing. As Rousseau put it so forthrightly in the beginning of *Le Contrat Social:* "Man is born free and everywhere he is in chains. How did this change come about? I do not know. What can make it legitimate? That question I think I can answer."

His answer was cast in terms of the famous doctrine of the general will which has been the fertile ground of extended controversy ever since. But whatever position one desires to adopt with regard to it—and ours will presently be developed—one will readily agree that the "general will," while not the will of the majority, nor even the will of all, presupposes a recognition of the common man as the source of all legitimate authority, since it is he who determines what the general will is. To be sure, it is he *collectively*, but then the belief in the common man is tenable only when the common man is taken collectively anyhow.[1] The firm faith in the common man's determination to

[1] See C. J. Friedrich, *The New Belief in the Common Man* (1942), p. 121ff. The general discussion contained in this volume is here assumed to be familiar.

act in accordance with what he considers "right" conduct provides the basis for the idea of "freedom under law"—the central tenet of constitutionalism, or, as Kant would put it, republicanism. Genuine peace, or legitimate restraint, is possible only within such a constitutional order, whether the community be a Swiss Canton or the wide world. Hence the problem of how to organize peace cannot be resolved without a consideration of the three interrelated issues of faith in man, the general will, and freedom under law.

The United Nations Charter provides in Article 13 that the progressive development of international law and its codification "shall be a concern of the United Nations by empowering the Assembly to initiate studies and make recommendations." In the same paragraph it also provides rather tamely for recommendations "assisting in the realization of human rights and fundamental freedoms for all without distinction as to race, sex, language, or religion." [2] These provisions of the Charter are a pale reflection of the hope shared by many Americans that an international bill of rights would be included in the Charter of the United Nations. The Commission to Study the Bases of a Just and Durable Peace, of the Federal Council of Churches of Christ in America, stipulated in their programmatic Statement on World Order, later elaborated into the Six Pillars of Peace, that "the peace must establish in principle, and seek to achieve in practice, the right of individuals everywhere to religious and intellectual liberty." In the Catholic, Jewish and Protestant Declaration on World Peace appended to that document, there is likewise included the proposition that "the dignity of the human person as the image of God must be set forth in all its essential implications in an international declaration of rights . . ." [3]

---

[2] Besides Art. 13 of the Charter, Art. 62:2 and art. 76(c) are important in this connection. See also the "Proposed Constitution of the United Nations" in *Federation—The Coming Structure of World Government,* ed. O. H. Eaton (1944), p. 211ff, which provides, in Arts. 22-27, for an explicit bill of rights.

[3] See *Statements on World Order* (1943), pp. 17, 20.

It is evident that the idea of freedom under law, as expounded in the "Four Freedoms," has receded to a rather minor place in the United Nations Charter—a mere echo of the key position assigned to it in the constitutions of the eighteenth century, especially the American ones. This idea is also central to Kant's approach, since it constitutes the real core of his first definitive article, which requires that the civil constitution in each member state shall be republican.[4] By this he means, as we have seen, that power is exercised according to well-defined laws, made with the consent of the citizens. True freedom is that freedom which is compatible with the freedom of all other free men, but the rules for realizing this true freedom are laws only if they are the result of agreement among the citizens. This problem of legitimate constraint had, of course, been at the very center of Jean-Jacques Rousseau's *Contrat Social,* and the question arises, for the historian of ideas, as to whether or not Kant went beyond Rousseau in stating his answer.[5] There is a good deal of

---

[4] See Chapter II, above, for a general discussion and evaluation of Kant's meaning.

[5] The relation of Kant to Rousseau has been the occasion of many general remarks, but has not been the subject of any really penetrating analysis. John Morley's fine *Rousseau* (1873) only notes that Kant was kept from his customary afternoon walk by his reading of *La Nouvelle Héloise.* Richard Fester, *Rousseau und die deutsche Geschichtsphilosophie* (1890), treats of Kant's relation to Rousseau in chapter iii (pp. 68-86) and again in an appendix especially devoted to the idea of eternal peace from Saint-Pierre to Kant. Konrad Dieterich, *Kant und Rousseau* (1878), is in reality little concerned with Rousseau. A brief but very valuable analysis has recently been offered by Ernst Cassirer in *Rousseau–Kant–Goethe* (1945), which relies for its estimate of Rousseau's moral and legal philosophy upon C. W. Hendel, *Jean-Jacques Rousseau, Moralist* (1934) and is sharply critical of Irving Babbitt, *Rousseau and Romanticism* (1919) and Ernest Seillière, *Jean-Jacques Rousseau* (1921). W. Kayser, *Rousseau, Kant, Herder über den ewigen Frieden* (1916), is especially addressed to the peace problem, but lacks precision and range. Cuno Hofer, *L'Influence de J. J. Rousseau sur le droit de la guerre* (1914), and Maxime Leroy, *La Guerre et la paix selon Jean-Jacques Rousseau* (1915), are quite inadequate on Kant, as is the otherwise valuable book by J. Texte, *J. J. Rousseau et les origines du cosmopolitisme littéraire au XVIIIe siècle* (1895; English ed. 1899). Cf. also J. C. Collins, *Voltaire, Montesquieu and Rousseau in England* (1908). For Rousseau's texts see C. E. Vaughan, *The Political Writings of Rousseau,* 2 vols. (1915).

confusion in the existing literature; it is often said that Kant, like Saint-Pierre, was a monarchist who based his hopes for peace upon an agreement among monarchs.[6] The opposite is the truth. Generally speaking, Kant's attachment to Rousseau was deep and lasting. In his otherwise unadorned study he always kept a picture of Rousseau. In his works, he time and again acknowledged his keen interest in and obligation to Rousseau, especially his *Emile* and his *Contrat Social.* It is to Rousseau that Kant admittedly owed his "belief in the common man." When about forty, he wrote:

I am myself by inclination a seeker after truth. I feel a consuming thirst for knowledge and a restless passion to advance in it, as well as satisfaction in every forward step. There was a time when I thought that this alone could constitute the honor of mankind, and I despised the common man who knows nothing. Rousseau set me right. This blind prejudice vanished; I learned to respect human nature, and I should consider myself far more useless than the ordinary working man if I did not believe that this view could give worth to all others to establish the rights of man.[7]

I learned to respect human nature: this central fact constituted the inspiration which obliged Kant to limit the importance of reason. For it was reason upon which the conceit of the rationalists of the eighteenth century had rested. It was reason which had provided the key to the "heavenly city of the eighteenth-century philosophers," all of them convinced that their "enlightenment" was the distinguishing mark of an intellectual elite whose contempt for the common herd knew no bounds.

---

[6] E.g., G. H. Putnam in his Foreword, p. viii, to *L'État de guerre and Projet de paix perpétuelle,* ed. S. G. Patterson (1920).

[7] *Immanuel Kant's sämtliche Werke* (ed. G. Hartenstein), VIII (*Fragmente aus dem Nachlass*) (1867-68), 624. This passage is quoted in the translation given it by Ernst Cassirer, who attributes central importance to it. I am very glad to have the support of so outstanding an authority on Kant to back up my view as here developed. It is shared by Karl Vorländer, *Immanuel Kant, Der Mann und das Werk* (1924), I, 148ff.

The passionate desire of Frederick of Prussia, of Catherine of Russia, of Joseph of Austria to be considered a member of the enchanted circle of enlightened philosophers testifies to the intensity of that sense of aristocratic superiority and seclusion which was the distinguishing mark of these high priests of "the age of reason."

Rousseau challenged all that. Stirred by his sensitiveness, urged on by his marvelous imagination and sustained by the depth of his feeling, Rousseau revolted against the conceit and self-satisfied smugness of the *philosophes*. His *Confessions* abound with unmistakable signs and recurrent incidents testifying to the genuineness of his attachment to the common man. The republican pride of his birthplace, Geneva, the simple handicraftsman's background of his family, his long periods of desperate poverty, his spontaneous and intense compassion with the suffering of others—these all combined to make him the natural democrat that he was. His accidental encounter at the age of twenty with a peasant near Lyons shows the strength of his feeling, since it is the only incident of this journey of 1732 that he remembered many years later:

After several hours of useless walking, tired and dying of hunger and thirst, I entered a peasant's hut . . . I begged him to give me dinner, and offered to pay for it. He offered me some skimmed milk and coarse barley bread, saying that that was all he had. I drank the milk with delight and ate the bread, husks and all; but it was not very invigorating fare for a man exhausted by fatigue. The peasant, who examined me closely, estimated the truth of my story by my appetite, and immediately afterwards declared that he could see that I was a good and honourable young man, who had not come there to betray him for money. He opened a little trap-door near the kitchen, went down, and came up a minute afterwards with a nice brown wheaten loaf, a very tempting-looking ham, although considerably cut down, and a bottle of wine, the sight of which rejoiced my heart more than all the rest; to this he added a substantial omelette, and I made a dinner such as none but a pedestrian ever enjoyed. When it came to the question of payment, his uneasiness and alarm returned; he would take none of my money, and refused it with singular anxiety; and the amusing thing was that I could not imagine what he was afraid of. At last, with a shudder, he uttered the terrible words, "Revenue-officers and excise-men." He gave me to understand that he hid his wine on account of the excise, that he hid his bread on account of the tax, and that he was a lost man, if anyone had a suspicion that he was not starving. All that he said to me on this subject, of which I had not the least idea, made an impression upon me which will never be forgotten. It was the germ of the inextinguishable hatred which subsequently grew up in my heart against the oppression to which these unhappy people are subject, and against their oppressors." [8]

John Morley, too, attaches central importance to this experience and comments: "It was because he had thus seen the wrongs of the poor, not from without but from within, not as a pitying spectator but as one of their company, that Rousseau by and by brought such fire to the attack upon the old order, and changed the blank practice of the elder philosophers into a deadly affair of ball and shell." [9] Kant, who also came from the home of a simple, impecunious handicraftsman, who had lived the life of a tutor—which was that of a servant of the rich in East Prussia as in royal France—who evidently like Rousseau had been struck with the frequent goodness of the poor and the equally frequent depravity of the rich and powerful, responded with unhesitating alacrity to Rousseau's revelation of the "true nature of man." In Rousseau, Kant found "an unusual penetration, a noble elevation of the spirit and a soul full of feeling in so high a degree as perhaps never was possessed by any other writer in

[8] *Confessions,* IV (Everyman's ed., I, 148-149).
[9] John Morley, *Rousseau* (2nd ed., 1878), pp. 45-46. The following sentence, too long to quote here, is a moving statement of the case. Altogether Morley's *Rousseau,* customarily referred to as a classic, is a curious compound of broad sympathies for the social and political side of Rousseau and tiresome mid-Victorian moralizing on his moral and psychological self. The fact that the two belonged together never ceased to baffle Morley. See for contrast C. W. Hendel, *Jean-Jacques Rousseau, Moralist.*

any other people or age." [10] He called Rousseau the Newton of the moral realm who first of all had discovered the deeply hidden nature of man under the variety of second natures adopted by human beings.

But this faith in "true human nature" is combined, in both Rousseau and Kant, with a mordant pessimism concerning the actual human beings who people the earth. This sentiment is clear from their general writings on law and government; it is more specifically indicated in their treatment of the problem of how to organize a lasting peace. In Rousseau, this dichotomy springs from feeling, from intuition, and is, as Kant puts it, "synthetic." In Kant, the contrast of the facts and the norms, of the phenomenal and the noumenal, has become a carefully elaborated central tenet of his philosophy.[11] The "revolt against reason" which Rousseau had initiated, and which Hume had seconded, albeit contradictorily, by an all-engulfing skepticism, Kant undertook to channel, as we have shown, by carefully delimiting the realm within which reason could serve.

These well-known facts contain, in a sense, the answer to our question as to how far Kant went beyond Rousseau.[12] Much light will fall upon the problem of war and peace, if we trace this out in terms of Rousseau's concept of general will which is held to be the foundation of every community and the source of all true law. But since the general will calls for genuine homogeneity, Rousseau found himself compelled to assert that representation was impossible in matters pertaining to the general will and that therefore only the smallest communities are likely to possess such a general will. This approach seems to bar completely the idea of a universal order under law such as Kant envisaged. Did Rousseau deny its possibility?

The answer to this question turns upon one's interpretation

---

[10] *Fragmente,* cited in footnote 7, p. 624.
[11] See above, Chapter III.
[12] See Ernst Cassirer, *Rousseau–Kant–Goethe.*

of Rousseau's approach to the work of the Abbé Saint-Pierre on the one hand, and upon one's concept of the general will on the other. A comparison of the Abbé's own work[13] with Rousseau's *Projet de Paix Perpétuelle* (1761)[14] discloses some sharp contrasts as well as basic agreements. Professor Vaughan says: "In a word, except as regards the mere kernel of the Project, there is much more of Rousseau than of Saint-Pierre in the whole statement."[15] Whether this be true or not, Vaughan is certainly right in feeling that Rousseau's *Project* was known to Kant.[16] I should like to add it as my own opinion that Kant was also familiar with Rousseau's *Jugement sur la paix perpétuelle* (1782) and with Abbé Saint-Pierre's own treatise. The reason for the latter opinion I derive from the unquestionable fact that Kant's *Eternal Peace* follows the Abbé's method of setting forth

[13] I have worked with an edition of 1712, entitled *Mémoires pour rendre la paix perpétuelle en Europe* (Cologne: Chez Jaques le Pacifique), with no author indicated. This edition is from the library of Christian Ernst Graf zu Stolberg, whose *ex libris* is dated 1721. Since the three-volume edition which is usually cited and has a longer title appeared in 1712-13 and 1717, the one I have used would seem to be an earlier version. See also Joseph Drouet, *L'Abbé de Saint-Pierre* (1912) and G. Derocque, *Le Projet de paix perpétuelle de l'Abbé Saint-Pierre comparé au pacte de Société des Nations* (1929), esp. pp. 55-134.

[14] For this essay I have used C. E. Vaughan's edition, *The Political Writings of Rousseau*, I, 364ff. G. Lowes Dickinson's introduction to Miss Edith Nuttall's translation, *A Project of Perpetual Peace, Rousseau's Essay* (1927), as well as the translation itself, is helpful. They breathe the hopefulness inspired in the twenties by the founding of the League of Nations. Thus Dickinson concludes his introduction with the following judgment: "The philanthropic zeal of the Abbé, the political genius of Rousseau and the persuasive charm of his words, have not been wasted. They helped to create an institution which, rightly used, should at last bring jarring races and warring nations into the calm and prosperous haven of perpetual peace." Would that the institution had been "rightly used"!

[15] I, 360. C. W. Hendel, accepting Vaughan's position, has given an extended summary of Rousseau's *Project* in *Jean-Jacques Rousseau, Moralist*, pp. 200-214. On p. 199 Hendel writes: "The great and fine thoughts were, however, transformed by his own thinking." This is a sounder position than Vaughan's.

[16] *The Political Writings of Rousseau*, I, 363. It is curious that Vaughan should believe this not to be generally recognized, as he suggests in a footnote which correctly calls attention to Kant's mention of Saint-Pierre in Kant's *Idee zu einer allgemeinen Geschichte* (1784).

his views in the form of "articles," that he divides these articles into preliminary and definitive ones, and that the actual articles of Kant coincide more nearly with Saint-Pierre's than they do with Rousseau's.

A comparison between the Abbé's work and Rousseau's presentation of it shows that Rousseau inserted a long introductory section for which no equivalent is found in the Abbé's treatment.[17] This is understandable enough, in view of the fact that Rousseau had to address himself to the question: "If the advantages of this union are so real, why then have the sovereigns of Europe not adopted it?"[18] To answer this question, Rousseau abandoned the basic assumption of the optimistic Abbé, that men, and more especially princes and their ministers, are rational and follow their true, long-range interest. "Let us distinguish real from Apparent interests," he suggests. Perpetual peace is the real interest; that the *Project* shows. But the apparent interest is a state of absolute independence which removes sovereigns from the reign of law.

This latter issue is of decisive importance. Rousseau questioned the Abbé's confidence in the "enlightenment" of princes. The platonic inclination to turn to a "teachable tyrant" had become for eighteenth-century rationalism the faith in an enlightened despot. It was the hope of Voltaire and the young Bentham, no less than of Bossuet and Fénelon. The good Abbé had shared it heartily. Not so Rousseau. He sarcastically remarked that the proposed Union would "take away from Sovereigns . . . the precious right of being unjust when they please," aggrandisement, conquest, search for glory, so why should they join such a Union? What would be the compensations for so many deprivations? The Abbé answered in typical rationalist fashion by appealing to the higher reason in princes.

[17] See Vaughan, *The Political Writings of Rousseau*, I, 360: "The long introduction, itself a brilliant historical essay, is all his own."
[18] See *Judgement* in *Political Writings*, I, 388.

Rousseau could not follow him. He did not deny that there might occasionally be a prince who would be thus motivated by a desire to secure the public good. In his *Judgement* he tells us, however, that "all the business of kings or of those to whom they delegate their duties, is concerned with two objects alone; to extend their rule abroad or to make it more absolute at home." [19] When they or their ministers talk about the public good, the happiness of their subjects, or the glory of their nation, the people may well tremble; for these are merely pretexts for hiding their true intentions, their interests as they see them. The issue here raised by distinguishing the subjective element in "interests" is, of course, ancient in philosophy. As applied to foreign policy, it is as real in a democracy as in other types of government. [20]

Walter Lippmann may be taken as typical of the many who plead with their fellow citizens to realize the "true interests"—as Lippmann sees them. If he is right that "for fifty years no nation has been more liberal in its words than has been the United States; none neglected its own interests so dangerously, or contributed less to realizing the ideals it so assiduously preached," then the American people know no more how to attend to their real interests than did the monarchs against whose folly Rousseau inveighs. And yet Lippmann himself observes: "Their own concept of their own interest is for all masses of peoples the motive which determines their actions." If that is so, and if their concept is so utterly foolish, then there is no hope except in finding some way to enthrone the select circle of wise men, the self-appointed elite who know the people's true interest, to take charge of their affairs. We are, in short, back with Plato and his eighteenth-century rationalist followers.

Of these, the Abbé Saint-Pierre was a striking example, as we

[19] *Political Writings,* p. 389. The earlier quotation is from the *Project* itself, and is found on p. 380.
[20] See Walter Lippmann's remarks in his *U. S. Foreign Policy* (1944), p. 166ff.

have seen. Rousseau's complete lack of sympathy with his approach made him suppress some of the characteristic features of his plan. Like Bentham, the Abbé had a decided penchant for working out things in minute detail. He organized his ideas in the form of three sets of articles: eight fundamental ones, seven necessary ones, and six useful (*utile*) ones. These twenty-one articles Rousseau compressed into five, which he compounded mostly from the eight fundamental ones, but he lifted an occasional idea from the others and embodied it in his general treatment.[21] While it would be tedious to undertake a detailed comparison, the omission of the Abbé's fundamental articles iii, iv, v, and vii by Rousseau invites a few comments.

The omission of Article iii is understandable enough; for it concerns itself with those causes of war so common at the time of the Peace of Utrecht, controversies over succession. It commits the union to protecting the existing "sovereign" against internal as well as external usurpers. Rousseau, bitterly hostile to the institution of monarchy as such, could not possibly be expected to sympathize with this provision.[22]

The elimination of the other three articles is much less defensible, and from our standpoint today the Abbé was more realistic and practical than his "editor." For in Article iv he provides against treaties between members of the union except with the consent of three fourths of the members, such treaties to be made publicly and at the international headquarters of the union. In Article v, it is provided that trade will remain on the

---

[21] This fact makes it impossible to agree with Vaughan's judgment cited above (note 15) about the introduction, for several elements, especially the favorable view of the Germanic federation, are found in the Abbé's work. A thorough comparison seems never to have been made.

[22] There are many other provisions of this type which show that the Abbé Saint-Pierre's ideas were more nearly akin to the legitimist Holy Alliance than to either the League of Nations or the United Nations. However, the latter have some decidedly legitimist aspects. Concerning the Holy Alliance see C. K. Webster, *The Congress of Vienna* (1919), and my comments in *Foreign Policy in the Making* (1938), p. 140ff.

same footing as before the war, unless and until three fourths of the members agree on a new treaty, which treaty must, however, provide equal and reciprocal rights and opportunities for all members. In view of the extended trade wars which filled the seventeenth and eighteenth centuries, such a provision was clearly designed to remove one of the patent causes of war. It finds its equivalent in the United Nations Charter, though in a modified and attenuated form.[23] Article vii, finally, organizes courts of the union to deal with quarrels involving any subjects of the several sovereigns, if the sums involved are above a certain amount. Since Saint-Pierre speaks of these as "Frontier Chambers," it is evident that he is vividly aware of the recurrent difficulties arising between neighbors. In his explanation, he exclaims: "Who does not know that one of the most ordinary occasions of war among neighboring peoples is the injustices which the subjects or citizens of one suffer or believe themselves to suffer from the subjects of another?" There are plenty of illustrations of this "cause" of war in our time, such as the extended controversies over national minorities in Europe. It is an admitted shortcoming of the United Nations Organization that it does not provide judicial methods for the settlement of disputes between individuals; only states are admitted as parties before the International Court of Justice.[24]

Like the United Nations Charter, the Abbé Saint-Pierre's

[23] See chapters ix and x of the Charter, providing for international economic and social coöperation and the establishment of an Economic and Social Council of the United Nations. However, the Charter only vests the power of promoting such trade agreements in the UNO (see art. 13) and fails to provide for clear-cut legislative power in this field, even if restricted by a three-fourths requirement like Saint-Pierre's.

[24] United Nations Charter, Article 92, makes the Statute of the Court an integral part of the Charter; Article 34 of the Statute provides that "only states may be parties in cases before the Court." It should be noted, however, that Article 95 of the Charter provides that member states may entrust "the solution of their differences to other tribunals by virtue of agreements." Such special tribunals have, of course, existed for many years. It is worth remembering that the good Abbé did not overlook their value as instrumentalities for reducing tensions and thus improving the chances of peace.

union has a distinctly conservative flavor in the sense that it primarily aims to preserve the *status quo*. Saint-Pierre's declared reason for this approach is the kind of utilitarian realism which permeates his entire work. He was trying to draw up a plan which would appeal to the good sense of the princes and ministers of the established monarchies of Europe. To do so, he felt that he must offer them effective security for their position and possessions. Not so Rousseau. For him, as we have seen, these men are selfish, short-sighted enemies of the people, who talk of the public good merely to cloak their aggressive designs to extend their rule abroad or to make it more absolute at home. They are despots. Hence the only possible chance of securing lasting peace will lie in securing a different pattern of government—a pattern in which the public good can be expected to prevail.

This problem is, of course, the central one in the *Social Contract*, and it may therefore be surmised that the reflection upon the inadequacies of the Abbé Saint-Pierre's work led Rousseau to develop his most important contribution to political thought. It is now generally known that Rousseau saw this work as part of a much more comprehensive plan of treating "Political Institutions." He has told us so himself in his *Confessions*[25] and has offered us his plan for this work in the *Emile*.[26]

The glittering generality of Rousseau's treatment in the *Contrat Social* and the many apparent contradictions have given rise to a great many conflicting interpretations. There can be little doubt that Rousseau loked upon the *Contrat Social* as offering a

[25] See *Confessions* (Hedouin edition, c. 1904), vol. ii, Bk. ix, p. 159.
[26] See *Emile,* Livre V. Cf. the extracts in *Political Writings,* ii, 142ff, and Vaughan's comments in his Introduction, p. 95ff. How Vaughan can say, in his introductory remarks to the extracts from the fifth book of *Emile,* that they do not treat of the *volonté générale* is incomprehensible to me, since the whole discussion revolves around it. Nor can I find the alleged difference between the doctrine of the *Contrat Social* and that of *Emile* which Vaughan professes to see; but this failure probably turns upon my disagreement with Vaughan's general interpretation of the *Contrat Social*. See also Vaughan's remarks, vol. ii, p. 137ff.

yardstick for evaluating existing governments rather than a prescription for reorganizing them. Thus he says in *Emile:*

> One has at all times disputed a great deal about the best form of government, without giving consideration to the fact that each is the best in some cases, and the worst in others . . . we conclude that in general democratic government fits small states, aristocratic medium-sized ones, and the monarchical type large states.

And again: "There does not exist a unique and absolute constitution for a government, but there must be by nature as many different governments as there are different sized states." [27]

But whatever the form of the government, the essence of sovereignty consists in the general will (*volonté générale*), so that any deviation from this general will, any manifestation of a particular will, is an infringement of sovereignty, because instead of producing true laws it merely produces particular measures. It is one of the central aspects of this doctrine that a true law consists in a rule of general application, and it is the great problem of government how to secure such laws.[28] The difficulty lies in the fact that all human beings incline to decide in accordance with their particular wills. The private interest tends always toward seeking special privileges, whereas the public interest demands equality. How can one make sure that a particular will, or wills, shall always be in accord with this general will? There is a definite inclination in Rousseau to believe that the larger the number of particular wills consulted the more likely we are to secure a reliable index as to what would constitute the general will, but this does by no means imply that the will of a majority is the general will. It is merely a somewhat more promising source under ordinary conditions. At the same time, Rous-

---

[27] Rousseau's emphasis upon size as a decisive criterion results from his concern with the real relationships between actual people and his decided preference for the rural way of life as he expounds it movingly in the section of the *Emile* just quoted. Cf. also *Contrat Social*, ii, viii.

[28] *Contrat Social*, ii, vi.

seau fully admits that under exceptional circumstances the individual who rises above his particular will and his private interest, the great legislator, may in fact be the lawgiver, as was Lycurgus of old.

The decided preference Rousseau shows for the small state and its capacity for democratic organization flows from his keen concern with individual liberty rather than from the small states' likelihood of realizing the general will. "The more the state grows in size, the more liberty is diminished," he feels, because the general *mores* are not as closely related to the laws as in a small community, which means that the particular wills are less closely related to the general will in the large state. It is the greater divergence between the two which bothers Rousseau, because it entails a greater amount of force and its consequent dangers to liberty. This aspect of Rousseau's ideas has frequently been overlooked, and an extreme interpretation of the meaning of the concept "general will" has resulted. A rather striking passage occurs in *Emile,* toward the end of the discussion, when Rousseau, the tutor, is seeking to persuade his pupil that he owes much to his *patrie* and its laws, regardless of the constitution. He there exclaims:

> There is always a government and the phantom [*simulacre*] of laws . . . That the social contract has not at all been observed, what does it matter if the particular interest has protected him as the general will would have done . . . Oh, Emile, where is the man of good will who does not owe much to his country? Whoever he is, he owes it what is most precious for man, the morality of his action and the love of virtue.

This is not an isolated passage, but one which is echoed in many parts of Rousseau's writings.[29] The duty of the citizen was to him a most sacred obligation, and he is so convinced of

[29] More especially his *Lettres écrits de la montagne* and his *Considérations sur le gouvernement de Pologne.* See *Political Writings,* II, 173ff and 369ff. But it is also clearly set forth in the *Contrat Social.*

the difficulty of giving true laws to a community that even their semblances should command the respect of the citizen. "It would take Gods to give men laws." Rousseau was convinced, as were the Middle Ages, that laws should primarily be declaratory: "What makes a constitution really solid and lasting is the due observance of what is proper so that . . . law only serves to assure, accompany and rectify [the natural relations]." It is the idea that the *mores* of a people ought to be closely related to and revealed in the laws, an idea which is popularly associated with Burke rather than Rousseau.

But if all this is true, whose will is the general will? We know that its realization consists in the *general* rule which has equal application to all. But who wills thus? The *corpus mysticum* that is the corporate body politic? There can be little doubt that Rousseau expressed from time to time a belief in such an "organic" superentity.[30] Moreover, he insists that the general will is not the will of all, but something else.[31]

Here are some of Rousseau's famous and bewildering passages concerning the general will:

The general will is always right and tends to the public advantage; but it does not follow that the deliberations of the people are always equally correct.

Our will is always for our own good, but we do not always see what it is (*Contrat Social*, Bk. II, ch. iii, II, III).

The general will . . . is always constant, unalterable and pure; but

[30] *Contrat Social*, III, xi. The controversy over organismic theories of community, state, and government is very extensive. See Francis W. Coker, *Organismic Theories of the State* (1910), for a general survey of this line of thought. That the groups are both organic and purposive is the contention of W. Y. Elliott, who suggested the term "co-organic" to describe this dual nature, in *The Pragmatic Revolt in Politics* (1928), esp. parts IV and V. In fact, most organic theories have included another element which is purposive, normative, teleological.

[31] At times he equates it with the will of the people, as in *Emile*, II, 304: "La volonté du peuple ou la volonté souveraine, laquelle est générale," he writes, contrasting it with the "volonté commune des magistrats," which he thinks one might call "volonté de corps."

it is subordinated to other wills which encroach upon its sphere. . . . Even in selling his vote for money, a man does not extinguish in himself the general will, but he only eludes it (*ibid.*, IV, i).

The constant will of all the members of the State is the general will; by virtue of it they are citizens and free. When in the popular assembly a law is proposed, what the people is asked is not exactly whether it approves or rejects the proposal, but whether it is in conformity with the general will, which is their will. Each man, in giving his vote, states his opinion on that point; and the general will is found by counting votes (*ibid.*, IV, ii).

Of itself, the people wills always the good, but of itself it by no means always sees it. The general will is always in the right, but the judgment which discloses it is not always enlightened (*ibid.*, II, vi).

From all this it has been concluded that the general will is a universal, and in the Kantian sense a "rational" will. This rational will has, of course, an underpinning of sentiment which springs from the mores, custom, the long-established habits of a people which Rousseau in one famous passage calls the "real constitution of the state," "not graven on tablets of marble or brass, but on the hearts of the citizens." This constitution is not a fixed and immutable thing, but "everyday takes on new powers . . . insensibly replaces authority by the force of habit." [32]

All this sounds as if the general will were the voice of reason, in the sense of judgments as to what is right. But while some writers have thereby been misled into interpreting the general will as simply the dictates of right reason in the tradition of natural law, we have already seen that Rousseau's doctrine of natural law is different, because these dictates of the higher will are not "rational" in the sense in which that word was used by the traditional natural law schools. Rousseau never succeeded in extricating himself from the difficulties into which his passionate insistence upon the need for higher norms plunged him.

---

[32] *Contrat Social,* Bk. II, ch. xii. Cf, also the interesting passage in the essay on *L'État de Guerre* as quoted by G. D. H. Cole in his Introduction to the Everyman's edition of the *Social Contract* (1935).

His employment of the word "will" rightly stressed the element of freedom or choice involved in all actions subject to normative judgments, but he failed to clarify the peculiar "reason" which such a "will" posits. This missing philosophical link Kant supplied with his concept of *practical* reason, or as we might say today, reason in action. In his famous opening sentences of the *Metaphysics of Morals*, Kant immediately stated his fundamental conviction that "will" and normative judgment of any kind whatsoever are mutually coördinated: "There is nothing anywhere in this world, nor can even anything be thought of outside this world, which could be considered good without exception, save only a *good will*." [33]

"Two things fill me with ever renewed wonder: the starred heaven above me, and the moral law within me," Kant was to say in the *Critique of Practical Reason*. The general will is an ever-changing thing, not static as the dictates of right reason were conceived to be. It responds to the everchanging situation in terms of sentiments the ultimate source of which is none other than God. It was the religious sentiment in both Rousseau and Kant which rejected the rationalism of the eighteenth-century *philosophes*.[34] It gives us the rule which is in accordance with our higher nature. Kant insisted upon converting this great inspiration into a carefully elaborated thought. He emerged with the categorical imperative.

Besides the formulation in the *Critique of Practical Reason* discussed in Chapter III,[35] Kant offers a more closely Rousseauistic one in these words: "Act in such a way that you are using man, whether it be your own person, or that of any other, at all times as an end in itself, never merely as a means." [36] This

---

[33] *Werke,* IV, 249.
[34] See above, Chapter III.
[35] At footnote 21.
[36] *Grundlegung der Metaphysik der Sitten,* second section (*Werke,* IV, 287). The *Grundlegung* is earlier than the *Critique.* Cassirer stresses this earlier formulation in his *Rousseau–Kant–Goethe.*

insistence upon the autonomy and worth of *all* men renders any form of government which fails to provide for the participation of all in the determination of the laws suspect in peace as in war. Kant's insistence upon the importance of republican constitutional government springs from this conviction, as does Rousseau's. When Rousseau writes: "I therefore give the name of Republic to every State that is governed by law, no matter what the form of its administration may be . . . ." [37] we readily recognize the kinship of his statement to the Kantian concept of republicanism.

How can a society evolve toward an order of freedom under law? Kant believes, as we have seen, that there exists a hidden plan of nature for utilizing the selfish and pugnacious propensities of man to make him enter into ever-widening social relationships. As families, groups, classes, and nations clash, they discover that more is to be gained by compromise and peace than by fighting. The categorical imperative actually operates within limits in determining the actions of men and leads them to group themselves together under laws.[38]

Kant further asserts that the evolution of a constitution according to natural law, though accompanied by wild struggles, tends toward a pacific institutional order which is precisely the "republican" constitution. Kant makes the concession, however, that such a constitution may exist "by analogy" in a monarchy. What this "analogy" amounts to is the idea that a monarchy may be governed through laws which are analogous to those which a people would give itself when acting according to general principles of right and law.[39] It may, in other words, be a

[37] *Contrat Social,* II, vi. In citing this, one should always bear in mind the highly normative concept of law involved which is characteristic for both thinkers; that is, laws are acts of the general will.

[38] See above, Chapter III.

[39] *Werke,* VII, 400. This idea of *Rechtsstaat* (*Rechtsstaat* is government according to law) became deeply rooted in German tradition and was realized through the enlightened action of a bureaucracy trained in law and justice for the making of laws. See C. J. Friedrich, "The Continental Tradition of Train-

Rechtsstaat. Related to this notion of a possible realization by analogy of the general will as a *composite* categorical imperative is Kant's critical view of the government of Great Britain after the war against the revolting American colonists. He predicted that this "despotic aristocracy" would head a coalition against the revolutionaries. If, in contrast to such potentialities, Kant urged Prussia to live in peace with revolutionary France, and to pursue the path of enlightened reform, he indubitably adopted a viewpoint closely akin to that of Bentham, who in his early period inclined to rely upon the enlightenment of princes, as the Abbé Saint-Pierre had done. But Kant's concession resulted not so much from an optimistic overestimation of the prince's reasonableness as it did from a general skepticism regarding human nature and its consequent failure to live up to a categorical imperative in the mass as well as in any kind of select group.

The implied authoritarianism may easily be exaggerated, and has often been given undue prominence.[40] There are many statements to the contrary, especially in Kant's *Reflections* and unpublished *Loose Leaves*,[41] such as that "the will of all is the source of all law," or that "the general will of the people without regard to person must be made the basis," or again that "the state is a people which governs itself." These and similar views give a clue as to how to interpret the more formal and restrained statements in his published works. It is unquestionably true that Kant hoped for progressive yet gradual evolution toward such a

---

ing Administrators in Law and Jurisprudence," *Journal of Modern History,* XI, 129 (June 1929).

[40] For example, see Reinhold Aris, *History of Political Thought in Germany from 1789 to 1815* (1936), p. 70. This interpretation often turns upon an exaggeration of Kant's regard for the state which is common to German literature on the subject. See below, Chapter VIII.

[41] *Reflexionen Kant's zur kritischen Philosophie,* ed. by Benno Erdmann (1882-84); "Lose Blätter aus Kants Nachlass," ed. by Rudolph Reicke in *Altpreussische Monatsschrift,* 1887-94.

state of affairs. For Rousseau, such an orderly evolution from monarchy to republic was hard to imagine. At the very end of his *Judgement* Rousseau had raised this issue. Having declared that there was "no prospect of federative leagues established otherwise than by revolutions," Rousseau hesitated. Revolutions, he seemed to think, are perhaps an even more formidable prospect than wars. "Which of us would venture to say whether this European League is more to be desired or feared?" he exclaimed.

Rousseau's antipathy to revolution was deep-seated. He had once in his youth been in the position of seeing two friends, father and son, rush out of the same house in Geneva to join opposing factions. This was in 1737. He made up his mind then and there, and thirty years later in the *Confessions* he wrote: "This terrible sight made so deep an impression upon me, that I took an oath never to take part in any civil war, and *never to defend liberty at home by force of arms*, either in my own person or by my approval, if I ever entered upon my rights as a citizen." [42] While this is a personal, rather than a political observation, it contrasts sharply with the views of Luther[43] as well as Kant—a fact worth noting regarding the supposed philosopher of revolution. While Kant entertained the doubts all reasonable and law-abiding men have felt when it comes to the use of violence in exercising the right of resistance, in the last analysis he stands with those who cried: "Give me liberty or give me death!" In *Der Streit der Fakultäten* (1798) Kant wrote:

The revolution of a gifted people which we have seen happening in our days may succeed or fail; it may be filled with misery and atrocities to such an extent that a well-intentioned man if he could hope to undertake it successfully a second time would never decide to make the experiment at such a cost—this revolution, I say, occasions in the mind

[42] *Confessions,* Book V.
[43] See above, p. 100.

of all spectators a sympathy for its intention which borders on enthusiasm, and which, since its showing was dangerous, can have no other cause than a moral propensity in man.[44]

This moral "cause" has two roots. One is the right which entitles a people to the freedom of giving itself a civil constitution which seems best to itself, and hence to its right not to be interfered with by other powers in this undertaking. We can see here clearly that Kant restricts and defines non-intervention (as required in his *Eternal Peace*) to the making of a *civil constitution*; conversely, Kant would probably have asserted the right of other powers to intervene when a people is being deprived of its civil constitution by a totalitarian *coup d'état*. The other root is this: A constitution is in accordance with this right and morally good only if it is so constructed as to avoid aggressive war. Conceptually, this requirement is fulfilled only by a republican constitution. But Kant was sufficiently wary of being considered a revolutionary to protect himself in a footnote which explains that this statement does not mean that a people which has a monarchical constitution would claim the right, or even harbor the secret wish, to have this constitution changed. The scattered realms of such a monarchy, he reasons, may make the monarchical constitution the only one under which such a people surrounded by powerful neighbors could survive.

There are many similar thoughts scattered through Kant's writings, but it is noteworthy that he acknowledges the sympathy for the revolution as a sign of the moral nature of man even at a date (1797) when the revolutionaries were discredited with most of their former partisans. It is part of his settled belief in the progress of mankind toward a better future, though he is fully aware that such a belief cannot be proved from ex-

---

[44] *Werke,* vii, 398. The danger to which Kant alludes he had recently experienced, when he was threatened with disciplinary action and denounced as a Jacobin. See Karl Vorländer, *Immanuel Kant,* ii, 210ff, and esp. pp. 221 and 279. See also Vorländer's comments in his preface in the Akademie edition of Kant (*Kant's gesammelte Schriften,* Berlin, 1900-38), vii, 337-342.

perience but must be inferred from signs which coincide with this moral premise: the revolution is such a sign. Whatever may be the personal factors in this equation,[45] Kant's sympathy for the American war of independence went so far as to turn him against the English government, whose constitution he had until then viewed sympathetically. He wrote of it: "For a hundred years we have had in England the system of the civil constitution of a great state." [46] He later came to feel that the attempt of the British to put the American Revolution down by force of arms was a denial of their cosmopolitanism. "They want them [the Americans] to become subjects of subjects" and it is despotism "to relieve subjects of all their own choice and judgment."

No wonder that Kant responded with enthusiasm to the news that a revolution was sweeping away the French monarchy. He had for long harbored anti-monarchical sentiments. In the *Reflexions* which he wrote down for himself he noted that

[45] The more extreme psychological theories of the interpretation of personality certainly should be regarded with suspicion by the historian of ideas. However, where it is a matter of determining which idea is the more intense concern of the thinker, biographical data may, as in this case, provide helpful clues. The study by Kurt Borries, *Kant als Politiker* (1928), ch. iii, stresses the personal elements in Kant's outlook and skillfully balances the contrasting considerations.

[46] This and the following quotations are from Karl Vorländer, *Immanuel Kant*, II, 213. They are taken from his *Reflexionen,* which are found in *Kant's Gesammelte Schriften* (Akademie Ausgabe), vol. xv. See also Vorländer's article, "Kant's Stellung zur Französischen Revolution," in *Philosophische Abhandlungen zu H. Cohen's 70. Geburtstag* (1912), pp. 247-269, and the same author's introduction to his *Kant's Kleinere Schriften zur Geschichtsphilosophie, Ethik und Politik* (1913), esp. pp. vii-lvii, and his *Kant und Marx* (1911), for which see below, Chapter VIII. While I cannot entirely agree with Vorländer's interpretation of Kant's political philosophy, especially regarding his view of the state, Vorländer has in my opinion gone further than any other German author in rightly emphasizing this side of Kant's philosophy. I do not believe that Vorländer is correct in describing Kant as an admirer of Frederick the Great. The sharp remarks about the patriarchal as the most despotic form of government, no matter how agreeable to the subject's material welfare, are clearly directed against Frederick the Great and his system. See also *Lose Blätter aus Kants Nachlass* (ed. Rudolph Reicke), *Altpreussische Monatsschrift,* 1889.

princes have no regard for rights, that "we have no monarch who wants to do anything for the well-being of mankind, nor even for his own people," that "he who himself makes laws thinks he is not bound by any laws."

The French Revolution appeared to him as an attempt to secure freedom under law through the establishment of a republican constitution. We have numerous testimonials showing that Kant in public and private spoke in favor of the revolutionaries. At the beginning of the revolution this was true of a great many German intellectuals. Even princes and ministers of state displayed a sympathetic interest and ladies of fashion decorated themselves with red, white, and blue. But their enthusiasm soon evaporated. As the Terror succeeded the early revolutionary idealism, poets and philosophers turned against the movement, not only in England, but on the Continent. Not so Kant. He held fast to his earlier convictions, even when it became dangerous to do so. He was known as a Jacobin. Some of the passages we have quoted above[47] were written in this period and later. Indeed, one Metzger, a medical colleague (and no friend of his at that), spoke after Kant's death of his "frankness and intrepidity" in defending his principles which were favorable to the French Revolution. "It was a time in Königsberg when anyone who judged the revolution not favorably but just mildly was put on a black list as a Jacobin. Kant did not allow himself by that fact to be deterred from speaking up for the revolution even at the table of the noblemen." Kant's friend and publisher F. Nicolovius reported a remark of Kant's from the year 1794 to the effect that "all the terror which was happening in France was insignificant as compared to the continued evil of despotism which had previously existed in France, and that very probably the Jacobins were right in all that they were now doing." Kant, Nicolovius said, was still an avowed "democrat." In all of Königsberg it was well known, even in 1798, that Kant "loved the French cause with all his heart, and was not swayed by the out-

[47] See p. 177.

burst of crimes in his belief that the representative system is the best form of government." [48]

This avowed republicanism of Kant we know to be essentially a belief in the moral ideal of a government according to laws of freedom, laws that are in accord with the categorical imperative. In this connection, attention needs to be drawn to a very significant passage in *The Critique of Judgment* (1790). In discussing the concept of a natural end or purpose (*telos, Naturzweck*) much as Aristotle had conceived it, Kant contrasts an organism with a mechanism by laying stress on the creative and re-creative capacity by which an organism organizes the materials of which it is compounded. This inscrutable quality is quite distinct from any causality which we know. Nor can it be thought of as analogous to art or be explained by it. He then (in a footnote) remarks that the recent total transformation of a great people (the French) into a state as well as the setting up of their magistrates, etc., has rightly by analogy with organic beings been spoken of as organization. For "each member shall indeed within such a whole be not only a means, but also an end; and by cooperating in making this whole possible, each member shall likewise regarding its place and function be determined by the idea of the whole." The concept of the state as a functioning whole of coöperating members is a remarkable anticipation of more modern sociological insights which incidentally shows once again that Kant conceived of the state as an ideal norm to which only a constitutional government (republicanism) corresponds to a certain extent.[49] Once again the French Revolution is seen as pointing toward that ideal norm.

---

[48] *Abbeggs Tagebuch* for July 1, 1798, quoted in Vorländer, *Immanuel Kant,* II, 222.

[49] See Chapter VIII, below. I owe to Karl Vorländer (*Immanuel Kant,* p. 219), the realization of the importance of this footnote, but I cannot entirely follow him in his interpretation, especially the suggestion that only here is the categorical imperative given a collective social, as contrasted with an individual, content (*ins Soziale umgebogen*). Cf. also the interesting comment in R. A. C. Macmillan, *The Crowning Phase of the Critical Philosophy* (1912), ch. vii, and Kurt Borries, *Kant als Politiker* (1928).

We are now ready to face the alternative between Rousseau and Kant which is of vital importance for the organization of peace, even today. Shall we assume with Kant that a constitutional, "peace-loving" republican regime is signalized by the greatest consonance of the constitution with the principles of right and law (*Rechtsprinzipien*) and that a categorical imperative obliges us to strive to establish such a regime? [50] Or shall we conclude with Rousseau that a close-knit communal democracy is the only truly lawful government, because only here can the general will be readily ascertained and made the basis of law-making? The latter view leaves little hope for the establishment of peace, because of the required revolutionizing of all political organization, and more especially the break-up of large states into smaller ones (for only in the latter could such a close-knit communal democracy be expected to function in accordance with Rousseau's principles). Kant's requirement of constitutionalism has the dual advantage of permitting a gradual evolution toward such republicanism and of being applicable to large as well as small states. Indeed, Kant's already quoted suggestion that a far-flung realm with widely scattered dominions may be better off under a monarchical constitutionalism, while unquestionably intended to appease his royal Prussian masters, could as readily be considered applicable to the evolution of the British Empire and its Crown during the nineteenth century.

It has, however, been urged that federation provides a way out for Rousseau's dilemma. Vaughan and others[51] have maintained that such small states could, in Rousseau's view, federate, and through such a union cope with the difficulties resulting

---

[50] *Metaphysische Anfangsgründe der Rechtslehre* (*Werke,* vii, 124).

[51] Vaughan, *The Political Writings of Rousseau,* i, 95ff; ii, 135-136ff. Official doctrine regarding the United Nations assumes that one can have an effective federation without limiting sovereignty. The theoretical problems are stated in historical perspective, albeit inadequately, by Otto von Gierke, *The Development of Political Theory* (1939), 257-298.

from their small size. In this connection, writers usually refer to the example of Switzerland, which was, of course, very much on Rousseau's mind in all his political speculations.

What is more, there are some definite indications that Rousseau had given elaborate thought to this solution. We are told that "it is almost certain that Rousseau wrote a fragment of some length—sixteen chapters—on the subject," but that "the friend to whom he committed it took fright in the early months of the revolution and destroyed it." [52] Presumably it was part of that comprehensive work on Political Institutions which Rousseau never wrote, except for the *Contrat Social* and the *Etat de Guerre*. There is a brief indication in *Emile* as to what these chapters might have contained: after discussing the unfortunate consequences resulting from the several communities being in a state of nature in their relation to each other, Rousseau there wrote:

We shall examine finally the kind of remedy that men have sought against these evils in Leagues and Federations, which, leaving each State master in its own house, arm it against all unjust aggression from without. We shall inquire what are the means of establishing a good form of federal association, what can give it permanence, and how far we can extend the rights of the Federation without trenching on those of Sovereignty.[53]

From these statements, Vaughan believes we can infer what Rousseau had in view, and that we can surmise what he considered the best means for attaining the end desired. As to the aim, purpose, or end, Vaughan tells us that it is double. Federation seeks to do for the several communities concerned what the Social Contract has already done for the individual himself: to substitute a state of freedom under law for the state of nature. Concomitant with this aim is the other one of freeing men from "tyranny and war," both caused by the partial and incomplete

[52] Vaughan, *Political Writings of Rousseau*, I, 95.   [53] *Ibid.*, I, 96.

association which the establishment of separate commonwealths entails.

But is this really a practicable way out within the framework of Rousseau's conception of the general will as the only acceptable basis of true laws? It is most significant that Rousseau wishes to limit the rights of the Federation by those of sovereignty. This issue is, of course, central to all present discussions of international organization. All the component units then remain sovereign, as indeed they would well-nigh have to if Rousseau's concept of the sovereign general will of the genuine community held together by common bonds of feeling, tradition, and belief as the only basis of true laws is to be retained. No true laws are possible for the federation as a whole, except in the form of agreements between the several component units. The large number of individuals comprised in such a federation would make their judgment regarding what is in the general interest too tenuous to serve as a reliable index of "what the general will wants." It is from this perspective that we can appreciate the skepticism, not to say despondency, with which Rousseau viewed the prospects of organizing lasting peace.

Not so Kant. We have already seen that Kant hesitates between a world republic and a league. Reason seemed to him, as we have noted, to demand the former. He recognizes, however, that the existing republics with the several sovereignties do not want to accept it, because of their idea of international law, and therefore "only the negative surrogate of a league which guards [men] against war and gradually expands can check the current of law-evading bellicose propensities." Significantly, Kant considers this only a *check,* and therefore explicitly adds—quoting Virgil's *Furor impius intus—fremis horridus ore cruento*—that a constant danger remains that these propensities will break loose. In a note he further urges that it would be highly proper for a people, after the end of a war, to declare a day of repentance and atonement for the great sin that mankind has committed in not

being willing to submit itself to a real constitution and laws.[54]
"Practical reason provides us with an irresistible veto: *there shall
not be war.*" The effort to eliminate war and to live in peace is
one of the most clearly indicated norms with which the categorical imperative provides us. And therefore it is possible to say
that the general and continuous establishment of peace constitutes "not only a part, but the full final end of law and its theory
within the limits of reason." After reiterating his conviction of
the importance of a constitution, Kant then quotes the saying
that "the best constitution is one where not men, but laws have
the power"—a saying which has "the most proven objective
reality." This radical affirmation once more strongly confirms
Kant's indubitable kinship to the ideas of the American (as well
as the preceding English) Revolution. He follows it with a
clear judgment in favor of evolution. "This idea alone may lead
us in continuous approximation toward the highest political
good, eternal peace, if it is attempted and carried through by
gradual reform according to firm principles rather than by revolution; that is to say, by violent overthrow of an existing, defective constitution," for in the latter case there would occur a
brief period during which all legal order would be destroyed.[55]
Still, to bridge this gap, Kant introduces the idea of a "natural
constitution" or constitution according to natural law which is
evolving in the midst of this revolution and which tends to
bring into existence a republican constitution.[56] He goes so far
as to insist that even if the revolution should fail, he would still

---

[54] *Zum Ewigen Frieden* (*Werke*, vi, 442). The passage occurs at the end
of the discussion of the second definitive article. Kant adds that celebrations
thanking God for victories are at variance with the moral idea of the Father
of man, because they not only neglect the means through which men have
sought to secure their right, but suggest delight at having destroyed a lot of
men and their happiness. For similar thoughts see *Rechtslehre* (*Werke*, vii,
161-162).

[55] *Rechtslehre* (*Werke*, vii, 162). Cf. the parallel passages in *Der Streit der
Fakultäten* (*Werke*, vii, 400ff).

[56] *Der Streit der Fakultäten*, p. 400ff.

make it the basis of prediction that mankind will eventually realize a universal constitution, because "such a phenomenon in the history of mankind [the revolution] will not be forgotten" (*ein solches Phänomen in der Menschengeschichte vergisst sich nicht mehr*), since "it proves in strictest theory the proposition that mankind has always been progressing toward a better world and will continue to do so."

Unlike Rousseau's uncritical conception of law as based upon an ill-defined general will, Kant's rigorous definition of the general will as the composite will of a civilized people, each member exercising his will in accordance with the categorical imperative, provides a firm foundation for a universal order of freedom under law. In the course of his philosophical deduction of the foregoing, Kant made a point, however, which is not only central to his own position, but calls for much more detailed examination. The *salus reipublicae,* the general public interest, which is progressively being realized under a constitution which provides for the three powers—legislative, executive, and judicial—does not consist in the happiness and well-being of the citizens as individuals; for subjects may conceivably be more comfortable and satisfied in the state of nature or even under a despotic government. What, then, does the general public interest consist in? Kant answers: In the greatest possible consonance between the constitution and the principles of law which the categorical imperative obliges us to strive for. To put it another way: The general public interest calls for the progressive realization of a moral and legal order in which all human beings are treated as ends in themselves, never as means. For only this means freedom under law. The contrast between this moral duty on the one hand and happiness on the other as final motivation for man we will turn to next.

But first it may be well to sum up the broad basic similarities and contrasts in the approach of Saint-Pierre, Rousseau, and Kant as far as reason, revolution and popular participation in

the making of law are concerned. We thus find that each of
our philosophers shares with each of the others one, but not both,
of these basic assumptions.

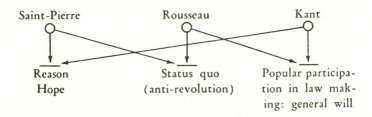

But Kant's belief in reason was tempered by the limits established by his critical method, and his belief in popular participation was similarly tempered by his realistic, unsentimental view
of all men, whether common or uncommon. But for that same
reason Kant could keep his perspective when confronted with
the Terror; the Terror was the same lapse from virtue as the
vices of princes, both to be expected from fallible men. Such a
failure was ever so much more readily to be forgiven in men
who were seeking to establish a true constitutional government,
a republic in the Kannatian sense, than in men whose avowed
purpose it was to hold other men in subjection and maintain
their despotic power. Thus Kant did not fall into the error of
Luther, who condemned participants in the popular movements
more severely because of their amoral behavior than he did their
oppressors whose behavior was no better. For Kant, a revolution
was a fact of nature, never to be morally or legally allowable as
such, but to be accepted as "natural" if directed toward a higher
moral goal, and more especially if directed toward the highest
moral goal—the establishment of a world republic of free men
living together in peace under law.

❦ VII ❦

THE UTILITY OF PEACE:
DUTY VERSUS HAPPINESS
AS MAN'S MOTIVATION

That it is the "duty" of man to work for the realization of peace is an ever-recurring thought in the philosophy of Kant. That this duty springs directly from the categorical imperative Kant likewise asserts without equivocation. Thus, the propensity to work for and establish peace would be the result of man's moral self. For from the categorical imperative: "Act in such a way that the maxim of your will could at all times be enforced [valid] as a principle of a universal legislation," there flows the conclusion that "pure reason is by itself practical and gives [to man] a general law which we call the moral law."[1] This concept of duty as a rational imperative is strictly antithetical to all views which link motivation with the search for happiness. For "it is the direct contrary [*Widerspiel*] of the principle of ethicality [*Sittlichkeit*] to make the principle of a man's own happiness the determining cause of his will . . ."[2] In keeping with this view, Kant goes so far as to suggest that people might be "happier" in the sense of being better off materially under a despot, but that this fact does not in any way absolve them from the "duty" of working for freedom under law.

In clear contrast, David Hume, as well as most of the philosophers of the Enlightenment, founded duty upon happiness and well-being. Characteristically, Hume would rather have England

---

[1] See above, Chapter III, as well as *Critique of Practical Reason*, §7 (*Werke*, v, 35-36).

[2] *Werke*, v, 40.

become a despotic kingdom than a democracy, because people would be happier. Hume is inclined to interpret duty as the response man makes to his environment in his search for happiness. There are two kinds of moral duties which we may respectively designate as instinctive or natural moral duties and as rational or prudent moral duties; besides these moral duties there is the civil duty of allegiance and obedience. The instinctive natural duties are "those to which men are impelled by a natural instinct or immediate propensity, which operates on them, *independent of all ideas of obligation, and of all views, either to public or private utility.*" [3] Love of children and pity for the unfortunate are two such instinctive duties. The rational moral duties are such "as are not supported by any original instinct of nature, but are performed entirely from a *sense of obligation.*" But what motivates this sense of obligation? How does it arise? It springs from a consideration of "the necessities of human society, and the impossibility of supporting it, if these duties were neglected." These duties, then, spring from reflection and experience by which man learns the pernicious effects of license. To measure the distance which separates Kant from Hume, consider the following sentence in Kant's *Critique of Practical Reason:*

The principle of happiness may yield maxims, but never such as would be serviceable as laws for the [general] will, even if the objective were the general happiness [of all]. For the knowledge [of general happiness] rests upon all kinds of data of experience which are in turn judged by everyone according to his opinion which is very changeable. Therefore, such judgments may give us general rules which apply on the average and most frequently, but not rules which must necessarily and always be valid [*gültig*]. Hence no practical laws can be founded upon such judgments. [4]

---

[3] "Of the Original Contract," in *Essays Moral, Political and Literary* (1742), xii (italics mine). All the quotations from Hume in this paragraph and the next are from the same essay.

[4] *Werke*, v, 42. Cf. also vi, 370. See also footnote 18, below.

Kant adds: "The moral law is thought of as objectively necessary only, because it is valid for everybody who possesses reason and will. The maxim of self-love [prudence] merely counsels; the law of ethical conduct [*Sittlichkeit*] commands."

Hume likens the appeal of the civil or political duty of allegiance and obedience to the rational moral duties. The duty to help maintain peace and public order springs from experience and reflection, for even "a small degree of experience and observation suffices to teach us that society cannot possibly be maintained without the authority of magistrates. The observation of these general and obvious interests is the source of all allegiance and of that moral obligation, which we attribute to it." Hume is fully cognizant of man's passions which incline him to "indulge in unlimited freedom" and which tempt him "to seek dominion over others," but reflection nevertheless suffices to sacrifice these strong passions. It is the utility of peace which will induce men to do what is requisite for the building of a peaceful order.

This position does not markedly differ from that of Hobbes, who had derived man's willingness and obligation to obey (duty of allegiance) from his desire for peace. However, Hobbes had derived this desire for peace from his fear of violent death, whereas Hume assigns a significant role to the operation of sympathetic emotions. In his discussion of "why utility pleases" he dwelt upon the "benevolent principles of our frame," the principles of humanity and sympathy which are the feeling from which the merit of social virtue is derived. There is here a clear link with Rousseau, who time and again dwelt upon the reality and force of such sympathetic emotions. Arguing, in *The Origin of Inequality*, directly against Hobbes, Rousseau speaks of "an innate repugnance at seeing a fellow creature suffer." And after giving a moving illustration of such compassion from the fable of the bees, where a savage is forced helplessly to witness a wild beast tearing a child from the arms of its mother,

Rousseau cries out: "What horrid agitation . . . what anxiety would he not suffer at not being able to give any assistance to the fainting mother and the dying infant! Such is the pure emotion of nature, prior to all kinds of reflection! Such is the force of natural compassion!" [5] Hume clearly expresses similar ideas, though in a less oratorical, more moderate fashion. It is a thought common to utilitarians. But whereas the recognition of compassion inclined Rousseau to accept it as an *emotional* restraint on selfish passions which he expands into a general disquisition on love, Hume sees it as the basis for arational conduct on the ground that the spectacle of the well-being of others is a source of happiness and pleasure.

But does Hume really believe that the average man clearly perceives what is requisite for a peaceful order of society? In view of what he says at the beginning of his discussion "Of Political Society" in *An Enquiry Concerning the Principles of Morals,* this may be flatly denied. For here we read: "Had every man sufficient *sagacity* to perceive, at all times, that strong interest which binds him to the observance of justice and equity, and *strength of mind* sufficient to persevere in a steady adherence to a general and distant interest, in opposition to the allurements of present pleasure and advantage; there had never, in that case, been any such thing as government or political society . . ." It is the failure of men to possess that sagacity and strength of mind which gives rise to government and laws. Hume, therefore, expects of the common man no more than obedience to established authority. He denies all contractual theories of government and suggests that we do not bother to concern ourselves with how authority arose.

[5] See Vaughan, *Political Writings of Rousseau,* I, 161. It may be noted in passing that certain authors in our time have expressed indignation at our American soldiers' showing such compassion at the sight of women and children of enemy nations being murdered and raped by their tormentors. The implied demand for "hardness" is, by Rousseau, described as a state of mind which "even the greatest depravity of morals has as yet hardly been able to bring about."

Hume's strong emphasis upon allegiance as the irreducible and basic underpinning of all order and government now becomes understandable. The emphasis of the later Utilitarians upon the coercive scheme of government is similarly to be understood as the essential substitute for any "moral" basis of obligation to law and government. "Make it painful for men to disobey, and their innate propensity to calculate pleasure and pain will do the rest," Bentham and his school seem to say.[6] But neither the sentiment of allegiance nor the calculation of pleasure and pain really meets the issue which was so sharply stated by Socrates' interlocutors in the *Republic* of Plato.[7] The "wave" which Socrates feared might engulf him is a statement of the issue in terms which eliminate all such external compulsions as morally irrelevant, but demand that the matter of "justice"— that is to say, morally right conduct—be discussed in terms of the man who reaps all the "advantages" of the man who acts unjustly, but who suffers none of the "disadvantages" of punishment because he manages to appear as completely just. For this, and only this, is the problem of ethical conduct in its pure form. The resolution of the problem in terms of the "beatitude" of the man who obeys his higher self, his conscience, is in no wise affected by Hume's or Bentham's argument. Its reappearance in the "categorical imperative" of Kant shows why it is possible to see the great argument between Hume and Kant as a resumption of the classic debate between the Sophists and the Socratics. But it is a resumption on a different plane, the level of critical rationalism. Both Socrates and Kant labored to argue the heteronomy of value judgments and existential judgments, the impossibility of arguing from facts to norms. The poignant sentence in which Kant rejects war as means for settling disputes as to who is right reveals the relevancy of this philosophical argument for any philosophy of peace: "The method by which

[6] See below, p. 198, for a more detailed discussion of Bentham.
[7] *Plato's Republic,* tr. by A. D. Lindsay (1935), Bk. I, pp. 25ff.

[sovereign] states pursue their right can never be a judicial process, but only war, and war cannot decide by its success and victory what is right." [8] In other words, might can *never* establish what is right. For Hume and the Utilitarians, there is no such incommensurability between might and right, and a government which exists and is in power is entitled to the allegiance of its subjects whose duty it is to obey.[9]

This juxtaposition of Hume and Kant reveals that neither is really able to account for the whole range of human experience involved in the problems "obligation" and "right." Hume's generalizations explain why most people fulfill their civic (as well as other) duties most of the time; Kant accounts for the intrinsic meaning of normativity and moral choice regardless of whether it is or is not realized in fact. To put it another way: Hume answers the question, Why do most men obey? Kant the question, Why does the morally conscious man obey? In keeping with his theory of law and republican government, Kant insists that all men ought to have a share in the shaping of law and in the building and maintaining of peace. But since he is even more aware than Hume of the limitations of the human mind, and since he fully realizes that the common man can not possibly be expected to perceive his true interest, Kant proceeds to draw a sharp distinction between the "ought" which every man can understand and the prudent calculation of happiness, well-being, and interest:

To obey the categorical command of ethical conduct [*Sittlichkeit*] is in the power of everyone at all times; to follow the empirically condi-

---

[8] *Werke,* vi, 404.
[9] Unfortunately, Kant himself adopted this view, or at least, seems to have adopted it, in his *Metaphysics of Morals, Werke,* vii, 178-180. It is not clear whether the highly authoritarian phrasing in these passages, belonging to Kant's old age, is restricted by the limitation that the duty to obey the constituted authorities applies only under a *Rechtsverfassung* or legal constitution, as was the case in his earlier works, or is meant to apply to any and all authorities.

tioned prescriptions of happiness is only rarely possible for everyone even in regard to a single purpose. The reason is that what matters in the first case is the general principle which must be genuine and pure, whereas in the latter case [what matters is] the resources and the physical capacity to realize the desired object.[10]

To illustrate: in the present world situation, Kant would urge that the common man in America should always try to act in such a way as to forward peace, because that is in keeping with the categorical imperative, and should not mind whether peace can be achieved or not, or what others would have to do to achieve it. Hume, on the other hand, would suggest that the common man obey the government, both national and international, for prudence suggests that the presumption lies in favor of the authorities' being right in whatever they are doing. Kant's is an active, practical, norm-creating approach, Hume's a passive, observing, norm-fulfilling approach.

The deeper philosophical issue involved in this divergence may be seen in Hume's concept of causation and Kant's critical evaluation and rejection of that skeptical notion. This argument in its general terms is familiar enough to philosophers.[11] Hume denied that we have any valid ground for speaking of cause and effect; that all we know by experience as occurring in nature is one phenomenon following another. He therefore defines a cause to be "an object, followed by another, and where all the objects, similar to the first, are followed by objects similar to the second." We may also define cause in relation to the mind and say it is "an object followed by another, and whose appearance

---

[10] *Critique of Practical Reason* (*Werke,* v, 42).

[11] See above, Chapter III, p. 000, for a discussion of some aspects. Cf. also the vital contribution to this problem by Robert M. MacIver, who in his *Social Causation* (1942) rightly commences his entire discussion with Hume, but to my regret fails to develop Kant's contribution. His only reference is to the *Critique of Pure Reason:* Transcendental Logic, I & II. Cf. also A. N. Whitehead, *The Concept of Nature* (1926), esp. pp. 30-41, and Morris R. Cohen, *Reason and Nature* (1931), p. 359ff, and passim.

always conveys the thought of that other." [12] It all is a matter of habit, this customary transition of the imagination from one phenomenon to another. We *feel* this connection in the mind, and this sentiment or impression is the basis upon which we form the idea of power or necessary connection.

In the course of this argument, Hume specifically rejected the common notion that the idea of cause or necessary connection (power) can be traced to the experience of our willing the motion of our limbs or the thoughts of our mind. For here, too, all we know is that the occurrence of one is followed by the occurrence of the other. We habitually experience this sequence and impute a power or causal capacity to our will which is not as such known or experienced. "That their motion follows the command of the will, is a matter of common experience, like other natural events: but the power or energy by which this is effected, like that in other natural events, is unknown and inconceivable." In order to get beyond this skeptical agnosticism, Kant asked the simple question, How is experience possible? Thus, Descartes's famous *cogito, ergo sum* became *cogito, ergo experio.*

Once experience was thus seen to be itself dependent upon mental activity, the inquiry turned to the question, What form does the process of cogitation, of mental activity, take? Or, in Kant's special words, How are synthetic judgments a priori possible? In answer to these questions Kant undertook to show that this process presupposes certain categories, such as space, time, and cause, without which no thought can be thought at all and no experience can be had. All this is familiar enough, and we merely mention it again because, without a grasp of Kant's concept of causation and necessity in nature, his rejection of experience as a basis of ethical conduct—and more especially as a basis for proclaiming peace as a command of the categorical im-

[12] *An Enquiry Concerning Human Understanding,* section VII. Cf. also *Essay on the Human Understanding,* section VII.

perative remains difficult to comprehend.[13] For if our reasoning is to be based upon experience, and our conduct is to be molded by conclusions arrived at in this process, why then war, rather than peace, will be the result, as indeed it had been in the argument advanced by Hobbes. There can be little doubt that Kant saw man's emotional selves as conflicting and quarreling. Not only the peace essay, but other writings, are quite explicit on this point.

This view is sometimes spoken of as "pessimistic," in contrast with the conviction that man is "naturally good," that is to say, friendly and coöperative. Modern psychology, curiously enough, is still divided on this score, in spite of the enormously increased range of observation and experience.[14] Even such views as that there is no "innate" propensity to aggression and conflict, and that all such propensities are the result of societal repressions and tensions, amount to something closely akin to "pessimism," since the prospect of eliminating, or even alleviating to any substantial degree, such social and environmental influences is problematical to say the least.

In any case, Kant, like Rousseau who has frequently been mis-

---

[13] In confirmation of what is said in the text above, I quote two passages from A. D. Lindsay, *The Philosophy of Immanuel Kant* (1919): "Reason, then, it is suggested, is concerned with the principles or conditions, according to which we can understand things" (p. 46). ". . . reason was not a method of observing objects as they really exist, but was concerned directly only with our ways of understanding objects" (p. 47). Cf. also Lindsay's masterly summary of Kant's conception of knowledge (p. 56): Space and time are "forms of our perception," "elements of what we perceive." And the principles of understanding, more especially the principle of causation, "are assumed in all scientific investigation," they are "the grounds of the possibility of experience." Therefore we "cannot deny them without denying elementary distinctions in our experience." But they "apply only to phenomena." The reality may be a continuous process, but this continuous process escapes us in our perceptions, which are fragmentary. Causal connection asserts that disconnected phenomena are outward signs of a connected reality. Hume proved too much in trying, on the basis of such fragmentary experience, to deny the validity of the causal hypothesis.

[14] Cf. the recent coöperative volume, edited by Gardner Murphy, entitled *Human Nature and Enduring Peace* (1945), especially pp. 21ff and 409ff.

interpreted on this score,[15] makes it abundantly clear that he considers man as torn between the social and asocial impulses. The latter impulse is the desire to arrange everything according to his own notions, which makes him anticipate resistance from others as well as it inclines him to offer resistance himself. It is this propensity in men to resist each other which rouses man's latent powers, surmounting his inclination to be indolent, so that, impelled by a mania for honor, power, and property, he seeks pre-eminence among his fellow men whom he can neither like nor leave.[16] It is the idea that struggle is the father of all things, but with a new and most decisive turn given to it. For Kant proceeds to show, as we have seen already, that this struggle is part of a "hidden plan of nature," by which man progresses toward ever more inclusive social organization. Without this assumption of a "plan," it would be necessary to agree with Rousseau that man was better off in the state of nature and virtual anarchy than in the present system of sovereign states with their constant and ever more violent wars.[17] But this very conflict becomes the agency for its eventual elimination. "Providence is justified in this expectation; for the moral principle in man is never extinguished, and reason which is pragmatically capable of executing the ideas of right in accordance with the principle [of morality] grows continuously as culture steadily progresses . . ." Clearly, Kant sees the deterministic sequences, the causal chain of human conflicts, as catastrophic and self-destructive forces which are being transcended by the moral forces in man. Without a recognition of the objective reality of the "ought," we are driven toward desperate conclusions. But just for that reason we are led to discover this objective reality, re-

[15] Cf. Vaughan, *Political Writings of Rousseau*, Introduction, p. 11.

[16] *Idee zu einer allgemeinen Geschichte* (*Werke*, IV, 155). Similar passages are to be found in *Theory and Practice* (*Werke*, VI, 397); *Zum Ewigen Frieden* (*Werke*, VI, 499ff); *Der Streit der Fakultäten* (*Werke*, III, 400ff); *Die Metaphysik der Sitten* (*Werke*, VII, 118); and elsewhere. Cf. Chapter II, above.

[17] *Idee zu einer allgemeinen Geschichte* (*Werke*, IV, 161); *Zum Ewigen Frieden* (*Werke*, VI, 467).

gardless of what empirical observation of politics may suggest. "The right of men must be held sacred, no matter what the cost to ruling powers."

Kant's fervent reassertion of the older view against the skeptical attacks of Hume did not prevent the Utilitarians in England from going forward on their predetermined path. Although it was in fragmentary notes only that Jeremy Bentham concerned himself specifically with the problem of international order, his entire approach to the problem of man in society was, so to speak, a disavowal of Kant in theory, and a demonstration of Kant in practice. For the central tenet of the Benthamite school, the calculus of pleasure and pain as the basic motivation of man, had been refuted by Kant before it was stated.[18] The idea that the greatest happiness of the greatest number should be used as a yardstick for public policy had been expounded before Bentham by such writers as the Abbé Saint-Pierre, Helvetius, Priestley, and others. But Bentham considered that the word "happiness" was rather vaguely used in writers like Priestley, for whom apparently it possessed moral connotations relating it to virtue. This ancient Aristotelian concept of happiness, comprising all states of well-being from the basal gratification of animal needs to the highest level of spiritual satisfaction (true happiness), called, from Bentham's viewpoint, for clarification. Virtue and its opposite, duty, obligation, justice, and the rest are, according to Bentham, mere fictions of language, empty names. The only true motives of conduct are the attraction of pleasure, the repulsion of pain.

[18] Kant's *Critique of Practical Reason,* carefully analyzing and destroying the arguments for any sort of hedonistic ethics, appeared in 1788; his *Metaphysics of Morals* even before that, in 1785. Bentham's *Introduction to the Principles of Morals and Legislation* was published in 1789, though written in 1780. Bentham's peace plan is included in his "Principles of International Law" (*The Works of Jeremy Bentham,* ed. by John Bowring, vol. II, 1843, pp. 535-571). The notes and fragments from which these principles stem, according to Bowring, bear the dates 1786-1789. A date mentioned in the peace essay shows that it was probably not composed before 1789.

Take away pleasures and pain: not only *happiness,* but *justice,* and duty, and *obligation,* and *virtue*—all which have been so elaborately held up to view as independent of them—are so many empty sounds. Destitute of reference to the ideas of *pain* and *pleasure,* whatever ideas are annexed to the words *virtue* and *vice* amount to nothing more than that of groundless approbation and disapprobation . . . empty declamation.[19]

Therefore Bentham's basic work, *An Introduction to the Principles of Morals and Legislation,* begins with the challenge:

Nature has placed mankind under the governance of two sovereign masters, *pain* and *pleasure.* It is for them alone to point out what we ought to do, as well as to determine what we shall do. On the one hand the standard of right and wrong, on the other the chain of causes and effects, are fastened to their throne. They govern us in all we do, in all we say, in all we think.

In throwing out this challenge, Bentham was well aware that he was depriving the moral realm of its autonomous status, that he was reducing all value judgments to existential judgments, that he was rejecting all ethics in favor of hedonistic calculation. "The principle of utility approves or disapproves every action whatsoever, according to the tendency which it appears to have to augment or diminish the happiness of the party whose interest is in question." The community is a "fictitious body," and the interest of this community is the sum of the interests of the several members who compose it. Therefore, the only parties whose interest can ever come into question are individual human beings. And in pointed argument against any and all autonomous ethics, Bentham chides: "Let him [who admits any other principle than that of utility as the basis of right and wrong] say

---

[19] Bentham, *Works,* I, 207. The boundless, if naive, enthusiasm of Bentham has at times inclined people to forget that the calculation of pleasure and pain has a clear antecedent in certain sophists, such as Eudoxus, whose views are mentioned by Aristotle in the *Nicomachean Ethics,* Bk. x, 1172b, and the discussion of Pleasure following it.

whether there is any such thing as a *motive* that a man can have to pursue the dictates of it: if there is, let him say what that motive is, and how it is to be distinguished from those which enforce the dictates of utility . . ." [20]

Unfortunately for Bentham and his entire school, Kant had already undermined the basis of this whole train of reasoning by pointing out that such arguments were concerned merely with natural necessity (*Naturnotwendigkeit*) but failed completely to face the underlying question of how men come to recognize an "ought" distinct from their pleasure and pain. Mockingly, as was his wont, Kant might have asked Bentham how he explained the fact that he, Bentham, had spent his life urging reforms which people rejected as painful? Or how would Bentham account for the further fact of his turning from enlightening princes to enlightening nobles, and finally to enlightening common men concerning their "true" interest without any of them listening to what he preached? And finally he might well have asked how Bentham would explain his frequent outbursts of moral indignation against the privileged, if after all they were doing no more nor less than he would admit they ought to do, namely consulting their own pleasure and pain? In other words, Bentham appealed to men as if they were free moral agents, after having denied most explicitly that they were. Kant was not unaware that there exist commands of prudence (*Gebote der Klugheit*), and he calls them *pragmatic imperatives*. But he insists that they are quite distinct from *technical imperatives*, which are rules of skill, and from *moral* or *categorical imperatives*, which flow from conviction and are valid regardless of the success attending them—"success may be, what it will." [21] He

---

[20] Bentham, *Works*, I, 1-4.

[21] *Grundlegung zur Metaphysik der Sitten* (*Werke*, IV, 274). This theme is so central that it recurs again and again in all of Kant's ethical writings. Cassirer has rightly insisted that these problems are primary in Kant's philosophy, and not subordinate to his theory of knowledge as contained in the *Critique of Pure Reason*. Cf. *Werke*, XI, 247.

then raised the question: How are these imperatives possible? and he adds: "This question does not demand to know how we can think [imagine?] the execution of the action which the imperative commands, but rather how we can think the compulsion of the will which the imperative expresses as the task." This philosophical issue Bentham never faced. He simply eliminated the categorical or moral imperatives by assimilating them to pragmatic imperatives which prudence dictated, and suggested that prudence be built upon a detailed analysis of what causes pleasure and pain. A close inspection of Bentham's analysis shows, of course, that the moral imperatives are included under the several pleasures and pains: "No. VIII—Pleasures and pains, of the Moral or Popular Sanction: viz., Pleasures of Reputation, or Good-repute; Pains of Bad-reputation, or ill-repute. No. IX —Pleasures and Pains of the Religious Sanction. Corresponding Interest—Interest of the Altar." We find, further, that the pleasure and pain of sympathy and antipathy are recognized.[22] Again, in considering sanctions, Bentham includes the religious and the moral (or popular) sanction along with the physical and political. But in all of his discussion, he is continually occupied with the problem of how to think of the execution of the action rather than how to think of the compulsion of the will. For he says: "Pleasures and pains which may be expected to issue from the *physical, political* or *moral* sanctions, must all of them be expected to be experienced, if ever, in the *present* life . . ."[23] illustrating his view with a man's house burning down "for want of any friendly assistance which his neighbour withheld from him out of some dislike to his moral character." Similarly, the religious sanction is essentially comprised in what *punishment* the deity provides for sinners. The crudity of this kind of Pharisee morals, where outward conformity is primary and the disposition of the mind, its convictions, and its charac-

[22] *Works,* I, 201ff. Other versions are given elsewhere, e.g., I, 17ff.
[23] *Works,* I, 14, 15.

ter count for little if anything, has been acknowledged in the deeper strands of doctrine of all the great world religions, including Christianity. Such reasoning would be considered by many including Kant a denial of the existence of true morality altogether. In any case, it can hardly be considered an account which provides an analysis of the process involved in genuine ethical conduct. Such an analysis needs to deal with those human actions which flow from a disposition to be good, to put it very simply. Kant, as well as Rousseau, was concerned with that process, when he dealt with the specifically moral. The categorical imperative is an attempt to state explicitly what is at the core of that process.

Pragmatic imperatives embodying rules of prudence are quite distinct from moral imperatives in this view. Indeed, there would be no need to differentiate them from technical imperatives, from rules which describe what means are required to secure a certain end, if what constitutes human happiness were not such a debatable matter, and if the means of securing whatever we decide would make us happy were not so uncertain. The reason for this situation Kant believes to be that "all elements which belong to the concept of happiness are empirical and must be derived from experience . . . and yet the idea of happiness is an absolute whole." Hence our finite minds cannot solve the problem. "If we seek riches, we bring upon us cares, envy and assaults . . . If we seek a long life, how do we know that it will not turn out to be a long misery? If we seek health, we may become reckless which a feeble constitution would have kept us away from, etc. In short, man is not able to determine in accordance with a principle and with complete certainty what would make him truly happy, because he would have to be omniscient." [24] Therefore, the pragmatic imperatives, these rules of

---

[24] Kant, *Grundlegung zur Metaphysik der Sitten,* II (*Werke,* IV, 275-276). See also note 4, above.

prudence, are not really commands at all; they are counsels and not "laws" in any true sense.

Applying this train of reasoning, Kant would urge that the pursuit of peace, if put in terms of the pursuit of happiness, is jeopardized by the uncertainties surrounding what constitutes happiness. He would point out that the arguments of men such as William James and H. G. Wells which urge that men are "happier" at war than at peace show, not that we must find a "moral equivalent," but that war is inherently immoral because it is manifestly contrary to the categorical imperative which bids us act only in accordance with a maxim which we can will to be a universal law.[25] From this imperative flows immediately the practical imperative which commands us never to use man merely as a means to an end. Since all warfare inevitably forces us to do just that, it is absolutely incompatible with the moral law.[26]

To test this dichotomy further, it will be desirable to present and analyze briefly the peace plan which Bentham himself worked out around 1789. In order to avoid being unjust to Bentham, we should bear in mind that the "plan" as published much later by Bowring was a "fragment," that it was prerevolutionary, and that it belongs to the period of Bentham's "Fragment on Government," when he was inclined toward a belief in the elite of the mind, and in an enlightened "patriot king." Like Voltaire and the Abbé Saint-Pierre, Bentham looked for the re-

[25] Kant, in order to drive home the rigid binding nature of this imperative, adds that the imperative may be formulated thus: "Act as if the maxim of your action were to become by your will a general law of nature" (*Grundlegung zur Metaphysik der Sitten, Werke,* iv, 279).
[26] The bitter ring of the title *They Were Expendable* illustrates the point well. This little book was written by W. L. White and published in 1942. More penetrating was the treatment in Rex Warner's haunting story *The Return of the Traveller* (1944), where the dead soldier tries to find an answer to the question: Why should I have to die? and where all the stock answers of patriotism, of reform, and the rest, including the will of God, are found hollow and wanting.

form of society from benevolent rulers rather than the will of the people.[27]

Bentham's plan is very simple. He would secure a lasting peace through two measures agreed upon between two powers, England and France. He would have them adopt these two fundamental propositions: First, the reduction and fixation of the force of the several nations that compose the European system, and second, the emancipation of the distant dependencies of each state. He feels that there can be no argument concerning the utility of an universal and lasting peace; that the only objection to it is its impracticability.

He then proceeds to formulate fourteen supplementary propositions which in fact may be reduced to nine, since VI-X merely repeat I-V but apply them to France instead of England. These nine propositions, besides restating the two fundamental ones, add the following: II, that it is not in the interest of Great Britain to have any treaty of alliance, offensive, or defensive, with any other power whatever; III, that it is not in the interest of Great Britain to have any treaty . . . of trade; XIII, that the maintenance of such a pacification might be considerably facilitated, by a common court of judicature . . . although such court were not to be armed with any coercive powers; XIV, that secrecy in the operations of the foreign department [is] . . . altogether useless, and equally repugnant to the interests of liberty and to those of peace.[28] It is apparent that this plan is largely a repetitive simplification of the plan of the Abbé Saint-Pierre, except for the stress laid upon colonies as causes of war. This early protest against the "inutility" of the colonial system is interesting. But Bentham's suggestion that this total inutility can be argued on the ground of the limited supply of capital is a travesty in its crudeness when compared with Adam Smith's

[27] For the "Fragment on Government" see John Bowring, *The Works of Jeremy Bentham*, i, 221ff. See Chapter V, above, for Bentham's criticism of the law of nature, and some bibliography.
[28] *Works*, ii, 546-547.

elaborate discussion of colonies in *The Wealth of Nations,* which had appeared more than ten years earlier, in 1776.[29] It turns essentially upon a rough approximation to the ideas of the Physiocrats, with their emphasis upon the utility of agriculture.

Bentham's plan contains one specific defect which requires especial mention and comment, however. It is obvious from what has been said that he does not envisage anything more than a disarmament treaty and a self-denying ordinance concerning colonies, with some very vague scheme of arbitration attached. In order to appreciate the significance of this approach it is necessary to recall the views of Bentham on state and sovereignty. They are as we have seen uncompromisingly absolutist. His diatribes against natural law are symptomatic of his impatience with any kind of restriction of the legislative sovereign. His reformist zeal rebelled against any fixed legal barriers preventing change. Defining political society and government as relative matters, he made the "habit of obedience" the prime criterion, and proclaimed the governor or governors wielding the legislative power to be unrestrained by any earthly superior. Although Bentham changed his ideas concerning those who might most usefully wield this legislative sovereignty, eventually arriving at a fairly radical democratic position, he never wavered in insisting upon the absolutism of the sovereign power, and more especially did he decry, as we have seen, the idea that a higher law, or a constitution could be admitted.[30] Bentham's view has well been summed up in the proposition that the state is a machine so well constructed that no individual, taken individually, can for one instant escape from the control of all the individuals taken

---

[29] See *The Wealth of Nations,* Bk. IV, ch. vii. Cf. also Klaus E. Knorr, *British Colonial Theories, 1570-1850* (1944), esp. ch. vi. Unfortunately for the topic here in hand, Knorr's excellent analysis does not include Bentham's peace plan.

[30] Elie Halevy, *The Growth of Philosophic Radicalism* (translated by Mary Morris, with a preface by A. D. Lindsay, 1928) esp. pp. 403-432. Bentham's concept of a "constitution" as adopted in the "Constitutional Code" (1827 and later—see *Works,* II, 270ff) is strictly legislative.

collectively. This artificial identification of interests, as Bentham called it, is the task of government and is needed to overcome the natural and necessary "love of self" which is universal. No natural identity of interests can be relied upon, as Payne and Godwin had been inclined to urge.

Such an approach is ill-adapted to world coöperation along constitutional lines. For its only *logical* solution of the problems of world government is a unitary scheme encompassing the globe. That such a radically democratic world republic was utterly visionary in Bentham's view may be inferred from the fact that Bentham argues that his *limited* plan is *not* impracticable. Even in our time, a plan of world government premised on radical majoritarian democracy is not advocated by even the most fervent apostles of world government.[31]

This blind alley of the utilitarian position on peace is not without deeper significance. Start with the greatest happiness of the greatest number in terms of a calculus of pleasure and pain, and you logically arrive at the conclusion of a rather *limited* community as the only manageable framework for legislation. Recalling Bentham's view of the community as a "fictitious body" (a view which incidentally would undo much of what Rousseau had recaptured in rediscovering the community), and his view of its interest as the sum of the interests of the individuals composing it, we can see how an enlargement of this community would make this "sum" ever more elusive an entity.[32] When you come to international life the matter is very complex. How the rival claims and interests of human beings belonging to different nations, such for example as the Jews and Arabs in Palestine and their sympathizers beyond the borders, can be

[31] The significance of Bentham's democratic acceptance of the belief in the common man should not be obscured by what has been said. Cf. my book, *The New Belief in the Common Man* (1942), p. 9ff.

[32] In mathematical terms, it would turn out not to be a sum at all, but a much more elaborate equation. Altogether, the use of mathematical metaphor is very crude not only in Bentham, but in many of the older members of the school.

"summed up" is indicated by neither Bentham nor his school. But it is clear enough that he unconsciously assumes a people which is as homogeneous as the English. On the other hand, a world republic would be most diverse in its heterogeneity.[33]

Thus Bentham's superindividualist and instrumentalist calculus of pleasure and pain, of the greatest happiness of the greatest number, leads him to as complete an impasse as far as world organization for peace is concerned as ever faced Rousseau. Though both are collectivist, Rousseau's belief in a general irrational will embodying the sentiment of a *real* community and providing the basis and motivation of social action finds no parallel in the Utilitarian collective will. Kant transcends both. He modifies Rousseau, as we have seen, by giving the general will a more rational content, interpreting it as a compound of the "rational" will of individuals—this compound rational will resulting ideally from their following the categorical imperative. And since the categorical imperative is simply spelling out the intrinsic meaning of the "ought" of acting men, it has universal application. Kant transcends the Utilitarians by insisting that there is this feeling of "ought," this inborn moral propensity to seek what is right, which the categorical imperative makes explicit as a basic motivation in man beyond the hedonistic wish for happiness. Important as this hedonistic principle is in the natural nexus of cause and effect in which human beings as parts of the world of nature are placed, it can never serve to "explain" the primary thesis of moral preference for what is believed to be right. Never could Kant have assented to Bentham's definition of duty.

That is my [political] *duty* to do, which I am liable to be *punished* for, according to law, if I do not do: this is the original, ordinary, and

---

[33] James Mill's "Law of Nations" (written for the *Encyclopaedia Britannica*) characteristically would found a peace order simply upon a code and tribunals for its enforcement. The problem of homogeneity is linked with the requirement of agreement on fundamentals so frequently urged in conjunction with constitutionalism and democracy. See *The New Belief in the Common Man,* ch. v, for a critical appraisal.

proper sense of the word *duty*. Have supreme governors any such duty? No: for if they are at all liable to punishment according to law . . . they are not, what they are supposed to be, supreme governors: those are the supreme governors, by whose appointments the former are liable to be punished.[34]

What becomes of the prime duty to work toward peace which Kant is never wearying of telling us about? The habit of obedience leads right to the opposite conclusion: "My country— right or wrong, my country!" There undoubtedly is a habit of obedience, and it is very important for the maintenance of government,[35] but it is transcended by the moral commandments embodied in the categorical imperative and the rules of action derived from it.

By taking this position, Kant provides himself with a tenable motivation for a world order under law which as derived from

[34] See "Fragment on Government," ch. v, para. vii. (*Works*, I, 293). There is an important footnote in which Bentham acknowledges the difference between political, moral, and religious duties; but, as previously noted, he gives the term "moral" a crudely pragmatic turn by linking it with community approbation or disapprobation. "Moral duty is created by a kind of motive, which, from the *uncertainty* of the *persons* to apply it, and of the *species* and *degree* in which it will be applied, has hardly yet got the name of punishment: by various mortifications resulting from the ill-will of persons *un*certain and variable—the community in general; that is, such individuals of that community as he, whose duty is in question, shall happen to be connected with" (italic in the original). The Kantian concept of duty (in line with Judeo-Christian ethics) asserts, of course, that duties call upon man to pursue a course of action regardless of consequences, although the intrinsic improbability of any man's following so repellant a path is reduced by promises *either* of internal bliss due to self-satisfaction resulting from having done "right" or of eternal bliss due to rewards in a life to come. Kant, like Aristotle and many other philosophers, leans toward the first, but basically rejects even this. In a very real sense, he is not concerned with the problem that Bentham deals with when he deals with pure practical reason. Instead he seeks to make explicit what the structure of this type of motivation may be, which he considers as given in basic feeling.

[35] It is clear that Bentham's principle of the supreme and arbitrary authority of the actual governors leaves no room whatever for such an undertaking as the trial of war criminals, except under their own law. Few of those who argue for the proposition that Goering and the rest should be tried by German courts realize that they are following the utilitarian and positivist position, even fewer of those arguing the opposite that they are abandoning it.

the categorical imperative impels the free individual to work for such a peace order, even while the conflicts and wars engendered by man's irrational and bellicose propensities propel mankind forward toward such an order against its conscious desire. There remain very serious difficulties, however, which have become explicit since Kant wrote. One is the emerging recognition of a class structure in society in which value judgments are concretely embedded, the other is the recognition of cultural, religious, and psychic (somatic) differentiations which are likewise apt to generate marked divergencies in the responses human beings will make to the categorical imperative. While these now generally recognized empirical antecedents do not, as often asserted,[36] necessarily destroy the Kantian position, they do raise real problems for anyone who seeks to determine what answer specific groups of human beings might give if confronted with a concrete situation, even though all acknowledged the cogency of the categorical imperative. Evidently wholly divergent responses would be made by members of different classes, as for instance, Hindus and Christians, Chinese and Europeans. Or would they be? The presumption at present is in favor of such contentions, and it is here that the deepest problems of a viable peace order present themselves.

Modern sociology, psychology, and anthropology have raised questions which the quest for peace and security must face. The approaches to the peace problem, epitomized in the work of Karl Marx and Friedrich Engels, of Thorstein Veblen and of Sigmund Freud, are pivotal to modern man. Class, religion. culture and somatic constitution—these and other preëxistent frameworks of man's approach to his duties have all been brought forward as so many obstructions to the realization of peace. Their true bearing on the political philosophy of peace will be our concern in the last chapter.

[36] E.g., John Dewey, *The Quest for Certainty* (1928), pp. 288ff, and Max Scheler, *Der Formalismus in der Ethik und die materiale Wertethik* (1913-1916), pp. 1ff.

❦ VIII ❦

PEACE

SOCIAL JUSTICE

AND CLASS STRUCTURE [1]

In all socialist thought, the problem of war has played a major role. Time and again, the idea of a universal reign of peace resulting from the establishment of social justice has cropped up, especially in the more utopian and anarchist strands. Thus Proudhon, the butt of Marx's *Communist Manifesto,* believed that only a gradual weakening of the state could reduce and eventually eliminate wars. This should be accomplished, Proudhon thought, by the building up of syndicalist and coöperative groups. Likewise Fourier, another "utopian" socialist, believed that the final stage of human development, when mankind is organized into composite associations, will bring a reign of universal peace. The ardent rationalism of these and other pre-Marxian socialists has often been commented upon; yet they were all rejected by the bitter doctrine of the *Communist Manifesto,* which declared that "all history is a history of class struggles."

It is well known that the *Communist Manifesto* treats explicitly of the several socialist systems and rejects them all as "unrealistic." Their lack of realism consists in their failure to

[1] The chapter here presented treats in broad outline the contrast between the Kantian and the Marxian approach to "inevitable" peace. It is programmatic in that it anticipates the results of a more elaborate analysis the author hopes to offer on the problems of war and peace in socialism and anarchism. It is manifestly impossible to do justice to the vast literature which has grown up around the writings involved in this chapter. The references are not meant to do more than suggest supporting evidence on special points, and are inadequate even for that purpose.

face the inexorable destiny of the proletariat as a class. Only the "scientific" socialists, that is to say, the Communists, squarely confront this destiny. "The Communists refuse to hide their views and purposes. They declare openly that their ends can only be achieved through the violent overthrow of the entire existing social order." That was, of course, almost a hundred years ago; in 1917, seventy years after the *Communist Manifesto* was first conceived, a social order, albeit not a strictly capitalist one, was overthrown by a party of Communists who believed themselves to be representing the emergent proletariat of Russia. As Russia was confronted by imminent defeat in war, the Bolsheviks made very effective use of the longing of the masses for peace to establish their ascendancy over the more numerous Mensheviks and to dislodge the Kerensky government.[2] But the seizure of power by the Communists brought on a violent civil war, as had been predicted by them ever since the *Communist Manifesto* identified "class war" as the inevitable outcome of any serious attempt of the proletariat or working class to achieve control of the state. Ever since then, the leaders of the Soviet Union have seen themselves surrounded by "class enemies" both within and without the Soviet Union; vast purges have been carried out to rid the USSR of these enemies of the working class—that is to say, enemies of the dictatorship of the proletariat; and wars have been fought against the class enemies without, more especially the Fascist exponents of world capitalism. The Five-Year Plan which the Soviet Union has launched since the end of World War II was clearly and openly linked by Marshal Stalin to the need to be ready for war in the interest of the "victorious" proletariat.[3]

[2] See Merle Fainsod, *International Socialism and the World War* (1935); F. Borkenau, *World Communism—A History of the Third International* (1939); John Reed, *Ten Days That Shook the World* (1919); Leon Trotsky, *My Life* (1930), and *The History of the Russian Revolution* (1936).

[3] See above, Introduction, p. 5, for quotation from Stalin. Cf. also the general view expounded in Victor Kravchenko, *I Choose Freedom* (1946), chs. xxv-xxvii for a very apprehensive interpretation. This view is shared by such writers as Louis Fischer.

As in the days of the *Communist Manifesto,* the various kinds of "bourgeois" socialism and utopianism are viewed with especial apprehension. The speeches of Stalin, Molotov, and other leaders of the USSR faithfully reproduce the essence of the *Manifesto,* which mercilessly dissected these dreamers.

To the degree that the class struggle develops and takes shape, the phantastic fight against the class struggle loses all practical value as it loses all theoretical justification. . . . The builders of these systems . . . were in many ways revolutionary, but their disciples always form reactionary sects. . . . They therefore seek persistently to soften the class struggle, and to conciliate the conflicts.[4]

Why recall these familiar facts? Because a full appreciation of the ideology of the Communist movement is the essential basis of the analysis of the conflict of ideas which has been undertaken. Marx and Engels,[5] like Kant before them, are firmly attached to a belief in eventual and lasting peace. They, like the philosopher of peace, were convinced of the fact that progress and struggle were linked to each other, that the nature of human beings compelled them to seek their own selfish interests. Like Kant, they were certain that such constant striving must have a

[4] Cf. *Communist Manifesto,* III, 3, and Charles Andler's interesting historical study, *Le Manifeste Communiste* (1901).

[5] The relation of Marx and Engels has been and will continue to be in controversy on many points. For the broad purposes of this chapter it is best to treat them as one. Although we shall at times, following long-established custom, speak of Marx alone, it is to be understood that Engels as well is meant. Besides the *Communist Manifesto,* their joint work *The German Ideology* is in some ways most interesting. The English edition published in 1939 by International Publishers, with an Introduction by R. Pascal, has been used here. It is noteworthy that among the list of "authors and works referred to" which the editor has prepared, Kant is not mentioned with a single work; this supports, we believe, our contention that Marx and Engels were very little acquainted with Kant, and knew of him almost entirely through Hegel, a most unsatisfactory source. Unfortunately, this tradition persists in England and America; among illustrations one might cite the learned and thoughtful Sidney Hook, *From Hegel to Marx* (1936) and *Towards the Understanding of Karl Marx* (1933). Hook follows in this regard his revered teacher, John Dewey, whose Hegelian approach to Kant is discussed above, Chapter II, footnote 2.

meaning. This meaning is a universal reign of peace. The state "withers away," "public power loses its political nature," and "in place of the old bourgeois society with its classes and class conflicts an association arises wherein the free development of each man is the condition for the free development of all." [6] But Kant saw the road to such a final and crowning achievement as a long and perilous journey in which various groups of human beings, nations, classes, states, fought over their interests only to discover that such struggle did not pay, while in more and more people a conviction grew that the categorical imperative demanded "There shall be no war." [7] Marx and Engels, on the other hand, stressed the task of the proletariat, whom they perceived as the class whose historical destiny it was to achieve a universal society. After noting that the national separation and conflicts were declining even under the bourgeoisie, they expressed the conviction that the rule of the proletariat will make them vanish. "To the extent that the exploitation of one individual by another is suspended, the exploiting of one nation by another will be suspended. With the conflict of classes inside the nations, the hostile attitude of nations against each other is removed." [8] Thus they preached war, the class war or class struggle, as the only road to peace. How would Kant—and like him those who subscribe to the ideology of the United Nations— deal with this "pessimism" which glorifies war as a necessary tool? How should anyone who believes in peace resolve the difficulty of a "peace-through-war" ideology?

[6] The striking similarity of this formulation of the final condition of mankind to Kant's formulation may be gleaned by comparing it with the discussion above, Chapter III. Cf. also the formulation below, p. 235. There is, however, óne very important difference. For Kant, this "free development of all" is conceivable only under law; no such condition is stated by Marx.

[7] Cf. Chapter III, p. 90 above.

[8] Cf. the *Communist Manifesto;* for an analysis of the potential threat of war among socialist states, compare the penetrating article by G. Lütkens, "Das Kriegsproblem und die Marxistische Theorie," in *Archiv für Sozialwissenschaft und Sozialpolitik* (May 1922), p. 467.

In the halcyon days of socialism before World War I, bitter battles were fought between the radical Marxists who believed in the war between classes as the central task of the class-conscious proletariat and the "revisionist" and "reformist" Marxists of many shades. Among these, Jean Jaurès occupied a preëminent position as a fighter for radical pacifism. In a brilliant pamphlet entitled *Le Proletariat, La Patrie et la Paix* (1902),[9] Jaurès expounded the view, reminiscent of Proudhon, that peace is a central concern of the proletariat but that the Marxian proposition that the proletariat has no country, no *patrie*, is wrong. Recalling the revolutionary tradition of the Jacobins,[10] he insisted that one's country provides the essential support of the revolution, and that the revolution constitutes the exaltation, even the fulfillment, of one's *patrie*. At the same time, he believed that Marx and Engels had rightly foreseen and formulated the decisive role which the proletariat would be called upon to play in the solution and suppression of the antagonism between nations. Jaurès was convinced that Marx and Engels, in their "juvenile simplicity," and their "a bit meagre brutality" had never, in spite of their dialectic and their erudition, grasped the revolutionary tradition of France. "No," he exclaimed, "the social revolution will be accomplished in each of the great modern peoples by an autonomous movement, and we will not be exposed to seeing the spirit of war, of domination, and of victory falsify the primary integrity of our common aspirations." [11] Animated by a primary sense of freedom—and that means free participation of the working classes in their own liberation—he formulated the

[9] These were originally articles in Juarès' journal, *La Petite République*. They are most readily accessible in the *Œuvres de Jean Juarès*, edited by Max Bonnafous, vol. i (1931). It is worth noting that Jean Juarès had ten years earlier written a doctoral dissertation entitled *De primis socialismi Germanici lineamentis apud Lutherum, Kant, Fichte et Hegel* (1891). Regarding this work and related French studies see Karl Vorländer, *Kant und Marx* (1911), pp. 106ff, and elsewhere.

[10] See Crane Brinton, *The Jacobins* (1930), esp. ch. vii.

[11] Juarès, *Œuvres*, i, 292.

strictly democratic view that it would instill an intolerable sense of defeat in a working class if it should be conquered by outsiders. Therefore, even if the conquering nation instituted communism in the conquered nation and abolished the capitalist tyranny, such a working class would feel itself violated in its very liberation and would be unable to enjoy its new-won freedom. Jaurès was firmly convinced that humanity would realize the unity of life within the framework of a free federation of autonomous and fraternal homelands. Jaurès took great pains to show that Marx and Engels themselves had recognized the role of the several nations in their liberation. He noted that the *Manifesto* had stated that the proletariat would rise as the sovereign national class and would constitute itself as the nation.[12] To him, the French proletariat could be faithful to its role only by heroically defending its republican homeland. Only in this way could the members of the proletariat remain faithful to the ideal of universal peace to be established by the victory of the working class in all countries.

In spite of his ardent profession of patriotism, Jaurès fell by a murderer's hand at the outbreak of hostilities between France and Germany in 1914. He had stood as a symbol of coöperation between the working classes of the two countries. Often he had argued the case of declaring a general strike to stop the outbreak of a war. He, who fought all his life for the recognition of labor's national attachment, hoped and worked for a grand demonstration of labor's international solidarity to avert a war. Some have suspected that he was put away by misguided nationalists as the uncompromising pacifist who might endanger France's defense against the onslaught of imperial Germany. If so, they were ill-informed about Jaurès. He had insisted often enough that the revolutionary tradition of France obliged the French worker to defend his *patrie*. Only a general strike on the part of the German socialists would have found Jaurès responding with

[12] *Ibid.*, pp. 301-302.

a similar call to French workers. Instead of doing any such thing, the majority of the German Social Democrats voted the war budgets of the German Empire until 1917. The more radical Marxists among them, faithful to their dialectic of war and revolution, met with French and Russian partisans, among them Nikolai Lenin. They sought to devise means of making the most of the bankruptcy of reformist socialism.[13] In the course of their deliberations, there reëmerged the central Marxian tenet of international civil war, of class war as the essential condition for the end of all wars. The Russian Revolution and the founding of the Third International ushered in a basic change in the development of universal peace through class war: henceforth the policy of a great state, backed by the traditional weapons of political power, would be at the center of the effort at uniting the world's proletariat. The decisive turn had occurred: class war and the war between organized states became intertwined in the issues confronting the Soviet Union and the world.

A fundamental issue, however, remained: Should the state power of the Soviet Union be employed to foster world revolution? Could universal peace and security be best promoted by placing such resources as were at the disposal of the victorious proletariat in the USSR behind the struggle for victory in as many lands as possible, more especially Italy, Germany, and China? Or should the Soviet Union and the Third International subordinate the exigencies of class war in other countries to the needs of the Soviet Union instead? This issue clearly stems from the central Marxist tenet of the world revolutionary solidarity of the proletariat in all countries. Since Marx and Engels had

[13] See Fainsod, *International Socialism and the World War*, esp. chs. iii-vi. For the personal aspect of Jaurès' fight for peace, see Margaret Pease, *Jean Jaurès, Socialist and Humanitarian* (1916), and (more penetrating) Charles Rappoport, *Jean Jaurès, l'homme, le penseur, le socialiste* (3rd ed., 1925). Emile Vandervelde and Lucien Levy-Bruhl also have given interpretations which attest Jaurès outstanding position among democratic socialists.

not foreseen it in all its fierce and dramatic urgency, it gave rise to the epochal fight for supremacy between Stalin and Trotsky.[14] After Trosky had lost, Stalin restated the Marxist position in terms which clearly showed that from then on the fate of the proletariat throughout the world, and the implied prospect of universal peace, would be shaped in terms of the survival and expansion of Soviet power. Stalin has returned to this theme again and again, and we may here add another passage to that quoted earlier; in his Report to the Eighteenth Party Congress, just before the outbreak of the war in Europe, Stalin criticized those who demanded that the "state wither away" in the Soviet Union, on the ground that the exploiting class had been abolished, and then said:

> These comrades have failed to understand the essential meaning of this doctrine . . . what is more they do not understand present-day international conditions, have overlooked the capitalist encirclement and the dangers it entails for the socialist country. . . . They likewise betray an underestimation of the role and significance of our socialist state and of its military, punitive and intelligence organs, which are essential for the defense of the socialist land from foreign attack.[15]

Then, after referring to the sin of all Bolesheviks in underestimating the danger and their blunder in not realizing the "espionage and conspiratorial activities of the Troskyites," he asked how they were to explain this blunder. And he answered thus:

> It is to be explained by an underestimation of the power and purpose of the mechanism of the bourgeois states surrounding us and of their

[14] Cf. L. Trotsky, *My Life,* pp. 329ff, Joseph Stalin, *Leninism* (International Publishers, 1942) pp. 83, 222ff, and elsewhere. According to Stalin, the "left" deviation *underestimates* the strength of capitalism. Cf. also the attempt at an objective evaluation of this conflict by Frederick L. Schuman, *Soviet Politics at Home and Abroad* (1946), pp. 196ff, which reaches conclusions favorable to the Stalinist position.

[15] "From Socialism to Communism in the Soviet Union," *Report to the 18th Congress of C.P.S.V.* (B), p. 50 (1939).

espionage organs, which endeavour to take advantage of people's weaknesses, their vanity, their slackness of will . . . It is to be explained by an underestimation of the role and significance of the mechanism of our socialist state and of its intelligence service . . . by the twaddle . . . that the Soviet intelligence service and the Soviet state itself will soon have to be relegated to the museum of antiquities.[16]

Stalin clearly recognized that in the matter of peace and war, of the relations between states, the Marxist doctrine of the state was incompletely worked out, and he called it "inadequate." He recalled Lenin's injunction that it is the mission of Russian Marxists "to further develop the Marxist theory." The theory that the state withers away cannot be applied in practice until socialism is victorious in all countries, or at least in the majority, or, as Stalin put it quite dramatically, until "a socialist encirclement exists instead of a capitalist encirclement." If, on the other hand, socialism is victorious in only one country, such a country "must have at its disposal a well-trained army, well-organized punitive organs, and a strong intelligence service—consequently, it must have its own state . . ."[17]

For Stalin, there is no doubt that the "state" will remain in the period of Soviet Communism until the capitalist encirclement is liquidated and the danger of foreign military attack has disappeared. But the state will "atrophy if the capitalist encirclement is liquidated and a socialist encirclement takes its place." Stalin strongly maintains the faith in the inevitability of the victory of the working class, based as it is upon a restatement of dialectical materialism. This faith, he holds, the bourgeoisie in the capitalist countries is trying to undermine and destroy. It has poisoned the minds of some of the working class. But the Soviet Union's foreign policy must be directed toward rousing their faith in the inevitable victory, which is at the same time a faith in the inevitable peace which will follow upon the establishment of the uni-

[16] *Leninism,* pp. 469-70.
[17] *Ibid.,* p. 471.

versal order of world-wide communism. Time and again Stalin and other leaders have made it clear that the inevitability of this event can be demonstrated from dialectical materialism, if rightly reinterpreted by taking into account the unforeseen, and perhaps unforeseeable, role of the Soviet Union, "Its growing economic, political, and cultural might," enjoying as it must "the moral support of the working people of all countries, who are vitally concerned with the preservation of peace . . . and friendship among nations." [18] From these and many similar remarks, it is clear that the linking of the class struggle and of world revolution with the expanding power and might of the Soviet state has converted the Marx-Engels-Lenin doctrines of "inevitable peace through class war" into a very ancient form of political philosophy: inevitable peace through conquest and dominion of the world by one state. This transformation has been the central fact pointed to by those who would convince us of the inevitability of war. It would, as we stated at the outset, be foolish to deny the seriousness of the issue. But it is easy to forget that the United States has its own tradition of the "war to end all wars," and its own manifest destiny by which the future of a united world and a universal order under law is intimately linked to the expanding power and might of the United States. So strikingly similar an outlook on peace and universal order must result from some common core of converging belief.

But before we undertake to develop these concluding ideas of a panhuman outlook, it is important to sketch in broad outline the approach to universal peace of an American thinker whose poignant analysis of the nature of peace has deeply influenced more recent American policy and ideology. In his remarkable book *An Inquiry into the Nature of Peace and the Terms of Its Perpetuation* (1917), Thorstein Veblen frankly acknowledged his kinship to Kant. He paid homage to the inspiration he had received from the Kantian essay *Eternal Peace:*

[18] *Ibid.,* p. 444.

It is now 122 years since Kant wrote the essay, *Zum Ewigen Frieden*. Many things have happened since then, although the Peace to which he looked forward with a doubtful hope has not been among them. . . . To Kant the quest of an enduring peace presented itself as an intrinsic human duty, rather than as a promising enterprise. Yet through all his analysis of its premises and of the terms on which it may be realized there runs the tenacious persuasion that, in the end, the regime of peace at large will be installed. Not as a deliberate achievement of human wisdom, so much as a work of Nature, the designer of things.[19]

It is now thirty years since Veblen wrote, and again many things have happened, although the peace whose necessary conditions Veblen outlined with mocking clairvoyance has not been among them. With retrospective irony, though hardly with surprise, Veblen might point out that he had insisted upon the necessity of eliminating the "Imperial military clique," and the consequent necessity of interfering in the internal affairs of Germany. In other words, he had advocated precisely that "liberation from outside" which Jaurès had rejected as insufferable and unacceptable to a class-conscious proletariat. Veblen anticipated the international class-warfare doctrine of the Soviet Union, and assigned this role paradoxically to the capitalist, albeit peace-loving, states of the West. Hence, Veblen argued that only an outright destruction of the German militarists (and the Japanese militarists in the bargain)—a liquidation of the "gentlemen-adventurers" engaged in the "dynastic enterprise of imperial conquest"—could lay the foundation of a lasting peace. But there is nothing inevitable about this happening. Indeed, one clearly gathers the impression that Veblen did not expect such a policy to be adopted. If it is not adopted, Veblen argued, war will inevitably follow. In other words, war is inevitable, not

[19] Veblen, *Inquiry into the Nature of Peace*, p. 1. Cf. also his *Imperial German and the Industrial Revolution* (new ed., 1942), which is encumbered with a rather questionable element of anthropological racialism which few, if any, anthropologists would today support.

peace. Time and again, Veblen suggests that there is no inherent reason why men should adopt such a policy. They can also assure peace by a policy of surrendering to the conqueror. But a "peace with honor" was not to be had on any other basis than liquidation of the ruling class of the "aggressor nation."

Unlike so many of his contemporaries who became intoxicated with phrases like "Make the world safe for Democracy," Veblen had no illusions about the undemocratic aspect of such international class warfare. Coldly he faced the problem of the victorious ideology imposing its policies. The uprooting of militarism, he wrote,

> means a serious intermeddling in the domestic concerns and arrangements of the fatherland, such as is not admissible under the democratic principle that any people must be left free to follow their own inclination and devices in their own concerns; at the same time that this degree of interference is imperative if the peace is to be kept on any other footing than that of eternal vigilance and superior armed force, with a people whose own inclinations and devices are of the kind now grown familiar in the German case,—all of which applies, with accentuation, in the case of Imperial Japan." [20]

In other words, Veblen was certain that a plan to enforce peace by concerted action of the pacific nations called for a policy of strict control and supervision of those peoples whose "pacific temper is under suspicion." We need not comment at length on the fact that precisely this approach characterizes the policy of the United States today. To quote one of many illustrations, the American Secretary of State, in paraphrasing the Potsdam Declaration, said:

> In agreeing at Potsdam that Germany should be disarmed and demilitarized and in proposing that the four major powers should by treaty

[20] *The Nature of Peace*, p. 240.

jointly undertake to see that Germany is kept disarmed and demilitarized for a generation, the United States was not unmindful of the responsibility resting upon it and its major allies to maintain and enforce peace under law.[21]

It is to be noted that in these and similar official declarations of the United States, even the hint of a class war is scrupulously avoided. A study of the American policy in the field of denazification reveals, however, that the meaning of demilitarization and denazification is in point of fact bound up with the destruction of the German ruling class. More specifically, the long list of major offenders, offenders, profiteers, and activists whose elimination from German public life our policy has persistently sought to bring about, includes the major portion of the "capitalist and militarist" class.[22]

It is important to consider fully the implications of such an approach to the problem of war and peace. Clearly, it transcends the conventional view of modern war as a war between nations. Yet it is a mistake to treat the two kinds of war as rigid alternatives as was done so often during the Second World War. It may have been several kinds of war at once.[23] This sort of confusion of basic motivations and causes has occurred before: both the American Civil War and the Thirty Years' War (1618-1648) furnish illustration for such intermingling of causal motives. Historically speaking, wars which were fought over issues involving the social and class structure of one or more of the combatant powers have been hard to bring to an end; in their

[21] Speech delivered at Stuttgart, Sept. 6, 1946, by James F. Byrnes, as given in *World Report,* Sept. 17, 1946, p. 42.
[22] For this problem, cf. ch. xi, entitled "Denazification," by Harold Zink, in *American Military Government in Germany* (1947).
[23] Cf. Paul M. Sweezey, *The Theory of Capitalist Development* (1942), p. 324, where *three* wars are identified—a war of redivision, a war between capitalism and socialism, and an anti-imperialist war. There are, of course, other ways of differentiating the intertwined skeins of the Second World War; the analysis turns upon one's theory of war and its causation.

aftermath, they have often been followed by a long-drawn-out period of "reconstruction." The Second World War appears to be no exception. Such efforts at reconstruction are in fact a continuation of the revolutionary process which flared forth into the war, but with altered means.

The long-range results of such "total" efforts are hard to gauge. Whether such revolutionary liquidation of a ruling class produces peace or spreads the seeds of further wars may be considered controversial. In the course of the incessant warfare between the cities of ancient Greece, the notion was ever present of insuring the ensuing peace by altering the class structure of the defeated city, more specifically by instituting either an "aristocracy" or a "democracy." These class struggles were, however, unmitigated by any conception of overall progress, or by any solicitude about the defeated "people" as contrasted with the class enemy. This contrast, which characterizes both the American and the Soviet approach, is of crucial significance. Stalin and Roosevelt, Molotov and Byrnes, speaking up for the German people or proletariat, give voice to one of the key conceptions which unite Kant and Marx: the belief in the ultimate universality of an order including the common man everywhere. Thorstein Veblen, too, belongs to this tradition, as contrasted with the jingoist and imperialist school of which Lord Vansittard became perhaps the most vocal exponent in our own time. Veblen's hard-headed analysis rested upon a ready appreciation of the fact that the German masses were the dupes of their imperial masters. He described with sardonic glee the nature of the imperialist class to which the Vansittards belong, and their Prusso-German counterparts—

the great distinguishing mark being that the German usufructuary gentlemen are, in theory at least, gentlemen adventurers of prowess and proud words, whose place in the world's economy it is to glorify God and disturb the peace; whereas their British analogues are gentlemen-investors, of blameless propriety, whose place it is more simply to glorify God and enjoy him forever.[24]

The rapacity and mendacity which Veblen noted as a distinguishing trait of both groups finds its ready counterpart in Soviet writings on the subject of the bourgeoisie and its capitalist exploiters. It is therefore not surprising that in the end Veblen turned away from such temporary expedients as the destruction of a pre-capitalist class of feudal warriors—gentlemen adventurers—by their capitalist enemies. For a lasting peace, he demanded a more radical step: the abolition of the price system. Without going into the details of how this proposal of Veblen is different from the Marxist doctrine of class war and the resulting liquidation of all exploiting classes, one may say that Veblen joined the great socialist strand of thought which subordinated the problem of peace to that of internal revolution and destruction of the capitalist economy.[25] It should be noted, however, that Veblen's peace program is primarily negative. It would seem clear that he thought that the abolition and destruction of two classes—first the militarist class in Germany and Japan, and thereafter the capitalist class in Britain, the United States and elsewhere—and the elimination of the price system would usher in a universal reign of peace. We do not find any explicit recognition of the governmental problems of a world-wide society, nor do we more especially find any insistence upon the need for a world constitution or world law. Veblen makes frequent reference to the concerted action of what he calls the

---

[24] *The Nature of Peace,* p. 250. The corresponding application of this pattern of analysis to Japan was attempted in my essay "International and Imperialist Problems—Democratic and Socialist Issues Involved in the International Settlement of the Japanese Empire," in *Japan's Prospect,* ed. by Douglas Haring (1946). Cf. the literature cited there.

[25] Cf. *The Nature of Peace,* ch. vii, entitled "Peace and the Price System"; its assumptions tend to invalidate the preceding analysis to the extent that German Socialists shared some such view.

pacific nations, but just how this action is to be had, how it should or might be organized, Veblen does not say.[26]

A disinclination to face the problem of government reveals an anarchist strand. Thorstein Veblen, like many other socialist thinkers, retained in substantial measure the nineteenth-century optimism about man. In the Rousseauistic tradition, most socialism assumed that once certain noxious obstructions were removed, the reign of universal peace would automatically come into existence as an "association in which the free development of each is the condition for the free development of all."[27] This is not the place in which to discourse at length upon the very difficult problems to which this notion of the "withering away of the state" and hence of the disappearance of war has given rise. In view of the sharp antagonism which a good many

---

[26] The ready acceptance of Veblen's *Inquiry into the Nature of Peace* by wartime propagandists in the early phase of America's participation, and their complete disregard of the work's ideology after November 1917, is undoubtedly traceable in part to its lack of "constructive" suggestions, but it is likewise related to the antirevolutionary outlook of the Creel organization and more especially its chairman. J. R. Mock and C. Larsen in their *Words that Won the War* (1939) failed to explore the fate of Veblen's book; in fact Veblen is not mentioned in their treatise. Joseph Dorfman, however, calls attention to this aspect in his introduction to the new edition of *Imperial Germany,* cited in footnote 19, although he is basically as uncritical as he had been earlier in his *Thorstein Veblen and His America* (1934), where the two works are treated in chs. xviii and xix. It is a pity that Dorfman's remarkable learning has kept him from achieving a greater perspective on his hero. A really penetrating study of Veblen's political theory remains to be written; Max Lerner's stimulating essay in *Ideas Are Weapons* (1939), pp. 117-144, suggests the need. Lerner rightly observes that Dorfman "gives us at least the resources for taking a new measure of the man." We note, with special reference to the issue we are dealing with, that Dorfman, out of the fullness of his knowledge, observes: "Kant held that critical philosophy has its origin in morality, in responsibility for actions, and this belief is implied in all of Veblen's work" (*Thorstein Veblen and His America,* p. 356).

[27] *Communist Manifesto,* ii, last sentence of section. It is to be hoped that this remark will not be misinterpreted, considering the analysis above in Chapter III. "Rousseauism" is a bird of a different feather from the thought of Rousseau himself. Like that of all seminal and influential thinkers, Rousseau's thought has meant different things to different men.

socialists—but more especially Marxists—have displayed toward anarchism, it is important to bear in mind that an element of anarchism is involved in their own views regarding the future society. Marx's and Engels' contemptuous references to the "utopianism" of their socialist predecessors and contemporaries are, to be sure, grounded in their appreciation of the difficulties and hazards of overthrowing the existing capitalist society and of the vast task confronting those who would have to undertake the direction of the transition from a capitalist to a socialist world. Marx and Engels themselves, however, were not sufficiently aware of the governmental problems of a socialist society, and in this sense were utopian themselves. The political thought developing in the Soviet Union is slowly groping toward a more realistic estimate of the situation. But the statements of Stalinist orthodoxy which we have cited earlier in this chapter[28] show clearly that a good deal of hesitation remains and that Stalin and his collaborators prefer the "conservative" approach of blaming the situation on the capitalist world outside.

In any case, Marxists are not anarchists in the more radical sense. Indeed, the thoroughgoing anarchist whom the nineteenth century produced is an arch individualist. It might even be said that he represents the *reductio ad absurdum* of individualism. The ordinary peaceful bourgeois has always been baffled by these doctrinaires who at one time refuse to bear arms in the defense of their country and at another are quite ready to throw bombs at a bank or an emperor. When Henry David Thoreau chose to go to jail in 1846, he did so because the government of the United States continued to protect slavery. "Under a government which imprisons any unjustly, the true place for a just man is also in prison," he wrote afterwards in "Civil Disobedience." [29]

---

[28] Cf. Chapter I.
[29] Quoted from *Walden and Other Writings of Henry David Thoreau* (Modern Library), p. 646. Consult also Henry Seidel Canby, *Thoreau* (1939), ch. xxiv.

To him, it made good sense to refuse to pay his poll tax, because a prison is "the only house in a slave state in which a free man can abide with honor." His was a case of direct and individual action. It was passive and non-violent action. In that respect it was sharply different from the bombs which European anarchists threw at their crowned heads (the Emperor Alexander II was killed by anarchists in 1881, Emperor William I of Germany was attacked by anarchists in 1878, Emperor Francis Joseph of Austria in 1853, etc.). But at the same time the essential inspiration of all these anarchist acts was an extremist individualism which felt justified in protesting against what it considered morally unjust by specific and individual defiance of the rulers of the state. Thoreau put the case quite well when he wrote that he could not without disgrace be *associated* with his government. "I cannot for an instance recognize that political organization as *my* government which is the *slave's* government also." The key notion here is that of an association of the individual with his government: government is a voluntary association of individuals which each individual assesses according to his own conscience as to its moral value. According to Thoreau men of probity are wanted, of genuine principle. He held that their probity is proven by the fact that they "recognize a higher law than the Constitution," a higher law than "the decision of the majority." [30] And when Thoreau spoke of "recognizing" such a higher moral law, he did not mean it in a purely intellectual sense, but evidently desired men to demonstrate their principle through appropriate action. "The chief want, in every state that I have been into, was a high and earnest purpose in its inhabitants," he wrote in "Life Without Principle." [31]

It can be seen from even these brief quotations that Henry David Thoreau and all like-minded men were radically asserting the binding force of the moral law which Kant had critically

[30] *Walden and Other Writings*, p. 674.
[31] *Walden and Other Writings*, p. 730.

examined and reconstituted in his "categorical imperative." And in so far as Thoreau's action in refusing the payment of the poll tax was explicitly related to the Mexican War (1846) it was part of the rising movement of those who would combat war by passive resistance to its protagonists, the government and the military. However, in Thoreau's own case, the objection for conscience's sake was restricted to an "unjust war." He not only did not object to the war which involved the abolition of slavery, but seems to have supported it. Like Marx and Engels, Thoreau was ready to condone a war of which the purpose was, or at any rate might be, to destroy a noxious social structure and the liquidation of an exploiting class, the slave-holders. The very fact that Thoreau often mentioned the wage slave in the same breath as the bodily slave, indeed at times expressed the view that subtle forms of slavery were even more vicious, reveals the important fact that his anarchist approach was largely the reverse side of the socialist medal. As far as war and peace are concerned, a more radical position would deny the possibility that any war could ever be just.

The view that no war in the contemporary world can ever be just, when coupled with the conviction that it is the individual's moral obligation to refuse to coöperate with any warlike enterprise, is, of course, the creed of the pacifist turned conscientious objector. It is essentially an anarchist position. It derives from the doctrine of the "inner light" which developed as a central tenet of the more radical protestant sects. The Quakers, as a group, have perhaps succeeded best in securing recognition for their belief that no man can or ought to be forced to kill other men against his religious conviction. They are not alone in their espousal of this cause; but it is evident that divergent moral convictions, when associated with the idea that faith is essentially a matter of divine guidance of the individual, of the "Christ within," imply an anarchist refusal to abide by the decisions of the majority. Rufus M. Jones has shown, in his *Mysticism and*

Democracy, how close to the center of democratic convictions this mystical doctrine of the "inner light" actually is. For, in its higher aspiration, democracy is a mystical fellowship of the "good" who share with each other the common ends through which the individual is "overpassed." [32] It is clear then that what appears as individualist anarchism from the standpoint of the state and its authorities is in fact a striving born of the longing for true community and fellowship. When that goal is being realized, the individual finds himself absorbed into a mystical order and through it transformed into a better man.

Such intense and mystical fellowship may, of course, be built around many ends, including even the fighting of wars. But for Quakers and other Christian pacifists the radical message of pacific devotion contained in the Sermon on the Mount is the decisive beacon of light. They may be deeply troubled by the intensity of national and class conflicts; they may feel that "we have grown so vast in these modern times, so complex, so heterogeneous, that it is of all things difficult to preserve the inward sympathy and solidarity of the group life," but they continue their search for the community even as they defy the decisions of the community to which they belong. Like Thoreau, they insist that there is "a higher law than the Constitution," "a higher law than the majority."

Such dogmatic pacifism has been a peculiar feature of Western civilization; in no other culture has it appeared in this sharply defined form. As such, it reveals a peculiar and very sharp conflict within this culture. There exist, of course, many strands of markedly pacific outlook elsewhere. The Chinese tradition, for example, is predominantly pacific in its outlook. Confucian, Taoist and Buddhist teachings resemble each other in this respect. But their anti-war sentiment is balanced by other values. As a recent Chinese writer has put it: "Confucius was not an

---

[32] See Rufus M. Jones, *Mysticism and Democracy in the English Commonwealth* (1932), esp. pp. 25-26 and ch. v.

ultra-pacifist; while he would nod to the Friends with approval, he would probably be the first to rush to enlist after the bugle call of a Lincoln, or a Wilson . . ." The Confucian readily recognizes that there are values worth fighting and dying for.

The moral objections to war should not be confused with general objections to the use of force. Only the particular kind of force which involves the wanton destruction of human life is condemned by the pacifist. What he objects to is "injurious coercion," [33] such coercion being held morally indefensible because it is incompatible with the paramount command of neighborly love. Pacifists have insisted that the law of love is absolute and that its moral command is inviolable. They point to their own sinfulness, and insist that "war never accomplishes anything." War, they insist, arouses such evil passions in the hearts of the men who fight it that both victor and vanquished are henceforth incapacitated for peace. Thus they challenge the very core of such idealistic appeals as "to save Democracy" by denying that violence and force can produce right and justice.

Such assertions turn, in part at least, upon questions of fact. It is no longer a question of right and wrong, but of success and expediency. It is important to face this issue of expediency squarely. Thoughtful pacifists do not deny that we have a moral duty to consider the results of our actions. They do not deny that the possibility exists that a refusal to fight may jeopardize decency and justice. But the radical pacifist concludes that on balance the chances are better if peace is maintained:

[33] Cf. the able defense of this position in Cecil John Cadoux's *Christian Pacifism Re-examined* (1940). This position has been controverted by two former Christian pacifists, Sir Norman Angell and Reinhold Niebuhr. The former set forth his new position in *Let the People Know* (1943), a clear plea for social as contrasted with individual action. Niebuhr developed the reasons why in his opinion the "church is not pacifist" in his *Christianty and Power Politics* (1940), esp. ch. i. A moving and imaginative exploration of the question of "why did I have to die?" is contained in Rex Warner's *Return of the Traveller* (1944).

The test of expediency shows that arguments based upon the positive power of love as a restraint upon wickedness and the chronic non-finality of repeated recourse to war constitute a strong and solid block of evidence. There is nothing palpably inexpedient about pacifism, because so many inexpedient results flow from war.[34]

In short, the doctrinaire pacifist simply refuses to believe that war, even if it is clearly a matter of resistance to aggression and tyranny, will accomplish its purpose. He finds the evidence against war of any kind conclusive.

This is not the place to argue this position. The obvious answer, offered in more orthodox Christian teachings, turns upon a more pessimistic estimate of the chances of accomplishing good. There is much submissiveness in Christian views on government and law, but there is also the corresponding recognition of spiritual value in "fighting for the Lord." Egotism and the pagan lust for power have recurrently been restrained by war. Magna Charta, constitutionalism, civil liberties—these and other relative goods have been secured, so it is said, by injurious coercion, that is to say, violence and force have been successfully opposed to the injurious coercion offered by the enemies of the godly. To speak in terms of the conflicts of our time, aggressive elements such as the Fascists, or the Nazis, have certainly been successfully restrained by war, and successful war may in that sort of situation be said to accomplish what the police accomplish with respect to criminals: this is, of course, the conception underlying the trial of war criminals.[35]

---

[34] Cadoux, p. 123.

[35] The already vast and steadily growing literature on this subject suggests its fundamental importance for our time. Too much of it neglects the point which Niebuhr put so well when he wrote: "Christianity should recognize that all historic struggles are struggles between sinful men and not between the righteous and the sinners; but it is just as important to save what relative decency and justice the Western world still has, against the most demoniac tyranny" (*Christianity and Power Politics*, p. 35).

In approaches such as this, where war is treated as a crime, the idea prevails that war is the result of willful and sinful choice by mortal man. There is nothing inevitable about it. The same idea underlies, of course, a good deal of radical pacifism. Yet this is not intrinsically necessary. Leo Tolstoy was profoundly convinced of the inevitability of history, and hence of war, while at the same time this very conviction of the insignificance of "leaders" made him urge the moral duty of each and every one of us to offer passive resistance. "Thou shalt not kill" is an absolute commandment flowing from the law of love imbedded in Christian teachings.[36] The combining of such a conviction with a belief in a deterministic and hence inevitable course of history brings Tolstoy close to Kant and the tradition from which his view is derived. It may be well, in order fully to grasp the implications, to quote one of the numerous passages in which Tolstoy elaborates this theme in *War and Peace*. "Rulers and generals are history's slaves," he asserts at the commencement of his description of the great war of 1812.

What produced this extraordinary occurrence? What were its causes? The historians tell us with naive assurance that its causes were the wrongs inflicted on the Duke of Oldenburg, the non-observance of the Continental System, the ambition of Napoleon, the firmness of Alexander, the mistakes of the diplomatists, and so forth and so on . . . To us, their descendants who are not historians and who are not carried away by the process of research and can therefore regard the event with unclouded common sense, an incalculable number of causes present themselves. The deeper we delve in search of these causes the more of them we find; and each separate cause or whole series of causes appears to us equally valid in itself and equally false by its insignificance compared to the magnitude of the events, and by its importance to occasion

[36] Tolstoy stated this view in many of his writings; in 1900 he wrote a special article entitled "Thou Shalt Not Kill," and in the next year two more, "A Soldier's Leaflet" and "An Officer's Leaflet," and in 1907 he expanded the first into "Thou Shalt Not Kill Anyone." Cf. for the setting and the relations to Tolstoy's other work the discussion by Ernest J. Simmons in his remarkable *Tolstoy* (1946), pp. 387-88, 491-92, 586-87, 600-601, 647-48, 667-70.

the event. To us, the wish or objection of this or that French corporal to serve a second term appears as much a cause as Napoleon's refusal to withdraw his troops beyond the Vistula and to restore the Duchy of Oldenburg; for had he not wished to serve, and had a second, a third and a thousandth corporal and private also refused, there would have been so many less men in Napoleon's army and the war could not have occurred . . . And so there was no one cause for that occurrence and the war had to occur because it had to. Millions of men, renouncing their human feelings and reason, had to go from West to East to slay their fellows . . . The actions of Napoleon and Alexander were as little voluntary as the action of any soldier who was drawn into the campaign by lot or by inscription . . .[37]

But this insight into the inevitable forward march of history, far from absolving the individual from responsibility, in truth reinforces his obligation to take things into his own hands and refuse to fight. War, thus seen as a natural catastrophe resulting from myriad causes, cannot in this view be brought under control by rational direction or coöperative organization. It is clear at this point how closely allied are anarchist and pacifist views which turn to the individual for combating war. The crucial weakness in Tolstoy's argument, as indeed in all pacifist arguments, is the "if" of the refusal of the corporals to fight. Such conditional refusal clearly contradicts the notion that "the actions of Napoleon and Alexander were as little voluntary as the action of any soldier . . ." For only if we assume that the action of soldiers and Napoleons alike is voluntary can any meaning be attached to the conditional refusal to act.[38] Without such an assumption, the conditional is unthinkable. Once again, we

---

[37] *War and Peace,* tr. by L. and H. Maude (1931), vol. ii, Bk. ix, ch. i. p. 255.
[38] Tolstoy, as far as I can discover, never succeeded in resolving this difficulty, any more than does Jerome Frank, in his *Fate and Freedom* (1946), when he embraces the other horn of the dilemma. Neither ever considered seriously the Kantian resolution of the difficulty. Tolstoy's enthusiasm for Schopenhauer (cf. Simmons, Tolstoy, p. 285) would be as effective a barrier as Marx's attachment to Hegel. In the face of the difficulties of fatalism, Tolstoy retreated into the faith that everything happens according to the will of the Lord.

are face to face with the unresolved difficulties which the critical examination of the limits of our rational faculties undertaken by Kant sought to resolve.

The very same problem is, in fact, presented by the Marxian doctrine of revolution within the context of an inevitable progress of historical evolution. That "freedom flowers in necessity" is an even more perplexing idea to expound on secular grounds than was the doctrine that the believer's freedom consisted in obeying the divine commands—a doctrine which has been offered as an answer to these perplexities from the Stoics down to Tolstoy. There is little doubt that Marx and Engels found little difficulty in thus picturing themselves as the "executioners" of the "dialectics of history." Speaking by analogy, they felt themselves as close to the divine commands of this great force as did Luther or Saint Augustine to the commands of a supernatural and revealed being. But lesser men have ever been troubled by the contradiction involved in acting to promote that which was bound to happen anyhow and at great inconvenience to themselves in the bargain. It was only towards the end of the nineteenth century that certain Marxian writers and thinkers, desirous of providing a more convincing basis for large-scale political action, turned to the critical rationalism of Kant for the purpose of reinforcing the Marxist position.

This is not the place to review the interesting doctrinal controversies which were associated with these efforts.[39] Suffice it here to remark that after a long period of pretty nearly complete

---

[39] The most informative general survey is found in Karl Vorländer, *Kant und Marx* (1911). Probably the most searching of all the efforts to implement Marx's position by the philosophy of Kant, especially in such matters as the concept of *Wissenschaft* and related methodological problems, was made by Max Adler, in "Kausalität und Teleologie im Streite um die Wissenschaft," in *Marx Studien,* vol. I (1904), pp. 193-433. Of general importance also is F. A. Lange's discussion of Kant and Marx in his *Geschichte des Materialismus* (3rd ed. 1876), vol. II. The legal aspects of Marxist materialism were examined in a most fruitful fashion by Rudolf Stammler, *Wirtschaft und Recht nach der Materialistischen Geschichtsauffassung* (1896).

neglect of Kant, a vivid interest in critical rationalism led certain important figures in the Marxist camp to adopt the view that for quite a few of the crucial doctrines of their movement Kant was a more useful philosopher than Hegel. More especially the brilliant Austrian group, led by Otto Bauer, was inclined in this direction. Their work was in part stimulated by the Neo-Kantian revival.[40]

It must be obvious from all that has gone before that reinforcement could be derived in part from Kant's doctrine of the autonomy of the ethical and normative sphere, once the specific content given it by Kant is appropriately modified, and the categorical imperative reinterpreted in socialist terms. Such an effort had once been made by Fichte in his Jacobin period.[41] But more specifically, the moral command "There shall not be war" could be meaningfully combined with the notion that the war of classes was an inevitable concomitant of the progressive development of mankind, and hence part of what Kant had called the "hidden plan of nature."

Such an analysis of the causes of war in terms of classes was only just barely foreshadowed in Kant's idea of republicanism. The quintessence of constitutionalism for Kant lay in the participation of every man in the making of laws, as we have seen, and in the organization of the government so as to make it responsive to the collective categorical imperative. But there is a link which lay dormant in Kant's approach to history and war. His view of history as the resultant of struggles between groups which are successively resolved by the formation of more in-

[40] Both Stammler and Max Adler based their special inquiries upon the Neo-Kantian philosophy as developed by Herrmann Cohen and Paul Natorp, especially the former's restatement of the problem of Kant's ethics, in *Kant's Begründung der Ethik* (1877). Cohen's analysis culminated in the conclusion that Kant's highest good is "political." Unfortunately, both he and Natorp were led to exaggerate the formalistic and cognitional aspects of Kant's philosophy. Natorp finally came to maintain that Kant, when he said that war should not be, did not really mean that—a view which we have rejected above, Chapter I.

[41] See H. C. Engelbrecht, *Johann Gottlieb Fichte* (1933), chs. ii-iii, and Reinhold Aris, *History of Political Thought in Germany, 1789-1815* (1936), ch. iii.

clusive groups (see above, Chapter II) contains the core of Marx's dialectic of history. Indeed it *is* this dialectic, before Hegel turned it upside down, as Marx said. It is therefore not surprising that Marx himself should provide a key to the reinterpretation of Kant, although he certainly did not intend it that way, but meant it as a criticism. In his criticism of the Hegelian philosophy of history, Marx refers to the categorical imperative as incidental to his criticism of all religion. He exclaims that the categorical imperative demands "that all conditions must be revolutionized in which man is debased, an enslaved, an abandoned, a contemptible being." [42] Since any form of slavery is evidently a condition in which man is being used as a means, not as an end, it is clearly incompatible with the categorical imperative (see above, Chapter III), and Marx is stating the Kantian position correctly. The two thinkers are, in a very real sense, complimentary to each other in their thought on peace. Kant, centrally concerned with the moral duty of man to carry out the imperative that "there shall not be war," treats the struggles of history as a "progressive realization" of order under law according to a hidden plan of nature. Marx, on the other hand, completely preoccupied with analyzing precisely this dialectic of the historical process, with its class struggles, refers only incidentally to moral and legal problems. It is part of the non-logical element in human make-up that Marx, the activist revolutionary, should thus have been preoccupied with "observing" and predicting the course of the evolution of human society, while Kant, the contemplative philosopher, stressed the central importance of the normative element in all decisions which determine action. To me, it seems clear that Marx and Engels, in a very real sense, carried out the "idea for a universal history with a cosmopolitan intent"—they undertook precisely what Kant had urged; they

---

[42] This statement is quoted by Otto Rühle, *Karl Marx, His Life and His Work* (tr. E. & C. Paul, 1929), p. 59, from Marx's *Zur Kritik der Hegelschen Rechtsphilosophie* (1843), which appeared in the first section of the *Deutsch-Französische Jahrbücher*.

showed that human activities are "like every other natural event, determined by general natural laws." The concluding proposition of Kant's essay was that a philosophical attempt to work out world history so as to show that it had gone forward according to a general plan of nature, and that it will culminate in a universal political order of mankind, was not only possible but would help to promote this predetermined end. Indeed, it is not too far-fetched perhaps to say that Marx and Engels were the only ones who attempted this task which Kant saw ahead, and of which he admitted that it would call for a man with a very good knowledge of history.[43]

*   *   *   *   *

We have reached the end of our analysis. We have examined one skein of the rich fabric of ideas which have gone into the institutional compromise that calls itself the United Nations. It is a central thread: the idea that mankind's destiny shall culminate in a universal order of peace. We have tried to show how the philosophy of man's history was combined with the idea of freedom and self-realization in a critical rationalism which enables us to resolve some of the most persistent ideological conflicts of our time. We have endeavored to sketch the unfolding and transformation of the concept of a universal right or law, until it could be made to serve as the basis of a universal "general will." The striving for peace, whether motivated by a sense of duty or a will to happiness, has been shown to posit the antagonism of class and cultural conceptions of either. Self-realization, whether looked upon as a duty or the fountain of true happiness, can become the basis of bitter and protracted conflict. On such grounds, war may become sanctified. The bitter doctrine of peace through war reveals the weakness of all notions of

[43] *Werke*, iv, 164-166. Very interesting comment on this is to be found in Karl R. Popper, *The Open Society and Its Enemies* (1945), vol. ii, chs. xv and xxii. For a contrasting view, cf. Vernon Venable, *Human Nature, the Marxian View* (1945), and especially chs. iii and iv.

inevitability which are not mitigated by a recognition of a freedom by which man may master his destiny. Freedom does not mean disobeying the laws of nature, but knowing and using them to avoid the explosions of war and to build the peace.

All this sounds very definitive. But it is not. In the beginning, I stated that I do not consider myself a Kantian. But then why this discourse? Because I believe that the Kantian critical evaluation of the rational capacities of man is an essential condition for escaping the skeptical uncertainty which is the philosophical counterpart of democratic corruption. It is likewise the essential condition for escaping the idealistic dogmatism which is the philosophical counterpart of Fascist violence. But Kant is not enough. There is more to man than his mind. There is, for instance, his economic well-being. I do not consider myself a Marxian. But I believe that without a full grasp of the Marxian understanding of man's material dependency it is likewise possible to escape neither the skepticism of democratic corruption nor the cynicism of Fascist violence. But Marx is not enough, even when reinterpreted by Lenin, Stalin, or their more moderate critics. There is also more to man than his economic well-being.

Peace is not merely the absence of war, whether of classes or nations, or cultures; peace flows from creative living.[44] I believe

[44] Both Kant and Marx excluded the "psychological" as of minor importance. Actually, the central significance which attaches to views of human nature in all speculation on peace makes the psychological aspect most important. Sigmund Freud and his school have taken a very pessimistic view. After quoting the old Latin proverb "Homo homini lupus," Freud in *Civilization and Its Discontents* (1930) states it as his conviction that "a powerful measure of desire for aggression has to be reckoned as part of their [men's] endowment" (p. 85). He had maintained earlier in *Beyond the Pleasure Principle* (1920) that there exists a "death instinct" which Eros is seeking to create. This thesis of the psychoanalytic school has been questioned on experimental grounds; see the symposium edited by Gardner Murphy, *Human Nature and Enduring Peace* (1945), esp. pp. 16ff and 409ff. See also, for a more general survey of contemporary theories concerning the causes of war, chapter v of the study entitled *War—The Causes, Effects, and Control of International Violence* (1943), no. 11 of the series Problems in American Life, published by the National Association of Secondary School Principals and the National Council for the Social Studies, Washington, D. C.

that both Kant and Marx knew it. But they were both enamored of "science." They both were intellectuals of the Western analytical tradition. Kant's famous "confession" of wonder and awe, "Two things fill me with ever renewed wonder: the starred heaven above and the moral law within," had little echo in the heart of Marx and Engels. Their greatest source of wonder was the exploitation of man by man. But these wonders could be what they were only because Kant and Marx and Engels were all shaped in their innermost aspirations by a universal sympathy for man. These three, and the others whom we find in their company in the never-ending quest for peace, loved man. Deep down below the bottom of their restless, energetic minds, there lived a faith which words cannot express. It is a faith which animates all the great world religions. It is a faith which all humanism seeks to salvage when faith declines. This faith provides the only real ground for believing in inevitable peace. It is inevitable only because man cannot escape his own destiny of fulfillment as man.

Immanuel Kant's Essay

ETERNAL PEACE

TRANSLATOR'S PREFACE

A new translation is here offered in spite of a number of existing translations, partly because they are difficult to secure, and partly because they do not satisfy the present writer. Some, while readable, are cast in nineteenth-century language which obscures the meaning; others are awkward and even quite misleading; still others are written in terms of an interpretation of Kant's philosophy which the writer does not share. Since the famous essay of Kant is central to our study of inevitable peace, it has seemed desirable to offer it here in a new garb, as far as the English language is concerned.

There are certain terms which present insuperable difficulties to the conscientious translator at any time. For example, and first of all, the German *Recht*, like the Latin *jus*, the French *droit* and the Italian *diritto*, are without a corresponding equivalent in English. The word, it seems to me, must at times be rendered by *right*, at times by *law*, and at still others by both *right* and *law*. Discarding false consistency, all three alternatives have at times been used. Where it has seemed necessary, the German has been put in parenthesis; this has been especially necessary in such combinations as *Rechtsgesetze* (i.e., statutes which are in keeping with the fundamental principles of right and law).

I have tried to avoid all unnecessary liberties in changing Kant's words. But there are times when some change is unavoidable, in order to have the meaning clear. Where additions are especially glaring, they have been enclosed in square brackets thus [   ]. Kant's habit of underlining certain words for special emphasis has been retained, in spite of its being unusual in English today. Anyone who has ever looked over a page of Kant's manuscripts in which these underlined words and phrases stand out with dramatic force, as if one heard him enunciate these items with special emphasis, will not want to miss them.

A very few footnotes (in square brackets) have been added by me for purposes of clarification; and a few of Kant's have been omitted, because they relate to now forgotten works of contemporaries, without elucidating what is said in the text. Kant's essay is redundant on several points. This redundancy has been interpreted as a sign of old age: maybe it was. But the repeated ideas play a central role in Kant's moral and political philosophy; they are developed and elaborated in other major works, and can truly be said to be quintessential. If it is true that all good propaganda is repetition, then Kant was well justified; for he surely wished to propagate these ideas to the fullest. It is one of the difficulties of the essay that its full meaning can often be assessed only by understanding the basic reasoning which Kant had set forth in his three great Critiques, that of Pure (Theoretic) Reason, that of (Pure) Practical Reason, and that of the Power of Judgment. Likewise, the Introduction to the Metaphysics of Morals and other works are of vital importance. For one thing, "morals" for Kant always embraced not only personal ethics but jurisprudence, that is the theory of law and right, as well. That is why a number of the translations which render "morals" as "morality" are completely confusing. But whatever one does, and however hard one tries, obscurities remain, and the deep disagreements concerning the true interpretation of Kant's philosophy remain likewise. I beg the forgiveness of the critical reader for such "errors" as he detects; I also beg him to remember that "truth" while real can only be realized by finite minds in infinite approximation. On this note the Kantian Essay Concerning Eternal Peace concludes. It is well to conclude this explanatory preface on the same note of diffidence. *Dum desint vires, tamen est laudanda voluntas*—I hope.

C. J. FRIEDRICH

ETERNAL PEACE

"To Eternal Peace."

Whether the above satirical inscription, once put by a certain Dutch innkeeper on his signboard on which a graveyard was painted, holds of men in general, or particularly of the heads of states who are never sated with war, or perhaps only of those philosophers who are dreaming that sweet dream of peace, may remain undecided. However, in presenting his ideas, the author of the present essay makes one condition. The practical statesman should not, in case of a controversy with the political theorist, suspect that any danger to the state lurks behind the opinions which such a theorist ventures honestly and openly to express. Consistency demands this of the practical statesman, for he assumes a haughty air and looks down upon the theorist with great self-satisfaction as a mere theorizer whose impractical ideas can bring no danger to the state, since the state must be founded on principles derived from experience. The worldly-wise statesman may therefore, without giving himself great concern, allow the theorizer to throw his eleven bowling balls all at once. By this "saving clause" the author of this essay knows himself protected in the best manner possible against all malicious interpretation.

FIRST SECTION

which contains the preliminary articles of an eternal peace between states

1. "No treaty of peace shall be held to be such, which is made with the secret reservation of the material for a future war."

For, in that event, it would be a mere truce, a postponement of hostilities, not *peace*. Peace means the end of all hostilities, and to attach to it the adjective "eternal" is a pleonasm which at once arouses suspicion. The preëxisting reasons for a future war, including those not at the time known even to the contracting parties, are all of them obliterated by a genuine treaty of peace; no search of documents, no matter how acute, shall resurrect them from the archives. It is Jesuitical casuistry to make a mental reservation that there might be old claims to be brought forward in the future, of which neither party at the time cares to make mention, because both are too much exhausted to continue the war, but which they intend to assert at the first favorable opportunity. Such a procedure, when looked at in its true character, must be considered beneath the dignity of rulers; and so must the willingness to attempt such legal claims be held unworthy of a minister of state.

But, if enlightened notions of political wisdom assume the true honor of the state to consist in the continual increase of power by any and every means, such a judgment will, of course, evidently seem academic and pedantic.

2. "No state having an independent existence, whether it be small or great, may be acquired by another state, through inheritance, exchange, purchase, or gift."

A state is not a possession (*patrimonium*) like the soil on which it has a seat. It is a society of men, which no one but they themselves is called upon to command or to dispose of. Since, like a tree, such a state has its own roots, to incorporate it as a graft into another state is to take away its existence as a moral person and to make of it a thing. This contradicts the idea of the original contract, without which no right over a people can even be conceived.[1] Everybody knows into what danger, even in the most recent times, the supposed right of thus acquiring states has brought Europe. Other parts of the world have never known such a practice. But in Europe states can even marry each other. On the one hand, this is a new kind of industry, a way of making oneself predominant through family connections without any special effort; on the other, it is a way of extending territorial possessions. The letting out of troops of one state to another against an enemy not common to the two is in the same class. The subjects are thus used and consumed like things to be handled at will.

3. "Standing armies shall gradually disappear."

Standing armies incessantly threaten other states with war by their readiness to be prepared for war. States are thus stimulated to outdo

---

[1] An hereditary monarchy is not a state which can be inherited by another state. Only the right to govern it may be transferred by heredity to another person. Thus the state acquired a ruler, not the ruler a state.

one another in number of armed men without limit. Through the expense thus occasioned peace finally becomes more burdensome than a brief war. These armies are thus the cause of wars of aggression, undertaken in order that this burden may be thrown off. In addition to this, the hiring of men to kill and be killed, an employment of them as mere machines and tools in the hands of another (the state), cannot be reconciled with the rights of humanity as represented in our own person. The case is entirely different where the citizens of a state voluntarily[2] drill themselves and their fatherland against attacks from without. It would be exactly the same with the accumulation of a war fund if the difficulty of ascertaining the amount of the fund accumulated did not work a counter effect. Looked upon by other states as a threat of war, a big fund would lead to their anticipating such a war by making an attack themselves, because of the three powers—the power of the army, the power of alliance, and the power of money—the last might well be considered the most reliable instrument of war.

4. "No debts shall be contracted in connection with the foreign affairs of the state."

The obtaining of money, either from without or from within the state, for purposes of internal development—the improvement of highways, the establishment of new settlements, the storing of surplus for years of crop failure, etc.—need create no suspicion. Foreign debts may be contracted for this purpose. But, as an instrument of the struggle between the powers, a credit system of debts endlessly growing though always safe against immediate demand (the demand for payment not being made by all the creditors at the same time)—such a system, the ingenious invention of a trading people in this century, constitutes a dangerous money power. It is a resource for carrying on war which surpasses the resources of all other states taken together. It can only be exhausted through a possible deficit of the taxes, which may be long kept off through the increase in commerce brought about by the stimulating influence of the loans on industry and trade. The facility thus afforded of making war, coupled with the apparently innate inclination thereto of those possessing power, is a great obstacle in the way of eternal peace. Such loans, therefore, must be forbidden by a preliminary article—all the more because the finally unavoidable bankruptcy of such a state must involve many other states without their

---

[2] [Presumably, the word "freiwillig" here refers to the citizens acting as a whole, and through a majority, not the individuals separately.—C.J.F.]

responsibility in the disaster, thus inflicting upon them a public injury. Consequently, other states are at least justified in entering into an alliance against such a state and its pretensions.

5. "No state shall interfere by force in the constitution and government of another state."

For what could justify it in taking such action? Could perhaps some offense do it which that state gives to the subjects of another? Such a state ought rather to serve as a warning, because of the example of the evils which a people brings upon itself by its lawlessness. In general, the bad example given by one free person to another (as a *scandalum acceptum*) is no violation of the latter's rights. The case would be different if a state because of internal dissension should be split into two parts, each of which, while constituting a separate state, should lay claim to the whole. An outside state, if it should render assistance to one of these, could not be charged with interfering in the constitution of another state, as that state would then be in a condition of anarchy. But as long as this inner strife was not decided, the interference of outside powers would be a trespass on the rights of an independent people struggling only with its own inner weakness. This interference would be an actual offense which would so far tend to render the autonomy of all states insecure.

6. "No state at war with another shall permit such acts of warfare as must make mutual confidence impossible in time of future peace: such as the employment of assassins, of poisoners, the violation of articles of surrender, the instigation of treason in the state against which it is making war, etc."

These are dishonorable stratagems. Some sort of confidence in an enemy's frame of mind must remain even in time of war, for otherwise no peace could be concluded, and the conflict would become a war of extermination. For after all, war is only the regrettable instrument of asserting one's right by force in the primitive state of nature where there exists no court to decide in accordance with law. In this state neither party can be declared an unjust enemy, for this presupposes a court decision. The outcome of the fight, as in the case of a so-called "judgment of God," decides on whose side the right is. Between states no war of punishment can be conceived, because between them there is no relation of superior and subordinate.

From this it follows that a war of extermination, in which destruction may come to both parties at the same time, and thus to all rights too, would allow eternal peace only upon the graveyard of the whole human race. Such a war, therefore, as well as the use of the means which might be employed in it, is wholly forbidden.

But that the methods of war mentioned above inevitably lead to such a result is clear from the fact that such hellish arts, which are in themselves degrading, when once brought into use do not continue long within the limits of war but are continued in time of peace, and thus the purpose of the peace is completely frustrated. A good example is furnished by the employment of spies, in which only the dishonorableness of others (which unfortunately cannot be exterminated) is taken advantage of.

Although all the laws above laid down would objectively—that is, in the intention of the powers, be negative laws (*leges prohibitirae*), yet some of them are strict laws, which are valid without consideration of the circumstances. They insist that the abuse complained of be abolished at once. Such are our rules number 1, 5, and 6. The others, namely rules number 2, 3, and 4, though not meant to be permitting exception from the "rule of law," yet allow for a good deal of subjective discretion in respect to the application of the rules. They permit delay in execution without their purpose being lost sight of. The purpose, however, does not admit of delay till doomsday—"to the Greek Calends," as Augustus was wont to say. The restitution, for example, to certain states of the freedom of which they have been deprived, contrary to our second article, must not be indefinitely put off. The delay is not meant to prevent restitution, but to avoid undue haste which might be contrary to the intrinsic purpose. For the prohibition laid down by the article relates only to the mode of acquisition, which is not to be allowed to continue, but it does not relate to the present state of possessions. This present state, though not providing the needed just title, yet was held to be legitimate at the time of the supposed acquisition, according to the then current public opinion.

SECOND SECTION

which contains the definitive articles for eternal peace among states

The state of peace among men who live alongside each other is no state of nature (*status naturalis*). Rather it is a state of war which constantly threatens even if it is not actually in progress. Therefore the state of peace must be *founded*; for the mere omission of the threat of war is no security of peace, and consequently a neighbor may treat his neighbor as an enemy unless he has guaranteed such security to him, which can only happen within a state of law.[1]

FIRST DEFINITIVE ARTICLE OF THE ETERNAL PEACE

The civil constitution in each state should be republican.

A republican constitution is a constitution which is founded upon three principles. First, the principle of the *freedom* of all members of a society as men. Second, the principle of the *dependence* of all upon a single common legislation as subjects, and third, the principle of the *equality* of all as *citizens*. This is the only constitution which is derived from the idea of an original contract upon which all rightful legislation of a nation must be based.[2]

[1] It is often assumed that one is not permitted to proceed with hostility against anyone unless he has already actively hurt him, and this is indeed very true if both live in a civic state under law, for by entering into this state one man proffers the necessary security to another through the superior authority which has power over both.—But man (or the nation) in a mere state of nature deprives me of this security and hurts me by this very state, simply by being near me, even though not actively (*facto*). He hurts me by the lawlessness of his state (*statu iniusto*) by which I am constantly threatened, and therefore I can compel him either to enter into a communal state under law with me or to leave my vicinity.—Hence the postulate which underlies all the following articles is this: all men who can mutually affect each other should belong under a joint civic constitution.

There are three kinds of constitution under law as far as concerns the persons who belong under it: (1) the constitution according to the law of national citizenship of all men belonging to a nation (*ius civitatis*); (2) the constitution according to international law regulating the relation of states with each other (*ius gentium*); (3) the constitution according to the law of world citizenship which prevails insofar as men and states standing in a relationship of mutual influence may be viewed as citizens of a universal state of all mankind (*ius cosmopoliticum*).

This classification is not arbitrary but necessary in relation to the idea of eternal peace. For if even one of these were in a relation of physical influence upon the other and yet in a state of nature, the state of war would be connected with it, and to be relieved of this state is our very purpose.

[2] [After explaining the customary definition of freedom as the right to do what does not deprive another of his right, Kant proceeds as follows:] External lawful *freedom* may be defined as follows: it is the authority [*Befugnis*] not to obey any external laws except those which I have consented to.—Likewise, external (lawful) *equality* in a state is the relationship of the citizens according to which no one can obligate another legally without at the same time subjecting himself to the law of being obligated by the other in the same manner.

This republican constitution is therefore, as far as law is concerned, the one which underlies every kind of civil constitution, and the question which we are now facing is, whether this is also the only one which can lead to eternal peace.

The answer is that the republican constitution does offer the prospect of the desired purpose, that is to say, eternal peace, and the reason is as follows: If, as is necessarily the case under the constitution, the consent of the citizens is required in order to decide whether there should be war or not, nothing is more natural than that those who would have to decide to undergo all the deprivations of war will very much hesitate to start such an evil game. For the deprivations are many, such as fighting oneself, paying for the cost of the war out of one's own possessions, and repairing the devastation which it costs, and to top all the evils there remains a burden of debts which embitters the peace and can never be paid off on account of approaching new wars. By contrast, under a constitution where the subject is not a citizen and which is therefore not republican, it is the easiest thing in the world to start a war. The head of the state is not a fellow citizen but owner of the state, who loses none of his banquets, hunting parties, pleasure castles, festivities,

---

(We need not explain the principle of lawful dependence since this principle is implied in the conception of any kind of constitution.)—The validity of these innate and inalienable rights which are implied in his very humanity is confirmed by the principle of the lawful relations of man to higher beings (in case he believes in them). For he imagines himself, according to these very same principles, as the citizen of a natural world.—For so far as my freedom is concerned, I have no obligation even with regard to the divine laws which I recognize by pure reason except insofar as I have given my own consent (for only in terms of the law of freedom of my own reason can I form a conception of the divine will). [Kant then argues that the principle of equality cannot be similarly confirmed because God has no equals.] Concerning the right of all citizens to be equal in their subjection to the law, the only thing which matters in regard to the question of the admissibility of a hereditary nobility is the following: whether the superior rank of one subject to another precedes merit or the latter the former, it seems obvious that it is most uncertain whether merit (ability and loyalty in one's office) will follow. Hence it is as if rank were attributed without merit to the most favored (to be commander). Clearly the general will of the people would never adopt such a provision in its original contract, which is the basis of all right, and in short a nobleman [Edelmann] is not necessarily a noble man [edler Mann]. As far as nobility derived from office [Amtsadel] is concerned, rank in that case does not attach as a position to the person but is connected with the post, and therefore the principle of equality is not violated, for when a man quits his office, he resigns his rank and returns to the people.

etc. Hence he will resolve upon war as a kind of amusement on very insignificant grounds and will leave the justification to his diplomats, who are always ready to lend it an air of propriety.

It is important not to confuse the republican constitution with the democratic one as is commonly done. The following may be noted. The forms of a state (*civitas*) may be classified according to the difference of the persons who possess the highest authority, or they may be classified according to the method by which the people are governed by their rulers, who ever they may be. The first method is properly called the form of rulership (*forma imperii*)[3] Only three such forms are conceivable; for either *one,* or a *few* associated with each other, or all who together constitute civil society possess the power to rule (*autocracy, aristocracy,* and *democracy*—the power of princes, of the nobility, and of the people).

The second method is the form of government (*forma regiminis*) and relates to the way in which the state employs its sovereign power— the constitution, which is an act of the general will by which a mass becomes a nation. The form of government in this case is either *republican* or *despotic.* Republicanism means the constitutional principle according to which the executive power (the government [*Regierung*]) is separated from the legislative power. *Despotism* exists when the state arbitrarily executes the laws which it has itself made; in other words, where the public will is treated by the prince as if it were his private will.

Among the three forms of state (or rulership), that of *democracy* is necessarily a *despotism* in the specific meaning of the word, because it establishes an executive power where all may decide regarding one and hence against one who does not agree, so that all are nevertheless not all—a situation which implies a contradiction of the general will with itself and with freedom. For all forms of government which are not *representative* are essentially *without form,* because the legislative cannot at the same time and in the same person be the executor of the legislative will; just as the general proposition in logical reasoning cannot at the same time be the specific judgment which falls under the

---

[3] [Kant here uses the term *Form der Beherrschung,* which is rulership—but further on down he shifts to *Staatsform* and *Staatsverfassung;* the essential point, however, is the distinction between form of rulership and form of government.—C.J.F.]

general rule.[4] The other two forms of rulership [*Staatsverfassung*] are defective also insofar as they give a chance to this (despotic) form of government. But it is at least possible that they provide a method of governing which is in accord with the *spirit* of representative system. Frederick II *said* at least that he was merely the highest servant of the state—while the democratic system makes this impossible, because all want to be ruler.[5]

It is therefore possible to say that the smallest number of truly representative rulers approximates most closely to the possibility of a republicanism and may be expected to reach it eventually by gradual reforms. Such an evolution is harder in an aristocracy than in a monarchy, while in a democracy it is impossible to achieve this kind of constitution— which is the only constitution perfectly in accord with law and right [*Recht*]—except through a revolution.[6]

The people are very much more concerned with the form of government in this sense than with the form of rulership [*Staatsform*], although a good deal depends upon the latter's adequacy to realize the former's end. But if the form of government is to be appropriate to the idea of law and right, it requires the representative system. For only in this system is a republican form of government possible. Without it the

[4] [It seems to be clear from Kant's analogy that the "cannot" of this sentence has a strictly logical connotation—i.e., All men have two legs; A is a man; therefore A has two legs.—C.J.F.]

[5] Many have criticized the high-sounding titles which are often given a ruler, such as "divinely anointed," "executor of God's will on earth," "God's representative," calling them coarse and flattering, but it seems to me without reason. Far from making the prince conceited, they should make him humble, if he has brains (which surely one must assume) and therefore is conscious that he has assumed an office which is too big for a man: to administer man's law, the most sacred thing that God has on earth, to hurt this prized possession of God in any way must surely worry any man.

[6] Mallet du Pan claims in his profound-sounding, yet hollow and empty language that after many years' experience he had come to accept the truth of Pope's well-known saying: "O'er forms of government let fools contest; that which is best administered is best." If that is to mean that the best-led government is the best led, then, to use a phrase of Swift, he has cracked a nut which rewarded him with a worm. If it is to mean that the best-led government is the best form of government, i.e. constitution, then it is very false; examples of good governing do not prove anything about the form of government. Who has governed better than a *Titus* or a *Marcus Aurelius?* Yet the one was succeeded by a *Domitian,* the other by a *Commodus.* This would have been impossible under a good constitution, since their incapacity to govern was known soon enough.

form of government is despotic and violent, whatever the constitution may be.

None of the ancient, so-called republics knew this representative system, and hence they were bound to dissolve into despotism, which is the more bearable under the rule of a single man.[7]

Second Definitive Article of the Eternal Peace

The law of nations (Völkerrecht) should be based upon a *federalism of free states*.

Nations may be considered like individual men which hurt each other in the state of nature, when they are not subject to laws, by their very propinquity. Therefore each, for the sake of security, may demand and should demand of the other to enter with him into a constitution similar to the civil one where the right of each may be secured. This would be a *union of nations* [*Völkerbund*] which would not necessarily have to be a *state of nations* [*Völkerstaat*]. A state of nations contains a contradiction, for every state involves the relation of a superior (legislature) to a subordinate (the subject people), and many nations would, in a single state, constitute only one nation, which is contradictory since we are here considering the right of nations toward each other as long as they constitute different states and are not joined together into one.

We look with deep aversion upon the way primitive peoples are attached to their lawless liberty—a liberty which enables them to fight incessantly rather than subject themselves to the restraint of the law to be established by themselves; in short, to prefer wild freedom to a reasonable one. We look upon such an attitude as raw, uncivilized, and an animalic degradation of humanity. Therefore, one should think, civilized peoples (each united in a state) would hasten to get away from such a depraved state as soon as possible. Instead, each *state* insists upon seeing the essence of its majesty (for popular majesty[8] is a paradox) in

[7] [It is readily seen that these rather involved thoughts are a restatement of the Aristotelian doctrine that all "good" forms of government are governments according to law and right—the quintessence of constitutional theory. But the ancients did not develop any "constitutional safeguards" for this "rule of law."—C.J.F.]

[8] [The German word *Majestät*, like the Latin *majestas*, was a term roughly equivalent to sovereignty; it was becoming obsolete in Kant's time—and yet, one ought not to translate it with *sovereignty* here, because the parenthesis becomes dubious then. It is worth notice, however, that Kant leans toward the idea of *state sovereignty*.—C.J.F.]

this, that it is not subject to any external coercion. The luster of its ruler consists in this, that many thousands are at his disposal to be sacrificed for a cause which is of no concern to them, while he himself is not exposed to any danger. Thus a Bulgarian Prince answered the Emperor who good naturedly wanted to settle their quarrel by a duel: "A smith who has prongs won't get the hot iron out of the fire with his bare hands." The difference between the European savages and those in America is primarily this, that while some of the latter eat their enemies, the former know how better to employ their defeated foe than to feast on them—the Europeans rather increase the number of subjects, that is the number of tools for more extended wars.

In view of the evil nature of man, which can be observed clearly in the free relation between nations (while in a civil and legal state it is covered by governmental coercion), it is surprising that the word *law* [*Recht*] has not been entirely banned from the politics of war as pedantic, and that no state has been bold enough to declare itself publicly as of this opinion. For people in *justifying* an aggressive war still cite HUGO GROTIUS, PUFENDORF, VATTEL and others (all of them miserable consolers). This is done, although their code of norms, whether stated philosophically or juristically, does not have the least *legal* force; nor can it have such force, since states as such are not subject to a common external coercion. There is not a single case known in which a state has been persuaded by arguments reinforced by the testimony of such weighty men to desist from its aggressive design.

This homage which every state renders the concept of law (at least in words) seems to prove that there exists in man a greater moral quality (although at present a dormant one), to try and master the evil element in him (which he cannot deny), and to hope for this in others. Otherwise the words *law* and *right* would never occur to states which intend to fight with each other, unless it were for the purpose of mocking them, like the Gallic prince who declared: "It is the advantage which nature has given the stronger over the weaker that the latter ought to obey the former."

In short, the manner in which states seek their rights can never be a suit before a court, but only war. However, war and its successful conclusion, *victory,* does not decide what is law and what right. A *peace treaty* puts an end to a particular war, but not to the state of war which consists in finding ever new pretexts for starting a new one. Nor can this be declared strictly unjust because in this condition each is the judge in his own cause. Yet it cannot be maintained that states under the law of nations are subject to the same rule that is valid for individual men in the lawless state of nature: "that they ought to leave this state." For states have internally a legal constitution and hence [their citizens] have outgrown the coercion of others who might desire to put them under a broadened legal constitution conceived in terms of their own legal norms. Nevertheless, reason speaking from the throne of the highest legislative power condemns war as a method of finding what is right. Reason makes [the achievement of] the state of peace a direct duty, and such a state of peace cannot be established or maintained without a treaty of the nations among themselves. Therefore there must exist a union of a particular kind which we may call the *pacific union* (*foedus pacificum*) which would be distinguished from a *peace treaty* (*pactum pacis*) by the fact that the latter tries to end merely *one* war, while the former tries to end *all* wars forever. This union is not directed toward the securing of some additional power of the state, but merely toward maintaining and making secure the *freedom* of each state by and for itself and at the same time of the other states thus allied with each other. And yet, these states will not subject themselves (as do men in the state of nature) to laws and to the enforcement of such laws.

It can be demonstrated that this idea of *federalization* possesses objective reality, that it can be realized by a gradual extension to all states, leading to eternal peace. For if good fortune brings it to pass that a powerful and enlightened people develops a republican form of government which by nature is inclined toward peace, then such a republic will provide the central core for the federal union of other states. For they can join this republic and can thus make secure among themselves the state of peace according to the idea of a law of nations, and can gradually extend themselves by additional connections of this sort.

It is possible to imagine that a people says: "There shall be no war amongst us; for we want to form a state, i.e., to establish for ourselves a highest legislative, executive, and juridical power which peacefully settles our conflicts." But if this state says: "There shall be no war between myself and other states, although I do not recognize a highest legislative authority which secures my right for me and for which I secure its right," it is not easy to comprehend upon what ground I should place my confidence in my right, unless it be a substitute [*Surrogat*] for the civil social contracts, namely, a free federation. Reason must necessarily connect such a federation with the concept of a law of nations, if authority is to be conceived in such terms.

On the other hand, a concept of the law of nations as a right *to make* war is meaningless; for it is supposed to be a right to determine what is right not according to external laws limiting the freedom of each individual, but by force and according to one-sided maxims. Unless we are ready to accept this meaning: that it serves people who have such views quite right if they exhaust each other and thus find eternal peace in the wide grave which covers all the atrocities of violence together with its perpetrators. For states in their relation to each other there cannot, according to reason, be any other way to get away from the lawless state which contains nothing but war than to give up (just like individual men) their wild and lawless freedom, to accept public and enforceable laws, and thus to form a constantly growing world *state of all nations* (*civitas centium*) which finally would comprise all nations. But states do not want this, as not in keeping with their idea of a law of nations, and thus they reject in fact what is true in theory.[9] Therefore, unless all is to be lost, the positive idea of a *world republic* must be replaced by the negative substitute of a *union* of nations which maintains itself, prevents wars, and steadily expands. Only such a union may under existing conditions stem the tide of the law-evading, bellicose propensities in man, but unfortunately subject to the constant danger of their eruption (*furor impius intus—fremit horridus ore cruento.* VIRGIL).

THIRD DEFINITIVE ARTICLE OF THE ETERNAL PEACE

"The Cosmopolitan or World Law shall be limited to conditions of a universal hospitality."

We are speaking in this as well as in the other articles not of philanthropy, but of *law.* Therefore *hospitality* (good neighborliness)

[9] After the end of a war, at the conclusion of a peace, it would not be improper for a people to set a day of atonement after the day of thanks so as to pray to heaven asking forgiveness for the heavy guilt which mankind is under, because it will not adapt itself to a legal constitution in its relation to other nations. Proud of its independence, each nation will rather employ the barbaric means of war by which that which is being sought, namely the right of each state, cannot be discovered. The celebrations of victory, the hymns which in good Old Testament style are sung to the Lord of Hosts, contrast equally sharply with the moral idea of the father of mankind; because besides the indifference concerning the manner in which people seek their mutual right, which is lamentable enough, they rejoice over having destroyed many people and their happiness.

means the right of a foreigner not to be treated with hostility when he arrives upon the soil of another. The native may reject the foreigner if it can be done without his perishing, but as long as he stays peaceful, he must not treat him hostilely. It is not the right of becoming a permanent guest [*Gastrecht*] which the foreigner may request, for a special beneficial treaty would be required to make him a fellow inhabitant [*Hausgendsse*] for a certain period. But it is the right to visit [*Besuchsrecht*] which belongs to all men—the right belonging to all men to offer their society on account of the common possession of the surface of the earth. Since it is a globe, they cannot disperse infinitely, but must tolerate each other. No man has a greater fundamental right to occupy a particular spot than any other.

Uninhabitable parts of the earth's surface, the oceans and deserts, divide this community. But *ship* or *camel* (the ship of the desert) enable men to approach each other across these no-man's regions, and thus to use the right of the common *surface* which belongs to all men together, as a basis of possible intercourse. The inhospitable ways of coastal regions, such as the Barbary Coast, where they rob ships in adjoining seas or make stranded seamen into slaves, is contrary to natural law, as are the similarly inhospitable ways of the deserts and their Bedouins who look upon the approach (of a foreigner) as giving them a right to plunder him. But the right of hospitality, the right, that is, of foreign guests, does not extend further than to the conditions which enable them to attempt the developing of intercourse with the old inhabitants.

In this way, remote parts of the world can enter into relationships which eventually become public and legal and thereby may bring mankind ever nearer to an eventual world constitution.

If one compares with this requirement the *inhospitable* conduct of the civilized, especially of the trading, nations of our continent, the injustice which they display in their *visits* to foreign countries and peoples goes terribly far. They simply identify visiting with *conquest*. America, the lands of the Negroes, the Spice Islands, the Cape of South Africa, etc., were countries that belonged to nobody, for the inhabitants counted for nothing. In East India (Hindustan) they brought in foreign mercenaries, under the pretense of merely establishing trading ports. These mercenary troops brought suppression of the natives, inciting the several states of India to extended wars against each other. They brought famine, sedition, treason and the rest of the evils which weigh down mankind.

China[10] and Japan, who had made an attempt to get along with such guests, have wisely allowed only contact, but not settlement—and Japan has further wisely restricted this privilege to the Dutch only, whom they exclude, like prisoners, from community with the natives. The worst (or viewed from the standpoint of a moral judge the best) is that the European nations are not even able to enjoy this violence. All these trading companies are on the point of an approaching collapse; the sugar islands, which are the seat of the most cruel and systematic slavery, do not produce a yield—except in the form of raising recruits for navies; thus they in turn serve the conduct of war—wars of powers which make much ado about their piety and who want themselves to be considered among the morally elect, while in fact they consume [the fruits of] injustice like water.

The narrower or wider community of all nations on earth has in fact progressed so far that a violation of law and right in one place is felt in all others. Hence the idea of a cosmopolitan or world law is not a fantastic and utopian way of looking at law, but a necessary completion of the unwritten code of constitutional and international law to make it a public law of mankind. Only under this condition can we flatter ourselves that we are continually approaching eternal peace.

FIRST ADDITION

On the guarantee of eternal peace

No one less than the great artist nature (*natura daedala rerum*) offers such a *guarantee*. Nature's mechanical course evidently reveals a teleology: to produce harmony from the very disharmony of men even against their will. If this teleology and the laws that effect it is believed to be like an unknown cause compelling us, it is called *fate*. But if it is considered in the light of its usefulness for the evolution of the world, it will be called *providence*—a cause which, responding to a deep wisdom, is directed toward a higher goal, the objective final end [*Endzweck*] of mankind which predetermines this evolution.[1] We do not

[10] [I am omitting a lengthy and obsolete footnote on the origin of the word *China,* in spite of its interest in showing Kant's keen personal delight in concrete historical detail.—C.J.F.]

[1] [In a lengthy footnote at this point, Kant discusses the concept of *providence* as something necessary to explain the basic "form" of events in their totality. He rejects the idea as illogical, when applied to specific events, but allows it as a general founding, governing, and directing providence. The discussion follows the treatment in the *Critique of Practical Reason.*—C.J.F.]

really *observe* this providence in the artifices of nature, nor can we *deduce* it from them. But we can and must *add this thought* (as in all relations of the form of things to ends in general), in order to form any kind of conception of its possibility. We do this in analogy to human artifices.[2] The relation and integration of these factors into the end (the moral one) which reason directly prescribes is very sublime in *theory*, but is axiomatic and well-founded in practice, e.g., in regard to the concept of a duty toward eternal peace which that mechanism promotes.

When one is dealing as at present with theory (and not with religion), the use of the word *nature* is more appropriate in view of the limits of human reason which must stay within the limits of possible experience as far as the relation of effects to their causes is concerned. It is also *more modest* than the expression *providence*, especially a providence understandable to us; for by talking of providence we are arrogantly putting the wings of Icarus on our shoulders as if to get closer to the secret of its unfathomable purpose.

But before we ascertain more specifically how the guarantee is worked out, it is necessary to explore the situation which nature has created for those who are actors upon its great stage, and which in the last analysis necessitates its guarantee of peace. Only after that can we see how nature provides this guarantee.

Nature's provisional arrangement consists in the following: (1) she has seen to it that human beings can live in all the regions where they are settled; (2) she has by war driven them everywhere, even into the most inhospitable regions, in order to populate them; (3) she has forced them by war to enter into more or less legal relationships. It is marvelous to notice that in the cold wastes of the Arctic Sea some mosses grow which the *Reindeer* scratches out of the snow thus being enabled to serve as food or as a draft animal for the Samoyeds. Such ends become even more apparent when one discovers that furred animals on the shores of the Arctic Sea, walruses and whales provide food through their meat and heat through their fat for the inhabitants. But nature's care causes the greatest admiration when we find that drift wood, the origin of which is not well known, is carried to these regions, since without this material the inhabitants could neither build boats and weapons, nor huts in which to dwell. In that situation they seem to be sufficiently occupied with war against the animals to live peacefully with each other.

[2] [Where the end shapes the means and tools.—C.J.F.]

But it was probably war which *drove* the inhabitants to these places. The first *instrument of warfare* among all the animals which man during the time of populating the earth learned to tame and to domesticate was the *horse;* for the elephant belongs to a later time, when established states made greater luxury possible. The same is true of the culture of certain kinds of grasses, now called *grain,* the original form of which we no longer know, as well as of multiplying and refining of fruit trees by transplanting and grafting—in Europe perhaps only two species, the wild apples and wild pears. Such achievements could take place only in established states with fixed property in real estate. Before this men had progressed from the lawless freedom of *hunting,*³ fishing and sheepherding to cultivating the land. After that *salt* and *iron* were discovered, perhaps the first articles of trade between nations which were in demand everywhere, through which they were first brought into a *peaceful relationship* with each other. This in turn brought them into understanding, community, and peaceful relations with the more remote nations.

Nature, by providing that men *can* live everywhere on earth, has at the same time despotically wanted that they *should* live everywhere, even against their inclination. This "should" does not presuppose a duty which obliged them to do it by a moral law. Instead, nature chose war to bring this about.

We observe peoples which by their common language reveal their common ancestry, such as the *Samoyeds* on the Arctic Sea and a people of similar language, about two hundred miles away, in the Altaic Mountains. Between those two a Mongolian, horse-riding and hence belligerent, tribe have wedged themselves in, driving one part of these people far away, and the rest into the most inhospitable regions of ice and snow, where they surely would not have gone by choice.⁴

³ Among all the ways of living the hunting life is unquestionably most at variance with a civilized constitution: because the families which are separated from each other soon become alien, and soon thereafter, dispersed in extended forests, hostile to each other, since each requires much room for its feeding and clothing. The Mosaic law forbids the eating of blood, Genesis 9:4-6, appears to have been originally nothing else but an attempt to forbid people to live as hunters; because in this life there often occur situations where meat must be eaten raw, and hence to forbid the eating of blood means forbidding a hunting life. This law, several times reenacted, was later, with a quite different purpose, imposed by the Jewish Christians as a condition upon the newly accepted heathen Christians.

⁴ Someone might ask: if nature did not intend these icy shores to remain uninhabited, what will happen to their inhabitants when no more drift wood

In the same manner the Finns in the northernmost part of Europe, called the Lapps, were separated from the Hungarians to whom they are related in their language by intruding Gothic and Sarmatian tribes. And what could have driven the Eskimos in the North, and the Pescheras in the South of America as far as it did, except war which nature uses everywhere as a means for populating the earth? War itself does not require a special motivation, since it appears to be grafted upon human nature. It is even considered something noble for which man is inspired by the love of honor, without selfish motives. This martial courage is judged by American savages, and European ones in feudal times, to be of great intrinsic value not only *when* there is a *war* (which is equitable), but also so *that* there may be war. Consequently war is started merely to show martial courage, and war itself invested with an inner *dignity*. Even philosophers will praise war as ennobling mankind, forgetting the Greek who said: "War is bad in that it begets more evil people than it kills." This much about what nature does in pursuit of its own purpose in regard to mankind as a species of animal.

Now we face the question which concerns the essential point in accomplishing eternal peace: what does nature do in relation to the end which man's reason imposes as a duty, in order to favor thus his *moral intent?* In other words: how does nature guarantee that what man ought to do according to the laws of freedom, but does not do, will be made secure regardless of this freedom by a compulsion of nature which forces him to do it? The question presents itself in all three relations: *constitutional* law, *international* law, and cosmopolitan or world law.—And if I say of nature: she wants this or that to take place, it does not mean that she imposes a *duty* to do it—for that only the non-compulsory practical reason can do—but it means that nature itself does it, whether we want it or not (*fata volentem ducunt, nolentem trahunt*).

1. If internal conflicts did not compel a people to submit itself to the compulsion of public laws, external wars would do it. According to the previously mentioned arrangement of nature, a people discovers a

---

comes to them (as may be expected). For it may be assumed that the inhabitants of the more temperate regions will, as culture progresses, utilize their wood better, and will not allow it to drop into the river and drift into the sea. I answer: the inhabitants of those regions, of the Ob, the Yenisei, the Lena, etc., will barter for it the products of animal life which the sea provides so plentifully in the Arctic—when nature has forced the establishment of peace among them.

neighboring people who are pushing it, against which it must form itself into a *state* in order to be prepared as a *power* against its enemy. Now the *republican* constitution is the only one which is fully adequate to the right of man, but it is also the hardest to establish, and even harder to maintain. Therefore many insist that it would have to be a state of angels, because men with their selfish propensities are incapable of so sublime a constitution. But now nature comes to the aid of this revered, but practically ineffectual general will which is founded in reason. It does this by the selfish propensities themselves, so that it is only necessary to organize the state well (which is indeed within the ability of man), and to direct these forces against each other in such wise that one balances the other in its devastating effect, or even suspends it. Consequently the result for reason is as if both selfish forces were nonexistent. Thus man, although not a morally good man, is compelled to be a good citizen. The problem of establishing a state is solvable even for a people of devils, if only they have intelligence, though this may sound harsh. The problem may be stated thus: "To organize a group of rational beings who demand general laws for their survival, but of whom each inclines toward exempting himself, and to establish their constitution in such a way that, in spite of the fact that their private attitudes are opposed, these private attitudes mutually impede each other in such a manner that the public behavior [of the rational beings] is the same as if they did not have such evil attitudes." Such a problem *must* be solvable. For it is not the moral perfection of mankind, but merely the mechanism of nature, which this task seeks to know how to use in order to arrange the conflict of unpacific attitudes in a given people in such a way that they impel each other to submit themselves to compulsory laws and thus bring about the state of peace in which such laws are enforced. It is possible to observe this in the actually existing, although imperfectly organized states. They approach in external conduct closely to what the idea of law prescribes, although an inner morality is certainly not the cause of it (just as we should not expect a good constitution from such morality, but rather from such a constitution the good moral development of a people). These existing states show that the mechanism of [human] nature, with its selfish propensities which naturally counteract each other, can be employed by reason as a means. Thus reason's real purpose may be realized, namely, to provide a field for the operation of legal rules whereby to make secure internal and external peace, as far as the state is concerned.—In short, we can say that nature *wants* irresistibly that law achieve superior force. If one neglects to do this, it will be accomplished anyhow, albeit with much inconvenience. "If you bend the stick too much, it breaks; and he who wants too much, wants nothing" (Bouterwek).

2. The idea of a law of nations presupposes the separate existence of many states which are independent of each other. Such a situation constitutes in and by itself a state of war, unless a federative union of these states prevents the outbreak of hostilities. Yet such a situation is from the standpoint of reason better than the complete merging of all these states in one of them which overpowers them and is thereby in turn transformed into a universal monarchy. This is so, because the laws lose more and more of their effectiveness as the government increases in size, and the resulting soulless despotism is plunged into anarchy after having exterminated all the germs of good [in man]. Still, it is the desire of every state (or of its ruler) to enter into a permanent state of peace by ruling if possible the entire world. But *nature* has decreed differently.—Nature employs two means to keep peoples from being mixed and to differentiate them, the difference of *language* and of *religion*.[5] These differences occasion the inclination toward mutual hatred and the excuse for war; yet at the same time they lead, as culture increases and men gradually come closer together, toward a greater agreement on principles for peace and understanding. Such peace and understanding is not brought about and made secure by the weakening of all other forces (as it would be under the aforementioned despotism and its graveyard of freedom), but by balancing these forces in a lively competition.

3. Just as nature wisely separates the nations which the will of each state would like to unite under its sway either by cunning or by force, and even in keeping with the reasoning of the law of nations, so also nature unites nations which the concept of a cosmopolitan or world law would not have protected from violence and war, and it does this by mutual self-interest. It is the *spirit of commerce* which cannot coexist with war, and which sooner or later takes hold of every nation. For, since the money power is perhaps the most reliable among all the powers subordinate to the state's power, states find themselves impelled

[5] *Difference of religion:* a strange expression! as if one were to speak of different *morals.* There may be different *kinds of faith* which are historical and which hence belong to history and not to religion and are part of the means in the field of learning. Likewise there may be different *religious books* (Zendavesta, Vedam, Koran, etc.). But there can only be one *religion* valid for all men and for all times. Those other matters are nothing but a vehicle of religion, accidental and different according to the difference of time and place.

(though hardly by moral compulsion) to promote the noble peace and to try to avert war by mediation whenever it threatens to break out anywhere in the world. It is as if states were constantly leagued for this purpose; for great leagues *for* the purpose of making war can only come about very rarely and can succeed even more rarely.—In this way nature guarantees lasting peace by the mechanism of human inclinations; however the certainty [that this will come to pass] is not sufficient to *predict* such a future (theoretically). But for practical purposes the certainty suffices and makes it one's duty to work toward this (not simply chimerical) state.

SECOND ADDITION

A secret article concerning Eternal Peace

A secret article in negotiations pertaining to *public* law is a contradiction objectively, i.e., as regards its substance or content; subjectively, however, i.e., as regards the quality of the person which formulates the article, secrecy may occur when such a person hesitates to declare himself publicly as the author thereof.

The sole article of this kind [in the treaty on eternal peace] is contained in the following sentence: *The maxims of the philosophers concerning the conditions of the possibility of public peace shall be consulted by the states which are ready to go to war.* Perhaps it would seem like belittling the legislative authority of a state to which one should attribute the greatest wisdom to suggest that it should seek instruction regarding the principles of its conduct from its *subjects* (the philosophers); nevertheless this is highly advisable. Hence the state will *solicit* the latter *silently* (by making it a secret) which means that it will *let them talk* freely and publicly about the general maxims of the conduct of war and the establishment of peace (for they will do it of their own accord, if only they are not forbidden to do so). The agreement of the states among themselves regarding this point does not require any special stipulation but is founded upon an obligation posited by general morality legislating for human reason. This does not mean that the state must concede that the principles of the philosopher have priority over the rulings of the jurist (the representative of governmental power); it only means that the philosopher be *given a hearing.* The jurist who has made the *scales* of law and right his symbol, as well as the *sword* of justice, commonly employs the sword not only to ward off all outside influence from the scales, but also to put it into one of the scales if it will not go down (*vae victis*). A jurist who is not at the same time a philosopher (morally speaking) has the greatest temptation to do this, because it is only his job to apply existing laws, and not to inquire whether these laws need improvement. In fact he counts this lower order of his faculty to be the higher, simply because it is the concomitant of power (as is also the case of the other two faculties).— The philosophical faculty occupies a low place when confronted by all this power. Thus, for example, it is said of philosophy that she is the *handmaiden* of theology (and something like that is said regarding the other two). It is not very clear however "whether she carries the torch in front of her gracious lady or the train of her dress behind."

It is not to be expected that kings philosophize or that philosophers become kings, nor is it to be desired, because the possession of power corrupts the free judgment of reason inevitably. But kings or self-governing nations will not allow the class of philosophers to disappear or to become silent, but will let them speak publicly, because this is indispensable for both in order to clarify their business. And since this class of people are by their very nature incapable of forming gangs or clubs they need not be suspected of carrying on *propaganda*.

APPENDIX

I

On the Disagreement between Morals and Politics in Relation to Eternal Peace

Morals when conceived as the totality of absolutely binding laws according to which we *ought* to act is in itself practice in an objective sense. It is therefore an apparent paradox to say that one *cannot* do [what one ought to do] once the authoritativeness of this concept of duty is acknowledged. For in that case this concept [of duty] would be eliminated from morals since *ultra posse nemo obligatur*. Hence there cannot occur any conflict between politics as an applied doctrine of right [*Rechtslehre*] and law [doctrine of right and law]. Hence there can be no conflict between theory and practice, unless theory were taken to mean a general *doctrine of expediency* [*Klugheitslehre*], that is to say a theory of the maxims as to how to choose the most appropriate means for the realization of self-interested purposes; in other words, altogether, to deny that morals exist.

Politics says: "Be ye therefore wise as serpents"; but morals adds as a limiting condition: "and innocent as doves." If the two cannot coexist in one commandment, there would be a conflict of politics with morals. But if the two are to be combined, the idea of a contrast is absurd, and it is not even possible to present as a task the problem as to how to resolve the conflict. Although the sentence *Honesty is the best policy* contains a theory which practice unfortunately (!) often contradicts, yet the equally theoretical sentence *Honesty is better than all politics* is completely above all objections; indeed, it is the inescapable condition of all politics. The god who guards the boundaries of morals does not yield to Jove who guards the boundaries of force; for the latter is yet subject to destiny. That is to say, reason is not sufficiently inspired to comprehend the range of predetermining causes which would permit it to predict with certainty and in accordance with the mechanism of nature the happy or bad result of the doings or omissions of men (although it may well hope for a result according with what is intended). But what needs to be done in order to remain within the groove of duty according to the rules of wisdom, and thus what is our final end, reason shows us quite clearly enough.

The practical man to whom morals is mere theory bases his cheerless rejection of our kind-hearted hope upon the notion that we never *want* to do what is necessary in order to realize the end leading to eternal peace, even when he concedes both that we *ought* and that we *can* do [what we should]. Of course the will of *all individual* men to live under a lawful constitution in accordance with the principles of liberty (which constitutes the *distributive* unity of the will of *all*) is not sufficient for this end. In addition it is necessary that all *jointly* will this state (which constitutes the *collective* unity of the united [general] will) which is the solution of a difficult problem. Only thus can the totality of a civil society be created. Since therefore there must come into existence, over and above the variety of the particular will of all, such a uniting cause of a civil society in order to bring forth a common will—something which no one or all of them can do—the *execution* of the idea [of an eternal peace] in practice and the beginning of a lawful state cannot be counted upon except by *force* upon the compulsion of which the public law is afterwards based. This fact would lead one to expect beforehand in practical experience great deviations from the original idea of the theory, since one can count little anyway upon the moral conviction of the legislator so that he would after he has united a wild multitude into a people leave it to them to establish a lawful constitution by their common will.

Therefore it is said: "He who has the power in his hands, will not let the people prescribe laws for himself. A state which is in possession of [the power of] not being subject to any external laws will not make itself dependent upon their judgments as far as concerns the manner of its seeking its right against such other states. Even a continent if it feels itself superior to another one, which may not actually be in its way, will not leave unutilized the opportunity of increasing its power by plundering or even dominating the other. Thus all theoretical plans for constitutional, international, and world-wide law dissolve into empty, unworkable ideals, whereas a practice which is based upon the empirical principles of human nature may hope to find a secure foundation for its structure of political prudence, inasmuch as such a practice does not consider it too mean to derive instruction for its maxims from the way in which the world is actually run."

Admittedly, if there exists no freedom and hence no moral law based upon it, and if everything which happens or may happen is simply part of the mechanism of nature, then politics as the art to use [the mechanism of nature] for the governing of men is the complete content of practical prudence, and the concept of right and law is an empty phrase. But should one find it absolutely necessary to combine the concept of law and right with politics, indeed to make it a limiting condition of politics, then the compatibility of the two must be conceded. I can imagine a *moral politician*—that is, a man who employs the principles of political prudence in such a way that they can coexist with morals—but I cannot imagine a *political moralist*, who would concoct a morals such as the advantage of the statesman may find convenient.

The moral politician will adopt the principle that if defects appear in the constitution or in the relations with other states which could not be prevented then it is one's duty, especially for the heads of states, to seek to remedy them as soon as possible; that is to say, to make such constitution once again commensurate with the law of nature as it is presented to us as a model in the idea of reason. He will do this even though it cost him sacrifices of selfish interests. It would be unreasonable to demand that such a defect be eliminated immediately and with impetuosity, since the tearing apart of a [constitutional] bond of national or world-wide community, before a better constitution is available to take its place, is contrary to all morals, which in this respect agrees with political prudence. But we may properly demand that the necessity of such a change be intimately appreciated by those in power so that they may continue to approach the final end of a constitution which is best in accordance with right and law. A state may be *governed* as a republic even while it possesses despotic *power to rule* [*Herrschermacht*] according to the existing constitution, until gradually the people become capable of realizing the influence of the mere idea of the authority of law (as if it possessed physical force) and thus are found able to legislate for themselves.[1] But should the violence of a *revolution* which was caused by a bad constitution have achieved illegitimately a more lawful one, then it should not be held permissible to bring the people back to the old one, even though during such a revolution everyone who got himself involved by acts of violence or intrigue would rightfully be subject to the penalties of a seditionist. As far as the external relation between states is concerned, it cannot be demanded of a state that it divest itself of its despotic constitution (which is after all the stronger in dealing with external enemies) as long as it runs the risk of being devoured by other states; thus even in this respect the delaying of the execution must be permitted until a better opportunity presents itself.[2]

It may well be true that despotic moralists who make mistakes in executing their ideas violate political prudence in many ways by prematurely adopting or advocating various measures, yet experience will necessarily, in case of such offenses against nature, by and by get them into a better track. On the other hand, moralizing politicians *make* progress *impossible* and perpetuate the violation of right by glossing over political principles which are contrary to right by pretending that human nature is not *capable* of the Good according to the idea which reason prescribes.

Instead of the practice on which these clever politicos pride them-

---

[1] [The last phrase is qualified by a parenthesis which reads "(welche ursprünglich of Recht gegründet ist)." This phrase is somewhat obscure, but probably means to suggest once more that legislation in the sense of true law is founded upon (natural) law and right in any system—an ancient doctrine of all natural-law thought.—C.J.F.]

[2] These are permissive laws of reason which allow a state of public law which is affected by injustice to continue until everything is ready for a complete revolution or has been made ripe for it by peaceful means: since a *legal*, even though only to a small degree lawful, constitution is better than none, and a premature change would lead to anarchy. Political prudence will therefore, in the state in which things are at the present time, make it its duty to effect reforms which are in keeping with the ideals of public law and right. At the same time it will utilize revolutions where nature produces them of itself, not for the purpose of camouflaging an even greater suppression, but rather consider it a call of nature to bring about by thorough reforms a legal constitution which is based upon the principles of freedom and therefore the only lasting one.

selves they employ *tricks* in that they are only intent upon sacrificing the people and even the whole world by flattering the established powers in order not to miss their private profit. In this they follow the manner of true lawyers—of the trade, not legislators—when they get into politics. For since it is not their business to argue, themselves, concerning legislation, but rather to carry out the present commands of the law of the land [*Landrecht*], therefore any presently existing legal constitution must seem the best to them; or should this one be changed by the "higher authorities," then the one following will seem the best. Thus all is right and proper in a formal order. But if this skill of being fit for any task gives such lawyers the illusion of being able to judge the principles of a basic constitution in accordance with concepts of law and right—that is, a priori and not empirically—they cannot make this transition except in a spirit of trickery. Likewise, if they boast of their knowledge of *men* (which may be expected, since they have plenty of dealings with them) without knowing *man* and what may be made of him (for which a higher standpoint of anthropological observation is required), and if they then, equipped with such principles, approach constitutional and international law as prescribed by reason, they cannot make that transition either, except in a spirit of trickery. For they follow their usual method [of reasoning according to] despotically adopted compulsory laws even where the concepts of reason will permit only a compulsion which is lawful within the principles of freedom, since only such compulsion will make possible a constitution according to right and law. The pretended practitioner believes he can solve this problem empirically—from experience, that is—with hitherto existing, largely unlawful constitutions which have worked best, while by-passing the basic idea [of basic principles of freedom]. The maxims which he employs for this purpose (though he does not pronounce them) are roughly the following sophistical ones:

1. *Fac et excusa.* Seize every favorable opportunity for arbitrary appropriation of a right of the government [state] over its people, or over a neighboring nation. The justification will be formulated and the use of violence glossed over much more easily and more decoratively *after the accomplished deed* than if one tried first to think up convincing reasons and await the counter reasons. This is especially true in the first of these cases where the higher authority becomes at once the legislative authority which must be obeyed without arguing. Such boldness itself produces a certain appearance of inner conviction of the

righteousness of the deed, and the God *bonus eventus* is afterwards the best legal representative.

2. *Si fecisti, nega.* Whatever [evil] you have committed—for example driving your own people to despair and into sedition—that you must deny and declare not to be your guilt. Instead you insist that what is to blame is the unruliness of the subjects. Or if it is a case of seizing a neighboring people, then blame it on human nature, since one can count with certainty upon being seized [by one's neighbor] if one does not forestall him in the use of force.

3. *Divide et impera.* This means: if there are certain privileged persons among your people who have merely elected you as their head as *primus inter pares,* then disunite them among themselves and set them at variance with the people; if then you will support the latter by pretending to favor greater liberties for them, all will depend upon your absolute will. Or, if it is a situation involving foreign countries, the creation of dissension among them is a relatively certain means to subject one after the other on the pretense of protecting the weaker.

No one is deceived by these political maxims, for they all are generally known. Nor is it a case of being too embarrassed, as if the injustice were too apparent. Great powers never worry about the judgment of the common crowd, but only about each other, and hence what embarrasses them is not that these principles become public, but merely that they *failed to work,* since they are all agreed among themselves on the morality of the maxims. What remains is the *political honor* which they can count upon, namely the *enlarging of their power* by whatever means are available.[3]

---

[3] If there may still be some doubt concerning the wickedness of *men* who live together in a state as rooted in human nature, and if instead the shortcomings of an as yet not sufficiently advanced culture may be cited as the cause of the lawless aspects of their frame of mind, this wickedness becomes quite obviously and unmistakably apparent in the external relation of *states* with each other. At home in each state it is veiled by the compulsion of the civil laws, because a greater power, namely that of the government, strongly counteracts the inclination of the citizens to employ force against each other. This not only gives to the whole a moral lacquer (*causae non causae*), but by putting a stop to the outbreak of lawless proclivities provides a real alleviation for the development of the moral predisposition for directly respecting right and law.—For everyone now believes of himself that he would honor and obey the concept of right and law if only he could expect the same from everyone else, and this latter the government secures for him to some extent; thus a great step (though not a moral step yet) is taken toward a morality when this

From all these serpentine turnings of an amoral prudential doctrine which seeks to derive the condition of peace among men from the warlike state of nature, one thing at least becomes clear: human beings cannot escape from the concept of right and law either in their private or in their public affairs, and they do not dare to base politics merely upon the manipulations of prudence and thus reject all obedience to a concept of public law—something which is particularly surprising in regard to the concept of a law of nations. Instead they show it all the honor that is due it, even if they think up a hundred excuses and camouflages in order to evade this concept in practice and to impute to a crafty force the genuine authority of being the origin and bond of all right and law.

In order to end this sophistry (although by no means the injustice which this sophistry glosses over) and to bring the deceitful *representatives* of the mighty of this world to confess that it is not right and law but force which they defend (and the tone of which they adopt as if they themselves had something to command in this connection), it will be well to uncover the fraud with which such persons deceive themselves and others, to discover the highest principle from which the purpose of eternal peace is derived and to show that all the evil which stands in the way of eternal peace results from the fact that the political moralist starts where the moral politician equitably ends. In short, the political moralist subordinates his principles to the end, i.e., puts the wagon before the horse, and thereby thwarts his own purpose of bringing politics into agreement with morals.

In order to harmonize practical philosophy within itself, it is necessary first to decide the question whether in tasks of practical reason we should start from its *material* [i.e., substantive] principle, from its end (as object of the will), or from its *formal* one, i.e., from the principle which relates to freedom in one's relation to the outside world which states: act in such a way that you could want your maxim to become a general law (whatever its purpose may be). Without a doubt, the latter principle must take precedence; for as a principle of right it possesses

---

concept of duty is accepted for its own sake and without regard to reciprocity. —Since everyone in spite of his good opinion of himself presupposes a bad character in all others, men mutually pronounce judgment upon themselves to the effect that they all as a matter of *fact* are not worth much (why this is so, considering that the *nature* of man, as a free being, cannot be blamed for it, we will leave undiscussed). But since the respect for the concept of right and law which man cannot abandon most solemnly sanctions the theory of an ability to measure to such a concept, everyone can see for himself that he must act in accordance with right and law, whatever others may do.

absolute necessity, whereas the material principle is compelling only on condition that the empirical conditions for its realization exist. Thus even if this purpose (e.g., eternal peace) were a duty, this latter would have had to be deduced from the formal principle of the maxims of external action.

The first principle, that of the *political moralist* (the problem of constitutional, international, and world law), is a mere *technical task* (*problema technicum*); the second, which is the principle of the *moral politician*, as an *ethical task* (*problema morale*) is therefore vastly different in its procedure for bringing about the eternal peace which is now desired not only as a mere physical good, but also as a condition resulting from the recognition of duty.

Much knowledge of nature is required for the solution of the first problem of political prudence, in order to utilize its mechanism for this purpose, and yet it is all rather uncertain as far as the result, eternal peace, is concerned, whichever of the sections of public one considers. It is quite uncertain whether the people can better be kept in obedience and at the same time in prosperity for any length of time by severity or by flattery, whether by a single ruler or by several, or by an aristocracy which devotes itself to the public service, or by popular government. History offers examples of the opposite happening under all forms of government, excepting the one truly republican form which, however, can only occur to a moral politician. Even more uncertain is an *international law* based upon a statute drafted by several ministries which is merely a word without a reality corresponding to it [*ein Wort ohne Sache*], since it would rest upon treaties which contain in the very act of their conclusion the secret reservation of being violated.

By contrast, the solution of the second *problem of political wisdom* readily presents itself, is evident to everyone, confounds all artifices, and leads directly to its end; yet with the reminder of prudence not to force it precipitately, but to approach it steadily as favorable opportunities offer.

Therefore it is said: "Seek ye first the kingdom of pure practical reason and of its *righteousness*, and your end (the well-being of eternal peace) will be added unto you." [4] For that is the peculiar feature of

---

[4] [This obvious paraphrase of a famous sentence of Jesus has a somewhat different flavor in German, because Luther speaks of *Gerechtigkeit* or justice, which is indeed nearer to the Greek original *dikaiosyne*. Those who are learned in the precise wording of Biblical texts will also note that Kant speaks of "its," that is the kingdom's righteousness, whereas the King James version

morals concerning its principles of public law and hence concerning a politics which is a priori knowable, that it harmonizes the more with an intended objective, a physical or moral advantage sought, the less it allows its behavior to depend upon it. The reason for this is that the a priori given general will (within a nation or in the relation between nations) alone determines what is right amongst men. At the same time this union of the will of all, if only the execution of it is carried out consistently, can be the cause within the mechanism of nature which produces the intended effect and thus effectuates the idea of law.

Thus it is a principle of moral politics that a people should unite into a state solely according to the natural-law concepts of freedom and equality. This principle is based upon duty, and not upon prudence. Political moralists may argue ever so much concerning the natural mechanism of a mass of people entering into society which (according to them) invalidates those principles and prevents their purpose from being realized. They may likewise try to prove their contention against those principles by giving examples of badly organized constitutions of old and new times (e.g., of democracies with a system of representation). They do not deserve to be listened to—the less so, since such a pernicious doctrine may even cause the evil which it predicts. For man is thereby put into the same class with the other living machines, and man then needs only to possess the conscious knowledge that he is not a free being to make him in his own judgment the most miserable of all creatures.

Fiat justitia, pereat mundus is a proverbial saying which sounds a bit pompous, yet it is true, and it means in simple language: "Justice shall prevail, even though all the rascals in the world should perish as a result." This is a sound principle of right and law which cuts off all the crooked paths of cunning and violence. However, care must be taken not to misunderstand this sentence as a permission to claim one's own right with the greatest severity, for that would conflict with one's ethical duty. Rather should it be understood to mean an obligation of those who have the power not to refuse or to infringe someone's right out of ill will or sympathy for others. [In order to achieve this result] there is required first of all an internal constitution of the state which is organized according to the pure principles of right and law, but then

---

has "his." In this case, the English translation is closer to the Greek *autou;* however, Luther no doubt intended the same with *seiner,* but unfortunately this may also be related to the kingdom and it is thus that Kant interprets the passage.—C.J.F.]

also the union of such a state with other states, either neighboring or more remote, for the purpose of settling their controversies legally (in analogy to what a universal state might do).

This sentence really does not intend to say anything more than that political maxims must not proceed from considering the welfare and happiness to be expected from their being followed, that is to say they must not proceed from the end which each of these maxims makes its object, nor from the will as the highest (but empirical) principle of political prudence. Rather such maxims must be derived from the pure principle of duty under natural law (from the Ought the principle of which is given a priori by pure reason) regardless of what might be the physical consequences thereof. The world will not perish because there are fewer bad men. The morally bad has a quality which is inseparable from its nature: it is self-contradictory and self-destructive in its purposes, especially in its relation to others who are like-minded. Therefore it yields to the moral principle of the good, though in a slow progression.

No conflict exists *objectively* (in theory) between morals and politics. Only *subjectively*, in the selfish disposition of men—which need not be called practice, however, since it is not based upon maxims of reason—such a conflict may remain [which is all right] since it serves as a whetstone for virtue. Virtue's true courage as expressed in the maxim *tu ne cede malis, sed contra audentior ito* consists in the present case not so much in standing up firmly against the evils and sacrifices which must be borne, but in facing the evil principle in ourselves and defeating its cunning. This principle is much more dangerous because it is deceitful and treacherous in arguing the weakness of human nature as a justification for all transgressions.

Indeed, the political moralist may say: ruler and people, or people and people are not doing *each other* an injustice when they fight each other with violence or cunning, even though they are committing an injustice by denying all respect to right and law. For while one violates his duty toward the other, who is just as lawless in his view toward him, it serves them both right if they exhaust themselves, as long as there remains enough of this species to continue this game till very distant times, so that a later generation may take them as a warning example. Providence [so they say] is justified in thus arranging the course of events; for the moral principle in man never is extinguished, and reason, which is capable pragmatically of executing the ideas of natural law according to this principle, is steadily on the increase because of the progress in culture; but so also is the guilt of such transgressions. It seems impossible to justify by any kind of theodicy the creation of such a species of corrupted beings upon this earth, if we are to assume that mankind never will be in a better state. But this standpoint of judging things is much too lofty for us—as if we could theoretically impute our notions (of wisdom) to the most supreme, inscrutable power.

We are inevitably pushed to such desperate consequences if we do not assume that the pure principles of right and law have objective reality in the sense that they can be realized, and hence that the people within the state and the states toward each other must act accordingly, whatever may be the objections of an empirical politics. True politics cannot take a single step without first paying homage to morals, and while politics by itself is a difficult art, its combination with morals is no art at all; for morals cuts the Gordian knot which politics cannot solve as soon as the two are in conflict.

The (natural) right of men must be held sacred, regardless of how much sacrifice is required of the powers that be. It is impossible to figure out a middle road, such as a pragmatically conditional right, between right and utility. All politics must bend its knee before the (natural) rights of men, but may hope in return to arrive, though slowly, on the level where it may continually shine.

II

On the Agreement between Politics and Morals According to the Transcendental Idea of Public Right and Law

If I abstract right and law from all the *substance* [*Materie*] of public law (as it exists in keeping with the various empirically given relations of men within the state or the relations between states, and as it is customarily considered by jurists) there remains the *formal quality of publicity*. For each law and rightful claim [*Rechtsanspruch*] carries with it the possibility of such publicity, since without publicity there cannot be justice (which can only be thought of as capable of being *made public*) and hence also no right, since that is only attributed by justice.

This capacity of publicity every law and rightful claim [*Rechtsanspruch*] must have. Therefore this quality provides a criterion which is easily applied and *a priori* discoverable through reason, because it is quite easy to determine whether it is present in a given case, i.e., whether it can be combined with the principles of him who is acting or not. If not, we can recognize the falsity (unlawfulness) [*Rechtswidrigkeit*] of the pretended claim (*praetensio juris*) quite readily and as by an experiment of pure reason.

After thus abstracting from all the empirical [substance] which the idea of constitutional and international law includes (of this order is the evil in human nature which necessitates coercion), it is possible to call the following statement the *transcendental formula* of public law: "All actions which relate to the right of other men are contrary to right and law, the maxim of which does not permit publicity." This principle should not only be considered as *ethically* relevant (belonging to the theory of virtue or ethics), but also as *juridically* relevant (concerning the right of men). For a maxim which I can not permit to become *known* without at the same time defeating my own purpose, which must be *kept secret* in order to succeed, and which I cannot *profess publicly* without inevitably arousing the resistance of all against my purpose, such a maxim cannot have acquired this necessary and universal, and hence *a priori* recognizable, opposition of all from any other quality than its injustice, with which it threatens everyone.

Furthermore, this [standard] is merely *negative*, that is, it only serves to recognize what is *not right* toward others. Like any axiom it is unprovably certain and easy to apply, as may be seen from the following examples of public law.

1. A question occurs in *constitutional law* (*jus civitatis*) which many believe to be difficult to answer, but which the transcendental principle of publicity easily resolves: "Is rebellion a right and lawful means for a people to overthrow the oppressive power of a so-called tyrant (*non titulo, sed exercitio talis*)?" The rights of the people are violated, and no injustice (*Unrecht*) is done to the tyrant by the deposition; there can be no doubt of that. In spite of that, it is nevertheless in the highest degree contrary to right and law (*unrecht*) to seek their right in this manner, and they cannot complain of injustice if after being defeated in such a conflict they have to submit to the most severe punishment.

Much can be argued both pro and contra in this matter, if one tries to settle the matter by a dogmatic deduction of the reasons in right and law [*Rechtsgründe*]; only the transcendental principle of the publicity of all public right and law can save itself this prolixity. According to this principle, the people ask themselves before the establishment of the civic contract whether they dare make public the maxim of allowing an occasional rebellion. It is easy to see that if one were to make it a condition of the establishment of a constitution to use force against the head of the government [*Oberhaupt*] in certain cases, the people would have to claim a right and lawful power over the head of the government. In that case the head would not be the head, or, if both [his being a head and the exercise of force against him] were to be made conditions of the establishment of the state, such establishment would not be possible, which was after all the objective of the people. The unrightfulness [*Unrecht*] of rebellion becomes evident by the fact that its maxim would vitiate its own purpose, if one *professed it publicly*. One would have to keep it secret.

Such secrecy would not be necessary for the head of the government. He could openly declare that he would punish every rebellion with the death of its ringleaders, even though these believe that he had violated the fundamental law first. For if the head of the government is convinced that he possesses the *irresistible* superior force (which must be assumed to be the case even under every civic constitution, because he who does not have enough power to protect each one among the people against the others, does not have the right to command him either), then he does not need to worry about vitiating his own purpose by letting his maxim become public. This conclusion is connected with another, namely, that in case of a successful rebellion such a head of government would return to the status of a subject, and hence he must not begin a rebellion to get himself restored, nor would he have to fear that he would be brought to account for his previous conduct of government.

2. *Concerning international law.* Only if we assume some kind of lawful state (i.e., the kind of external condition under which a man can secure his right), can there be talk of international law, because as a public law it contains in its very concept the publication of a general will which determines for each man what is his own. Such a *status juridicus* must result from some kind of treaty which can not (like the one establishing a state) be based upon compulsory laws, but at most can be a state of *continuous free* association, like the above-mentioned one of a federalism of different states. For without some kind of *lawful state* which actively links the various physical and moral persons (i.e., in the state of nature) there can only be a private law [and rights of individual persons]. In these cases [of international law] a conflict between politics and morals (morals in this case meaning

theory of law or jurisprudence) occurs again, but the criterion of publicity of the maxims [of prospective actions] likewise is easily applied
[to resolve it]. There is this restriction, however, that a treaty binds
the states only as concerns their intent of maintaining peace among
themselves and toward other states, but not for the purpose of making
conquests.

The following instances [which we shall outline] of an antinomy
between politics and morals may present themselves, together with their
solution. (a) "If one of these states has promised something to another,
whether it be assistance or the cession of a certain territory, or sub-
sidies, etc., it may be asked whether such a state can free itself of keeping its word in a case where the state's safety depends upon it by [its
head] declaring that he must be considered as a dual person, namely
first as a *sovereign* who is not responsible to anyone in his state, and
second merely as the highest *servant of the state* [*Staatebeamte*] who
must give an account to his state: wherefrom it is concluded that he is
absolved in his second capacity from what he has promised in his first."
But if a state (or its head) were to make public such a maxim, every
other state would avoid it, or would unite with others in order to resist
such pretensions. This proves that politics, with all its cunning, would
upon such a footing [of candor] vitiate its own purpose; hence such a
maxim must be contrary to right [*unrecht*].

(b) "If a neighboring power having grown to tremendous size
(*potentia tremenda*) causes anxiety, may one assume that such a power
will *want* to oppress, because she *can* do it, and does that give the less
powerful a right to make a united attack upon such a power, even without preceding insult?" A state which would publicize such a maxim
affirmatively would merely bring about the evil more certainly and
rapidly. For the greater power would forestall the smaller ones, and
as for the uniting of the latter, this would prove a weak reed against
him who knows how to use the *divide et impera*. This maxim of political prudence, if publicly declared, vitiates its own purpose and is therefore contrary to justice [*ungerecht*].

(c) "If a smaller state, by its location, divides the territory of a
larger one which this larger one requires for its security, is the larger
one justified in subjecting the smaller one and incorporating it into its
territory?" It is easily seen that the larger should certainly not publicize such a maxim; for either the smaller ones would soon unite, or
other powerful ones would fight over this prize. Therefore such pub-

licizing is inadvisable, which is a sign that the maxim is contrary to justice and may be so in a very high degree. For a small object of injustice does not prevent the injustice from being very large.

3. As concerns the *world* law, I pass it over with silence: because its analogy with international law makes it easy to state and appreciate its corresponding maxims.

The fact that the maxims of international law are not compatible in principle with publicity constitutes a good sign that politics and morals (as jurisprudence) *do not agree.* But one needs to be informed which is the condition under which its maxims agree with the law of nations. For it is not possible to conclude the reverse: that those maxims which permit publicity are for that reason alone also just, simply because he who has the decided superiority need not conceal his maxims. For the basic condition of the possibility of a [true] law of nations is that there should exist a *lawful state.* For [as we have pointed out] without such a state there can be no public law, rather all law and right [*Recht*] which one can imagine outside such a state (in the state of the nature, that is) is merely private right. We have seen above that a federative state among the states which has merely the purpose of eliminating war is the only *lawful* [*rechtliche*] state which can be combined with the *freedom* of these states. Therefore the agreement of politics with morals is possible only within a federative union (which therefore is according to principles of law and right *a priori* given and necessary). All political prudence has only one lawful ground upon which to proceed, namely to establish such a union upon the most comprehensive basis possible. Without this purpose, all its arguments are unwisdom and camouflaged injustice.

This sort of false politics has its own *casuistry* in spite of the best teaching of the Jesuits [*sic*]. There is first the *reservatio mentalis:* to word public treaties in such terms as may be interpreted in one's interest as one sees fit, e.g., the distinction between the *status quo de fait* and the *status quo de droit;* secondly, there is guessing at *probabilities* [*Probabilismus*]: to think up evil intentions of others, or to make the probability of their possible predominance the legal ground for undermining other peaceful states; finally there is the *peccatum philosophicum* (*pecatillum, bagatelle*): the absorption of a *small* state, if by that a much *larger* one gains in the pretended interest of the world at large.

This argument is favored by the duplicity of politics in regard to morals, and its use of one branch of morals or another for its own purposes. Both charity for other men [*Menschenliebe*] and respect for the *right* of others is a duty. But charity is only a *conditional* duty, whereas respect for the right of others is an *unconditional*, and hence absolutely commanding duty. He who wishes to enjoy the sweet sense of being a benefactor must first make sure that he has not transgressed this duty. With morals in the first sense (as ethics) politics is readily agreed, in order to sacrifice the rights of men to their superiors. But with morals in the second sense (as a theory of right and law or jurisprudence [*Rechtslehre*], to which politics should bend its knee) politics prefers not to have any dealings at all, and prefers to deny it all reality and to interpret all its duties as mere charities.[1] This cunning device of a secretive politics could easily be thwarted by philosophy through publicizing its maxims, if only politics would dare allow the philosopher to publicize his own maxims.

To this end I propose another transcendental and affirmative principle of public law the formula of which would be this: "All maxims which *require* publicity in order not to miss their purpose agree with right, law, and politics."

For if they can only achieve their purpose by such publicity, they must be in accord with the general purpose of the public, namely happiness, and it is the essential task of politics to agree with this—that is, to make the public satisfied with its state. But if this purpose can *only* be achieved by publicity—that is, by removing all mistrust of its maxims—such maxims must be in accord with the rights of such a public; for only in this right can the purposes of all be united. I must, however, leave the further elaboration and discussion of this principle to another occasion. But it is recognizable that this principle is a transcendental formula, [since it can be stated] by abstracting from all empirical conditions of happiness [*Glückseligkeitslehre*] as affecting the substance of law, and by merely taking into account the form of universal legality [*Gesetzmässigkeit*].

If it is a duty, and if at the same time there is well-founded hope that we make real a state of public law, even if only in an infinitely gradual approximation, then the *eternal peace* which will take the place of the peacemakings, falsely so-called because really just truces, is no empty idea, but a task which, gradually solved, steadily approaches its end, since it is to be hoped that the periods within which equal progress is achieved will become shorter and shorter.

[1] [This is presumably a sharp attack upon all utilitarian approaches to government and law, as expounded by Hume, Bentham, and others.—C.J.F.]

INDEX